ROUTLEDGE LIBRARY EDITIONS:
IDEALISM

Volume 3

NEOPLATONISM OF THE ITALIAN RENAISSANCE

NEOPLATONISM OF THE ITALIAN RENAISSANCE

NESCA A. ROBB

LONDON AND NEW YORK

First published in 1935 by George Allen & Unwin Ltd.

This edition first published in 2021
by Routledge
2 Park Square, Milton Park, Abingdon, Oxon OX14 4RN

and by Routledge
52 Vanderbilt Avenue, New York, NY 10017

Routledge is an imprint of the Taylor & Francis Group, an informa business

© 1935 Nesca A. Robb

All rights reserved. No part of this book may be reprinted or reproduced or utilised in any form or by any electronic, mechanical, or other means, now known or hereafter invented, including photocopying and recording, or in any information storage or retrieval system, without permission in writing from the publishers.

Trademark notice: Product or corporate names may be trademarks or registered trademarks, and are used only for identification and explanation without intent to infringe.

British Library Cataloguing in Publication Data
A catalogue record for this book is available from the British Library

ISBN: 978-0-367-70445-2 (Set)
ISBN: 978-1-00-315602-4 (Set) (ebk)
ISBN: 978-0-367-72255-5 (Volume 3) (hbk)
ISBN: 978-0-367-72272-2 (Volume 3) (pbk)
ISBN: 978-1-00-315414-3 (Volume 3) (ebk)

Publisher's Note
The publisher has gone to great lengths to ensure the quality of this reprint but points out that some imperfections in the original copies may be apparent.

Disclaimer
The publisher has made every effort to trace copyright holders and would welcome correspondence from those they have been unable to trace.

NEOPLATONISM OF THE
ITALIAN RENAISSANCE

by

NESCA A. ROBB, M.A., D.Phil.(Oxon)

LONDON
GEORGE ALLEN & UNWIN LTD
MUSEUM STREET

FIRST PUBLISHED IN 1935

All rights reserved
PRINTED IN GREAT BRITAIN BY
UNWIN BROTHERS LTD., WOKING

TO

C. R.
A. M. R.
G. M. R.

συνεργοί φίλοι

CONTENTS

CHAPTER		PAGE
	Introduction	11
I.	Petrarch	17
II.	Petrarch to Ficino	31
III.	Marsilio Ficino and the Platonic Academy of Florence	57
IV.	The Medici Circle (1): Poliziano, Lorenzo de' Medici, Girolamo Benivieni	90
V.	The Medici Circle (2): The *Poema Visione*	135
VI.	The Trattato d'Amore	176
VII.	Neoplatonism and the Arts	212
VIII.	The Lyric: Michelangelo	239
	Conclusion	270
	Appendix	279
	Bibliography	296
	Index	311

INTRODUCTION

THE title of this study may need some explanation. It is customary to speak of the "Platonism" of the Italian Renaissance, but for two reasons I have preferred the term "Neoplatonism" as less misleading when applied to the teaching that emanated from Florence in the latter part of the fifteenth century.

For the earlier Italian humanists Plato was a figure more venerated than understood. Petrarch and his immediate successors knew little or no Greek, so that their ideas of Platonism were pieced together from Latin authors and from the few dialogues then existing in Latin translations.[1] As the fifteenth century advanced Greek scholarship advanced with it; but manuscripts of the *Dialogues* were rare and had mostly to be obtained by the slow and perilous expedient of going to the East to look for them; and when they were found definitions, commentaries, and the whole ground-work of systematic study had still to be prepared. External difficulties apart, it was not easy for the scholars of a world just emerging from the Middle Ages to form a clear estimate of Greek thought. Even those who were able to study Plato at first hand came to him, as was only natural, with many preconceptions. Their interest in him was indeed mainly, though by no means exclusively, a literary one. There was no commanding philosophic intellect among them; but there was the need, more or less urgently felt, of setting up reasoned principles of thought and conduct in the face of the waning of mediaeval ideals. The many treatises on moral philosophy that appeared during the first period of humanism reveal, if not a deep understanding of Plato, a distinct Platonic colour.

The coming of the Greeks in 1438 gave a powerful impetus to Platonic studies, but complicated the issues by the prominence

[1] Only one, the *Timaeus* (trans. Chalchidius, fourth century), was at all widely known, but the *Meno* and *Phaedo* were translated by Henricus Aristippus in the twelfth century.

it gave to the works of the Neoplatonists. Through the influence of Gemisthus Pletho especially they came to be generally accepted as the truest interpreters of Plato. Marsilio Ficino, though he spent many years in the close and loving study of the *Dialogues*, drew almost as freely on Plotinus and the Alexandrian School when he came to elaborate his own philosophy. The same may be said, with varying degrees of truth, of his associates. On this account alone one should be cautious in speaking of Renaissance Platonism.

There is, however, a further consideration. Modern Italian scholarship has gone far towards a fuller understanding of the philosophical background of the period; and it is no longer possible to regard the work of the Florentine "Academy" as a mere antiquarian revival. It met, or tried to meet, the specific needs of its own age, ceasing by that very fact to be a simple reproduction of Alexandrian models, though its external likeness to them is sometimes so great as to obscure real differences of aim and feeling. If it was not always consistent or satisfactory as a system of philosophy it was certainly the affirmation of a faith that informed more than one phase of the spiritual and intellectual life of the time. It contained, along with much that was worthless, real elements of originality.

Some of its popular developments were so foolish that they have somewhat overshadowed its more valuable qualities just as, perhaps, the glamour that surrounds Ficino and his circle has done their reputation some harm. It has tempted the romantic to rhapsody and soured the scientific by reaction.

My own aim has been first to give a clear outline of Florentine Neoplatonism, and then to consider its influence on art and literature during a period that extends roughly from the age of Lorenzo de' Medici to the middle of the sixteenth century and the beginnings of the Counter-Reformation. No rigid divisions of time have been fixed, but with few exceptions the works discussed may be placed between these bounds.

Even within these limits it would require a work of greater dimensions than the present to exhaust so large a subject in all its bearings. The leaven of Neoplatonism had penetrated the thought of the age in many directions; this study is confined to such of its manifestations as were, in a somewhat narrow sense, artistic and literary and to the use and abuse of philosophical ideas for aesthetic purposes. For this reason, in the chapter on Ficino some aspects of his thought, such as the theory of love and the conception of the dignity of man, have been discussed at length, while others which had fewer literary echoes have been much more summarily treated.

Except for a few very general remarks in the opening of the first chapter no attempt has been made to trace the transmission of the Platonic heritage through the Middle Ages. The large and complex problems here involved are outside the scope of this inquiry, which does not primarily seek to assess the speculative value of Neoplatonism or to view it historically in relation to the systems of philosophy that preceded and followed it. The same considerations account for the exclusion of the philosophical developments of the latter part of the sixteenth century and of so great a name as Bruno's.

With Petrarch begins what may fairly be called the Renaissance attitude to Plato, and his work provides a suitable starting-point.

The two preliminary chapters deal respectively with his philosophical writings and with those of his successors down to the beginning of Ficino's literary career. The third chapter contains an analysis of the latter's Neoplatonism and of such variations of it as were introduced by Pico della Mirandola, and seeks to present a coherent view of such of their ideas as passed into common usage.

The Medician circle has been treated as a homogenous group. Though its influence and prestige were great, it stands by itself in the literary history of the age, living its own independent and well-rounded life in the days of Lorenzo's ascendancy, and passing away almost entirely before the end of the century. Its members lived on terms of unusual intimacy, sharing in many common interests and enthusiasms that lend a distinctive character to their work. They were, moreover, the personal friends and disciples of Ficino and Pico, and provide some of the most marked and interesting examples of Neoplatonic influence as well as some little-known material.

Their work has been discussed in some detail, but the chapters on the Lyric and on the "Trattato d'Amore" are arranged on more general lines. To make a separate analysis of every individual treatise, of every one of an innumerable array of sixteenth-century "canzonieri," would be well-nigh impossible and of rather doubtful value. Several exhaustive works on the "Trattato d'Amore" and some others of slighter proportions on the lyric are noted in the bibliography. Here it has seemed sufficient to treat the questions broadly, but with plentiful illustrations and references for each point brought forward.

In the chapter on art centres the chief difficulty of the work. To many it may seem unjustifiable to include art at all in a study of this kind. To trace an influence in literature, though an invidious task is a perfectly defensible one, but to try to establish the relation of any abstract mode of thought to the plastic arts is to follow, like Christian, a path between the fiends and the quagmire. Yet it may be generally conceded that between different periods and schools of art there exist certain broad distinctions other than those of individual temperament, of technical resources, or of purely aesthetic merit that correspond to fundamental differences of outlook. This does not, of course, imply that an artist must necessarily have a formal philosophy, but only that he can hardly, whatever his personal endowments, succeed in withdrawing himself entirely from the common cultural heritage to which he was born, the somewhat vague background of general ideas that makes up in any age the philosophy of the average unsystematic mind. During the Italian Renaissance Neoplatonism formed an important part of that background; and in few other periods has the connection between artists and men of letters been closer or more fruitful. The influence of the arts on literature has often been noted; but the amount of literary inspiration in art is almost as remarkable, though more difficult to estimate with precision. The Neoplatonists' theories were almost universally known; and it may not be useless to examine how far, if at all, those theories were applied and how much of their peculiar idealism is reflected in the art of the time. The conclusions reached may perhaps appear too slight to justify the energy expended on them. I can only hope to present a debatable point of view soberly and without arrogance.

In the final chapter on the lyric, Michelangelo has been given a place by himself. He was, in spite of the frequent obscurity of his verse, perhaps the greatest Neoplatonic poet; and he forms a link between the idyllic days of the "Academy" and the stormy close of Italy's golden age. His genius, at once so representative and so individual, requires special treatment; and a study of it may fitly round off this survey.[1]

The main portion of the work is analytical in character, but a final chapter has been added in which are summed up such general conclusions as the material collected seems to warrant.

A word should perhaps be said concerning the translations. These are my own, with one or two exceptions which are noted where they occur. In my renderings of verse I have tried throughout to follow my texts faithfully, though here and there obscurely worded lines have caused me some uncertainty as to the author's real intentions, and at other times I have had to confront the problem, ever awaiting the translator, of whether fidelity consists in adherence to the letter or to the style and spirit of an author's work. As to how far these difficulties have been satisfactorily met the reader must be my judge. I sincerely hope that the versions here presented may be readable, but am well aware that they cannot be faultless.

The labour of writing this book has been lightened and its completion made possible by the help and advice of many scholars for whose generous assistance I am deeply grateful. I much regret

[1] Biographical detail and the facts of external history have been introduced throughout only where they seem strictly relevant.

that one of their number, the late Professor Gargano of Florence, is no longer here to receive this expression of gratitude. My special thanks are due to Professor G. Saitta, Professor G. Mazzoni, Professor Mario Praz, the Director of the Biblioteca Nazionale of Florence, Sir Robert Tate, F.T.C.D., Dr. Henry Guppy, Professor J. A. Smith, Signorina Adelaide Conti, Miss V. Farnell, and Miss M. Mann. Above all I have to thank Professor C. Foligno of Oxford, whose wide learning and unfailing kindness and encouragement have placed me, like so many other British students of Italian letters, for ever in his debt.

NOTE.—Throughout, in copying from MSS. and contemporary editions, I have preserved the original spelling, except for:—

(*a*) Writing out abbreviations in full; and
(*b*) Adding apostrophes or inverted commas where these would be used in modern Italian and where they make for immediate ease of reading.

ABBREVIATIONS

Arch. St. It.	Archivio Storico Italiano.
G.S.	Giornale Storico della Letteratura Italiana.
MS. Magl.	MS. Magliabecchiano.
MS. Laur.	MS. Laurenziana.
MS. Laur. Plut.	MS. Laurenziana fondo Plutarchiana.
Cod. Ricc.	Codice Riccardiana.
Cod. Vat. Lat.	Codice Vaticano Latino.
Cod. Urb. Lat.	Codice Urbinate Latino.
N.A.	Nuova Antologia.
o.c.	Opera citata.

NEOPLATONISM OF THE ITALIAN RENAISSANCE

CHAPTER I

PETRARCH

THE Neoplatonism of the Italian Renaissance was no new thing in the sense of having no roots in the philosophies that immediately preceded it. The contacts of the early doctors of the Church with the Neoplatonists of Alexandria brought into Christian philosophy elements which became so inextricably mixed with it that even those philosophers who professed themselves rigid Aristotelians could not always succeed in discarding them. Plato himself was scarcely known to the Middle Ages, which were in any case too far removed from Greek modes of thought to have understood him.

The stream of thought that flowed from the Alexandrian philosophers ran, roughly speaking, in two main channels: the naturalistic and the mystic. The first, deriving from the Neoplatonic conception of the Universe as a series of emanations from the ineffable godhead tended to seek for truth in the study of the cosmos as a manifestation of the divine, and therefore to the cultivation of mathematics and the natural sciences. The second, which came from the belief that true knowledge cannot be attained but can only be revealed to the soul, tended to emphasize the inwardness of religious experience and hence the independence of the individual who does not need an external authority to show him what he can only know by immediate revelation.

The naturalistic current appeared most notably in the Arab philosophers like Avicenna; the mystic had its most famous exponents in the pseudo-Dionysius and St. Augustine. The latter, with his doctrines of self-knowledge as an essential in the approach

18 NEOPLATONISM OF THE ITALIAN RENAISSANCE

to truth and of the will as the ultimate power in moral life, prepared the way for the dynamic conception of personality peculiar to the period of humanism.

Augustine's teaching was perpetuated by a long series of followers, and it was not until the thirteenth century that Aristotelianism, as interpreted by Aquinas, became the official system of the Church and displaced its rivals, Augustinian and Avicennist. Even so, the Neoplatonic tradition was not eradicated, but lingered in the schools of Europe, and especially of Italy, to emerge once more into full life in the fifteenth century.

In Dante, although the framework of his thought is Aristotelian, there are many Neoplatonic elements. In the *Vita Nuova* he elaborates ideas that were already common among the poets of the "stil nuovo" (e.g. that love is a means of moral perfection, an ascent through successive stages of contemplation towards a celestial vision) when he speaks of his passing from "amor sensitivo" aroused by the sight of Beatrice, to "amor intellettivo," and hence to the universalized and depersonalized emotion of "Oltre la sfera che piu largo gira." In the *Convivio* and still more in the *Commedia* his debt to Neoplatonic sources is apparent and has often been pointed out.[1] His theory of creation shows affinities with that of the *Timaeus*; the world was created by the whole Trinity, Power, Wisdom, and Love, so that all creatures might participate with God in the joys of conscious existence.[2] The divine ideas, "splendore e pitture delle cose contingenti in Dio," are reflected in the creation.[3] The primal matter, which receives the forms of all things, came from the hand of God in the same

[1] His sources were mainly Dionysius and Augustine. He probably knew Chalchidius' translation of the *Timaeus*. See for the Platonic and Neoplatonic elements in his work E. Moore, *Dante Studies*, Oxford, 1st series, pp. 156-64, 282-8, 291-4. A. Carlini *Del Sistema, Filosofico Dantesco nella D.C.*, Bologna, 1902. E. Gardner, *Dante and the Mystics*, London, 1913. G. Gentile, *La Filosofia, Storia dei Generi letterarii*, Milan, Vallardi (in continuation), Vol. I, p. 122. P. Wicksteed, *Dante and Aquinas*, London, 1913. V. Fornari, "Il Convito di Dante" in *Dante e il suo secolo*, Florence, 1865.

[2] *Paradiso*, VII, 64-6; XXIX, 13-18.

[3] *Par.* XIII, 52-78; *Convito*, III.

creative act as did the angelic orders and the heavens, as three arrows might fly from a three-stringed bow, a view that suggests the theories of emanation of the Alexandrian school.[1] The angels move the heavens and by the virtue of the heavens all earthly existences are generated. Only into man God breathes an immortal soul, gifted with free will by which, with the aid of grace, he may order and purify his affections. Love, which moved God to create and draws His creatures back to Him, is the vital activity of the universe. It is the root of good and evil, the inspiration of poetry, philosophy, and art, the means by which the soul rises through various grades of being until it is satisfied at last by the Beatific Vision.[2]

It was scarcely surprising that the Platonic Academy of Florence should have seen in Dante an illustrious forerunner. It was Petrarch, however, who first definitely linked the name of Plato with the ideals of Italian humanism. He was not himself a systematic or deeply original thinker, though he managed to give a certain personal quality to the ideas that he borrowed freely from his favourite authors. His philosophical writings contain in germ most of the motives that appear in the thought of the fifteenth century. Stoic ideals of virtue and glory; the first justification of Epicurus, that scapegoat of the Middle Ages; Augustinian conceptions of voluntarism and self-knowledge; a vein of scepticism and a passionate love for the serenity and beauty of the classics, are all combined in him in a Christian setting, and are directed towards the revaluation of man and his achievements that characterizes the Renaissance.[3] Of this movement Plato became, for Petrarch and for those who followed him, a symbol and rallying cry. Petrarch's literary life covered all the middle years of the fourteenth century, a time in which the spiritual forces of

[1] *Par.*, XXIX.
[2] *Purg.*, XVIII, 34–75. *Par.*, V, 19–24. The moral system of Purgatorio is based upon the conception of sin as diseased love—love of evil object, love defective, love excessive.
[3] The Platonism of his *Rime* is derived from the "stil nuovisti" and from the Ciceronian conception of rational love.

mediaevalism were losing their vigour. The religious idea as the Middle Ages conceived it was no longer satisfying to a people in whom the sense of human values was growing steadily stronger. The dominion of mediaevalism in Italy had never been as complete as it was in other countries. The existence of the free communes had kept alive the ideal of civic autonomy in the face of that of universal authority, and the presence of Roman antiquities and the persistence of the Latin language and traditions had preserved that strain of humanistic and even pagan feeling that never wholly vanished from the art and literature of Italy during the Middle Ages.

By the fourteenth century these tendencies were well defined and were becoming increasingly self-conscious, but theoretically they lacked any real justification. Since reality was regarded as entirely beyond the reach of the human mind the activities of that mind could not be considered as a part of it. The division between religious revelation and human knowledge had grown painfully acute and no conciliation of the opposing terms had been found. The result was a general slackening of religious sentiment and of moral restraints. Active unbelief was not common but was exemplified in some of the Averroists of the University of Padua against whom Petrarch launched some of his fiercest invectives. They, like Petrarch himself, were moved by the desire for intellectual liberty, and numbered among them such a notable political thinker as Marsilio da Padova.

Philosophy as a whole was passing through a dead period. After the *Summa contra Gentiles* of Thomas Aquinas there had been little real creative thought. Thomism, in which the philosophical implications of Christian dogma were developed on an Aristotelian basis, had become the accepted system of the Church; and the later Schoolmen, revolving continually within the same circle of ideas, tended with a few honourable exceptions to reduce their work to an arid and abstract dialectic. The oligarchic and ecclesiastical character of mediaeval learning had equally made a closed system of the other branches of knowledge. The various sciences, formalized into "Summae" and "Summulae," threatened to become mere repetition of verbiage, and were protected against free criticism by the "Ipse dixit" of Aristotle's infallible authority. By translating the bulk of contemporary learning into the vulgar tongue Dante had gone far towards encouraging a more liberal spirit; but he made no intentional break with the mediaeval tradition. Aristotle was for him "il maestro di color che sanno"; and it remained for Petrarch, with his somewhat aggressive individualism, to challenge the schools that founded themselves on Aristotelianism. His lifelong desire to be a man apart and to separate himself from the herd had, no doubt, its share in his attitude; but he was sharply conscious of the need of a re-tempering of all intellectual life at the well-heads of ancient civilization, and of some moral force strong enough to be of practical worth to himself and his contemporaries. Yet it was hard for him, a professed lover of antiquity, to set himself against the cult of Aristotle. He saw the difficulty and met it at first by saying guardedly that his adversaries knew their Aristotle only through the medium of corrupt translations, and that in any case he was only a man and no more infallible than another. Later, under the influence of his favourite Latin authors, and especially of Cicero and St. Augustine, he frankly declared that Plato was the prince of philosophers and so confronted the Aristotelians with another great but still mysterious figure of the ancient world.[1]

Petrarch himself could not read Greek and knew only the scantiest translations of Plato, who was so little known during the Middle Ages that he was commonly supposed to have written only two works. One of these, the *Timaeus*, in the fourth-century Latin version of Chalchidius, was fairly widely diffused, and this

[1] See *De Suiipsius atque multorum ignorantia* in *Opera*, Basle, 1581, pp. 1052–3. *De Vera Sapientia*, ibid., p. 323. *Lettere Familiari ed Fracassetti*, 5 vols., Florence, 1863, Vol. IV, p. 15. The edition of the *Lettere Senili* cited hereafter is also that of Fracassetti, Florence, 1863, 2 vols.

Petrarch certainly possessed.[1] In later life he may also have seen the *Meno* and the *Phaedo* in the translation made about 1157, by Henricus Aristippus, Archdeacon of Catania. It is possible that Barlaam, the Calabrian monk who taught him the rudiments of Greek, may have expounded for him some passages from other dialogues. It is, however, more probable that the manuscripts he eagerly collected remained to the last unknown to him. He had in his library at least sixteen works of Plato in the original, and cherished them though he could not read them, a fact that is almost symbolical of his attitude to their author.

The bar of language would have kept him in equal ignorance of the work of the Neoplatonists had these been available. The whole Platonic school, however, shared in his commendation of their master, and he makes several references to Plotinus and Porphyry among the great men who honoured "the divine Plato."[2] His chief sources of knowledge were, therefore, the so-called "Latin Platonists." Two of them, Cicero and St. Augustine, were the objects of his special veneration, so their tribute to the greatness of Plato carried peculiar weight. Both were also masters of style, and may have helped Petrarch to divine some of the aesthetic qualities that afterwards endeared Plato to the Renaissance. The glamour of a great name and of literary excellence might have attracted him even if the need for a prophet to set against Aristotle had been lacking. On the testimony of Augustine, strengthened by his own reading of the *Timaeus* and of the *Tusculan Disputations* of Cicero, Petrarch formed an idea of Plato as the philosopher whose teaching approached most nearly to Christianity.

[1] His copy, inscribed "Felix miser qui hoc sciens unde ista nescisti," is preserved in Paris. For his sources see P. De Nolhac, *Pétrarque et l'humanisme*, Paris, 1892. R. Sabbadini, *La Scoperta dei Codici nel secolo XIV e XV Florence* (2 vols., I, 1905; II, 1914), Vol. I, p. 219. G. Saitta, *La Filosofia di Marsilio Ficino*, Messina, 1923, Ch. III, p. 44. G. Gentile, "I dialoghi di Platone posseduti dal P.," *Rassegna critica della let. it.*, tom. IX, 1904, pp. 193-219. Voigt, *Il Risorgimento dell'antichità classica*, Florence [trans. D. Valbusa], 1888, 2 vols., Vol. I, p. 84.

[2] *De Suiipsius atque multorum Ignorantia. Opera*, p. 1052.

The doctrines of the immortality of the soul and of the creation of the world in time; and the idea of life as a continual preparation for death and the final vision of "il sommo ed unico bene" all seemed to him to be foreshadowed in the Platonic dialogues. The value of Platonism as a weapon against unbelief was manifest in his eyes, and he pointed it out to his friends and successors.[1] It was not, however, the purely speculative aspects of Platonism that appealed to him most strongly. Abstract thought for its own sake interested him very little. His mind worked in terms of the individual and the concrete both by natural inclination and from fidelity to the Latin tradition. The idea of personality which had been obscured during the Middle Ages was central to his thought. Scholasticism, based as it was on a belief in an impassable gulf between the Infinite mind and the finite mind of man, had arrived at a conception of human personality as of something essentially static. The "voluntarist" schools of mediaeval thought emphasized man's free will, though the freedom they described was severely limited by the frailty of its possessor; but the fundamental belief in a humanity whose only hope of rising from its degradation lay in the gift of an external power lessened the importance of the individual, who appeared simply as a vessel to be filled or abandoned by grace from a transcendent source. This belief in its fervour had created all that is still vital in mediaeval art and thought; but by Petrarch's time it had lost its early vigour and passed into a stereotyped culture and a philosophy of abstract reasoning divorced from the immediate life of man. It was this cleavage between theory and life that Petrarch struggled to remedy. Philosophy for him was the art of virtuous living; and all systems that failed to teach that art he regarded as no more than splendid chains and sounding weights on the soul.[2] Cicero and Augustine and Plato, as seen through their works, appeared to him as true philosophers whose first and final aim was the good of their

[1] E.g. to Luigi Marsigli, whom he urged to take up the struggle against the Averroists.
[2] *De Sui. Opera*, p. 1039.

readers.[1] His own purpose in writing his philosophical works was mainly ethical. His range of speculation was narrow; and he ignored or only perfunctorily noticed many major problems.

He was primarily concerned with the moral life of the individual, and it is his treatment of this favourite theme that gives him his chief interest and importance as a philosophical writer.

From Augustine he derived his chosen form of moral philosophy, based on psychological observation. The two men were in many ways curiously alike. Both were restless and introspective with an exquisite sense of their own fleeting moods and inward contradictions and a rare power of fixing them in words. "Mihi quaestio factus sum" might have been said with equal truth by both of them; but where Augustine solved his problem by a final surrender of faith Petrarch remained unsettled to the end. There is no need to doubt the sincerity of his religious beliefs; but he was never, like Augustine, completely absorbed in religion. One may find evidence in his works of genuine devotional feeling, but nothing to match in kind or intensity with Augustine's cry to "the Beauty of Ancient Days" or his last conversation with Monnica. Petrarch himself recognized the deficiency. In his prose as in his verse there is a continual tension between the man of the Middle Ages, who believes his true life to be in another world, and the man of the Renaissance, whose deepest interest centres in the world of human experience.

He follows Augustine closely in the place which he gives to self-knowledge and to the power of the will. Yet in his treatment of the former there is a difference which is almost one of atmosphere rather than of actual words; one feels that the centre of gravity has shifted. Augustine entered into his own soul in order to pass beyond himself to an eternal spirit outside and above him. Ostensibly Petrarch wished to do the same; but in comparison

[1] Hi [Cicero and Augustine] sunt ergo veri Philosophi morales et virtutum optimi magistri quorum prima et ultima intentio est bonum facere auditorem et lectorem, quique non solum docent quid est virtus aut vitium praeclarumque illud hoc fuscam nomen auribus instrepunt sed rei optimi amorem studium pessimique rei odium fugamque pectoribus inferunt. *De Sui. Opera*, p. 1052.

he deals very perfunctorily with the divine vision, and lingers rather on the greatness of the human spirit as an active force in the world.

Man's chief end is to live so that he may ultimately enjoy the knowledge of God. This is not attainable under earthly conditions, since God is above all that we can imagine or postulate of Him "aeterna sapientia per qua ex qua et in qua omnia."[1] None the less it is possible for a man to approach true knowledge even in this life if he sets himself to seek it; and his first endeavour must be to know himself, or in other words to recognize his own ignorance and free himself of all false opinions, arrogance, and foolishness.[2]

No knowledge of things external to itself can compensate the soul for ignorance of its own true nature. Man is a stranger on the earth "quasi hospes in domo aliena" and possesses nothing but the spirit within him. If he cannot hold that inner world he has nothing, for external things possess him instead of his possessing them.[3] In the *De Remediis Utriusque Fortuna* Petrarch puts this inward struggle into the form of a dialogue between Reason and the passions, in which Reason proves by argument the unreality of all pains and pleasures, while the passions do not argue but repeat the same phrases again and again. Finally, Reason shows how most of our troubles could be avoided by the exercise of virtue and of a certain philosophic detachment. So far the thought is Platonico-Ciceronian, but Petrarch could not accept the purely intellectual ideal of the ancients. For Plato the man who continues to be the sport of passion is ignorant. If he could be brought to use his reason properly and recognize his true good he

[1] *De Ver. Sap.*, II, *Opera*, p. 328.
[2] Ibid. Cf. p. 325. Igitur si velis fieri noli ut iam dixi te ipsum opinari sapientiam.
[3] Ibid., II, *Opera*, p. 325. Quid tibi prodest universum lucrari mundum teipsum perdens? Noveris licet omnia mysteria, noveris lata terrae profundo maris, alto caeli si te nescieris similis eris viro aedificante absque fundamento, ruinam non structuram faciens. Non est sapiens qui sibi non est sapiens: in acquistione enim salutis tuae nemo tibi germanior neque propinquior.

could not do otherwise than follow it, and in so doing become righteous.[1]

Petrarch, with his background of Augustinian culture and bitter experience, knew otherwise. He was not ignorant of what to do; his trouble was that he did not do it. The solution of his difficulty he saw in Augustine's teaching with regard to the will as the final arbiter of moral life. No man, he says in the *Secretum*, ever fell into sin except by his own voluntary act. It is vain to plead that one cannot help oneself; when one says "I cannot" one ought rather to say "I will not" (ut ubi te non posse dixisti ultra te nolle fatearis). All sin is due to a misdirection of the will; and mere compunction without a change of volition is useless for moral progress.

Mens immota manet, lacrimae voluunt inanes,[2]

Full knowledge of our own shortcomings should produce an ardent desire to forsake them. Such desire is in itself a great part of virtue, capable of annihilating all lesser wishes and opening a way through all difficulties. It is not easy, while one is in the body, to achieve a single-hearted love of the Good. If the soul of its own will rises towards heaven the lusts of the flesh drag it back to earth, and so, balanced between two desires, we fail of both. From the body proceed the phantasms that perturb the soul, and so clog and hinder it that it forgets its divine origin and its creator, and quenches its own brightness in the dust of mortality.

It is the work of a great soul to withdraw itself from outward things and to be wholly at one with itself and choose to see with the inward eye rather than with the eye of flesh. Yet if the choice is made, the joy of the search is so great that it never brings satiety. The soul becomes like the man who found treasure in a field and sold all that he had that he might buy it. The object of desire is the sovereign good which is present in the world as "delectatio in omne delectabile, pulchritudo in omne pulchro," but man

[1] For the *De Remediis* see F. Fiorentino, "La Filosofia di F. P.," in *Scritti varii di letteratura, filosofia e critica*, Naples, 1876, pp. 114 et seq.
[2] *Secretum*, Bk. I, *Opera*, p. 334.

cannot rest content with the image, but seeks to possess the truth itself.[1]

This incessant spiritual movement is the inner law of the soul and cannot be disregarded. The will for Petrarch is neither desire nor inclination nor acceptance, but a dynamic force that cannot of its very nature be inactive. A man's inner life is a continual process of self-creation consciously and deliberately undertaken.

". . . ita et nos oportet voluntatem ostendere, navigamus enim et nostraim navigationem non eam quae a terra in terram, sed eam quae a terra in caelum. Construamus igitur mentem nostram ad aptem gubernationem quae sursum fert et nautas ei obedientes et navem solidam ut neque circumstantia neque tristitia submergatus mundiale neque elationis elevetur spiritu sed bene praecincta sit et levis; si sic quidem navium si sic vero gubernatorem et nautas praeparabimus cum aptitudine ventorum navigabimus et filium Dei qui verus est gubernator attrahemus ad nosipsos qui non dimittet submergi navem nobis sed, et si infiniti flaverint venti et ventos increpabit et marem et pro fluctatione multum tribuit tranquillitatem."[2]

Petrarch, as this paragraph shows, certainly did not look upon humanity as completely autonomous or deny the need for the gift of grace. He speaks frequently of the helplessness of man; and his personal sense of the vanity of mortal things was too strong to allow him the jubilant confidence that characterized his suc-

[1] *Sec.*, I, p. 339. *De Ver. Sap.*, p. 329. Cf. Aeterna sapientia in omne gustabile gustatur, ipsa est delectatio in omne delectabile, ipsa est pulchritudo in omne pulchro, ipsa est appetito in omne appetibile et sic in cunctis delectabilibus vel desiderabilibus dicito. Hinc non aliud in omne desiderio intellectualis vitae desideras quam ceteram sapientiam, quae est desiderii tui complementum, principium medium et finis. Sapientia enim infinita est indeficiens vitae pabulum de quo aeternaliter vivit spiritus noster qui si rectus est, non nisi sapientiam et veritatem amare potest. Omnes enim intellectus appetit esse, suum esse est vivere, suum vivere est intelligere, suum intelligere est pasci sapientia et veritate. Unde intellectus qui non est degustans claram sapientiam hic est ut oculus in tenebris. . . . Sola enim aeterna sapientia est in qua omnis intellectus intelligere potest.

[2] *De Ver. Sap.*, p. 326, et seq. See also *Let. Sen.*, Bk. X, Vol. II, p. 121, where P. says that morality is the struggle to remake oneself.

cessors. Yet by placing the remedies against fortune in the human mind itself he was preparing the way for the doctrines of the self-sufficiency of man whom he regards within limits as the architect of his own soul and as a creator in his own human world.[1]

Petrarch developed his theme farther in his picture of the philosophic life. The solitude described in the *De Vita Solitaria* and the *De Ocio Religiosorum* is only superficially monastic. There is nothing in it of the negation of individuality or of the passive obedience to the will of a superior that are the distinguishing marks of monastic discipline. Petrarch's philosopher labours to perfect his soul for its immortal destiny by a free and conscious preparation of which it is itself the author.

His solitude is not idle or empty. It is primarily a flight from sin and carnal preoccupations; an inner solitude in which the rational soul understands itself, governs itself, and remains unperturbed among the shocks of circumstance. Retirement from the world is good but not essential, since the true philosopher possesses himself too completely to be shaken from his serenity by any outward accident. "Quod si, inquam, intestinus tumultus tuae mentis conquiesceret fragor iste circumtonans (mihi crede) sensus quidem pulsaret sed animum non movet."[2] Through the four stages of virtue that Macrobius and Plotinus defined as political, cathartic, spiritual, and superhuman, the soul returns to its true self. The apparent inaction is really the exercise of that "mentis actio" which is alone pure and unimpeded activity. All philosophic studies must tend not simply to the acquisition of the knowledge of virtue, but to an act of will by which the mind assimilates itself to virtue, and in a sense becomes what it knows. Philosophy that does not result in such an assimilation is worse than vain.[3]

The true philosopher is in fact the true Christian, but the Christian who has known how to use all culture as a means of moral growth. Petrarch seems to have had in mind a hero of

---

[1] *De Sui.*, p. 1052.
[2] *Sec.*, II, p. 350. Cf. *Let. Sen.*, II, Letter 2, Vol. I, p. 98.
[3] *De Sui.*, p. 1051.

scholarship in whom learning had helped to form a kind of sanctity. Many, he says, have achieved sanctity without the aid of learning, but learning has never hindered anyone from becoming holy.[1] On the contrary, it gives its possessor a store of remedies against temptation in the form of wise thoughts that sooth the mind and temper wrath.[2] There emerges a new conception of culture as the growth of the soul towards a balance of all faculties in full development. The idea of learning, as the memorizing of rigid sciences, breaks up before the claim of every man to perfect himself freely in the single art of virtue and truth.[3] The liberal arts are no longer ends in themselves, but means to one great end. The Scholastics had regarded knowledge as a fixed quantity which the individual mind could receive, but could not modify. For Petrarch the mind was a living organism and knowledge the food that it transforms into its own substance. In other words, every man re-creates knowledge for himself, and must test the statements of authority by the light of his own consciousness before he can accept them as true.

Man's supreme greatness lies in the creativeness of his spirit, which realizes itself by its own continual and spontaneous activity, and leaves the fruit of its life as a precious heritage to the future.[4] His sense of the originality of the human mind led Petrarch to glorify poetry as the creative art which excels all others because it includes and transcends them all.[5] His continued brooding on

[1] *Let. Sen.*, I, Letter 5, Vol. I, p. 47.
[2] "Mollitque animos et temperat iras," *Sec.*, II, p. 351.
[3] *Let. Sen.*, XII, Vol. II, p. 62. *Sec.*, II, p. 351.
[4] "Operosa ac difficilis res est fama et praecipue literarum." Omnes in eam vigiles atque armati sunt etiam qui sperare illam nequeant, habentibus nituntur eripere, habendo calamus semper in manibus, intento animo erectisque auribus semper in acie standum erit (*De Sui.*, p. 1041).
[5] *Let. Sen.*, I, 3; IV, 4; XIV, 11. *Sec.*, II, 351. P. was at the same time faithful to the mediaeval view of poetry as

"La dottrina che s'ascose
Sotto il velame degli versi strani."

His own eclogues are good examples of involved allegorical writing. (See his expositions of them, *Let. Fam.*, Vol. V, Lettere Varie No. 49, p. 416.)

the subjective aspects of true knowledge and true nobility made him place the mind of man at the centre of all philosophic speculation; and in this he foreshadows that central motive of the Florentine Neoplatonists, the deification of man.

TRANSLATIONS

Page 25. aeterna sapientia . . .
eternal wisdom by which, from which, and in which are all things.

Page 26. Mens immota manet . . .
The mind remains unmoved and tears flow in vain.

Page 26. delectatio in omne delectabile . . .
The delightfulness in all things delightful, the beauty in all things beautiful.

Page 27. . . . ita et nos oportet . . .
. . . and thus it behoves us to make manifest our will, for we are voyaging, and our voyage is not from one earthly country to another, but from earth to heaven. Let us therefore fit our mind for the right steering that leads on high, and let the sailors be obedient and the ship solid, that it may neither be swamped by circumstances nor by sorrow, nor lifted up by a worldly spirit of elation, but be well-framed and light; and if we thus make ready the pilot and crew of the ship we shall sail with favouring winds and shall draw unto ourselves the Son of God, that true pilot who will not suffer the ship to sink with us, but however the infinite gales may blow, will rebuke the winds and the sea, and give for tempest a great calm.

Page 28. Quod si . . .
For I say that if the internal tumult of thy mind should quiet itself, the uproar raging around thee would indeed strike upon the sense, but (believe me) would not move the soul.

CHAPTER II

PETRARCH TO FICINO

THE period following Petrarch's death is generally known as the philological stage of humanism. The revival of Greek learning which he had desired was pushed forward by his successors, and simultaneously the prestige of Plato grew among Italian scholars. Petrarch's two most notable disciples, Luigi Marsigli and Coluccio Salutati, were, like their master, dependent on Latin sources for the Platonic elements in their work; but after the sojourn of Manuel Chrysoloras in Venice and Florence [1394–9] the numbers of humanists capable of reading Plato in the original increased rapidly.

Their interest in him was at this time mainly linguistic and literary, nor was such an attitude without its value. It promoted such essential preliminaries as the search for manuscripts, the close study of the original texts, and the definition of philosophical terms. In the years between Petrarch's death and the appearance of Ficino's versions (1374–1483) Platonic and Neoplatonic manuscripts were eagerly collected and some fragmentary translations were made.[1] The greatness of Plato's art, and the beauty and variety of his style laid their spell on the humanists before his ideas had penetrated very deeply into their thought.

Pleasure in literary and philosophical discussion was very general all through the fifteenth century and was fostered in courts and the homes of private citizens and in a number of more or less informal "academies" or literary circles. One of the earliest

[1] For an instance of this philological labour see Leonardo Bruni, *Epistolae*, ed. Méhus, Florence, 1741, 2 vols., Vol. II, Bk. V, pp. 1 et seq.
Bruni defends himself for translating ταγαθον as "summum bonum," while his critics maintain that he should have rendered it simply by "bonum." For the Renaissance enthusiasm for the aesthetic aspects of Plato one might instance L. Bruni, *Ep.*, Vol. I, p. 16, or Bessarion, *In Calumniatorem Platonis*, Bk. I, esp. Chs. 3, 4, 5.

of these centred around Petrarch's friend Marsigli and met in the cloister of Santo Spirito in Florence.¹ Marsigli, himself an Augustinian monk, lives chiefly by his personal influence, for his literary remains—a few scattered letters and some slight commentaries on Petrarch, written in "volgare"—give only scanty indications as to his teaching. In his youth he met Petrarch at Padua and was told by him to cultivate his gifts for a great struggle against the Averroists and other false philosophers, but nothing is known of his attitude towards them in later life. He was reputed a learned theologian and was given to the allegorical interpretation of mythology. He may have extended his methods to the Scriptures, and if he did, he was following a practice common to the Florentine Neoplatonists and to the Reformers who derived it from them. While he lived he gathered about him the best intellects of Florence, men like Salutati, Niccolo Niccoli, and Roberto de Rossi; and after his death he seems to have become almost a legend. No contemporary records of his circle exist, but it is probable that the discussions ranged over a wide selection of subjects and that they were conducted with considerable freedom. The spirit if not the letter of them may survive in the *Dialogum ad Petrum Paulum Histrum* of Bruni and the *Paradiso degli Alberti* of Giovanni da Prato, in the second of which Marsigli is one of the principal speakers. The latter book, with its strange mingling of philosophical debate and Boccacciesque story-telling, set in a framework of Florentine social life, shows how widely diffused

¹ For Luigi Marsigli see Voigt, o.c., Bk. II, Ch. II, pp. 180–207. Saitta, *Educazione dell'Umanesimo*, Ch. II. C. Casari, *Notizie intorno a L. M.*, Lovere, 1900. C. Salutati, *Epistolae*, ed. Novati, Vol. I, pp. 243–5; 314; II, pp. 174, 462–3, 469; IV, pp. 120–38, 174. Poggio Bracciolini in "Oratio in funere N. Niccoli" [in Martène-Durand, *Veterum scriptorum et monumentorum amplissima collectio*, Paris, 1724, Vol. III, p. 729] gives an impression of his fame with a younger generation. [Cf. Salutati's praise in *Ep.*, IV, 138. S. says that L. M. left no writings, but neither did Pythagoras nor Socrates nor Christ.]

Boccaccio contributed much to the revival of letters but did not fully share Petrarch's enthusiasm for Plato. In so far as he had a formal philosophy he was an Aristotelian and gave Plato second place. See *Amorosa Visione*, Ch. IV. *De genealogia deorum*, XIV, Ch. 9; XVI, Ch. 13.

was some degree of philosophic culture and how readily and unconventionally a lay assembly was prepared to handle it.

In the early fifteenth century the tradition of Marsigli's academy was carried on, with a fuller equipment of hellenic learning, by Ambrogio Traversari, Carlo Marsuppini, and others. Later in the century, after the coming of the Greeks, the more famous Academies—Pomponio Leto's group in Rome, Pontano's circle in Naples, and, above all, the Platonic Academy of Florence—came into being. But before the period of the Councils, Italy already possessed a sound foundation of Greek culture, a fair stock of MSS. and translations, and a number of informal societies intent on discussing and developing these new discoveries.

The fifteenth century was rich in vigorous thinkers, but their work, though often remarkable, was unsystematic. Before Ficino there is no attempt at a large philosophic synthesis, though there is an abundance of original suggestions. From this scattered and fragmentary material it will be necessary to attempt not a complete analysis of humanistic thought, but a general sketch of those aspects of it that most affected the development of Florentine Neoplatonism.

The direct influence of Plato and the Neoplatonic writers was comparatively slight in the first half of the century. Plato was rather a symbol of the peculiar humanity and wisdom of the ancient world than a philosopher scientifically studied. The humanists divined in him the qualities that they themselves prized most highly; freedom from the rigidity of the schools, and delight in the beauty and variety of the world, combined with serenity and self-command. They aspired towards the fusion of two ideals hitherto regarded as irreconcilable; the classic ideal of beauty and the Christian ideal of moral perfection. Their thought, which takes a form half aesthetic and half moralistic, embodies itself in a large number of educational and ethical treatises whose chief purpose is to depict types of perfect manhood. The writers were on the whole, even more impatient of metaphysics than Petrarch had been, and concentrated their attention primarily on the sphere of human activity.

Among the earliest of them Coluccio Salutati holds a high place.[1] He was a vigorous defender of the new learning, whose life-long contact with practical affairs kept him from a too-slavish devotion to antiquity. Throughout a busy and responsible public career he maintained his youthful taste for moral philosophy; and contrived to write voluminously on very varied topics. He admired and corresponded with Petrarch, but seems otherwise to have had no outstanding teacher and to have forged for himself his ideal of morality and culture. Like his predecessor he knew no Greek, but he shows a somewhat wider acquaintance with Platonic sources than Petrarch, a fact that his friendship with Leonardo Bruni might go far to explain. He was one of those who welcomed Chrysolaras to Florence and though his own plan for learning Greek in his old age never materialized he was an enthusiastic collector of manuscripts and an encourager of younger scholars. Without possessing great genius, he was a fine type of the early humanist, independent, energetic, and dignified, with a genuine love of liberal culture and intellectual freedom.

In the mass of his works, written over a period of many years and probably hastily put together in the intervals of State business,

[1] For Salutati see *Epistolae*, ed. F. Novati, 5 vols., Rome, 1891–6. F. Novati, *La Giovinezza di C. S.* [1331–53]. *Saggio di un libro sopra la vita, le opere ed i tempi di C. S.*, Turin, 1888. Voigt, o.c., Bk. II. F. Fiorentino, *Il Risorgimento Filosofico del'* 400, Naples, 1888, p. 183. Gentile, *Storia della Fil.*, Vol. I, p. 196. G. Saitta, *L'Educazione dell'Umanesimo*, Venice, 1928, pp. 1–17, and the essay on Giovanni Dominici, Salutati's monkish opponent, p. 120. E. Emerton, *Humanism and Tyranny*, Cambridge [Mass.], Harvard U.P., 1925, pp. 25 et seq., which contains an English translation of Salutati's tract *De Tyranno*. An MS. essay on Salutati by Lamberto Borghi of the University of Pisa, kindly lent me by Professor Saitta has also proved helpful. Alfred von Martin's *C. S. und d. humanist Lebensideal*, München, 1916, and *Mittelalterliche Welt u. Lebensanschaung im Spiegel der Schriften Col. Salutatis*, München, 1913, contain references to S.'s unpublished works, *De Saeculo et Religione, De Fato et Fortuna*, etc.

By courtesy of the officials of the Vatican Library I have been enabled to obtain a photographic reproduction of the *De Hercule Eiusque Laboribus*, Urb. Lat. 201, and hope in the near future to edit it wholly or in part.

it would be easy to point out inconsistencies and contradictions, yet it is possible to trace in them a fairly coherent scheme of thought. They give in the main the impression of a mind moving from a youthful philosophy of rather rigid self-sufficiency towards a fuller humanity and a more ideal view of the universe. Coluccio links himself with the Platonic tradition in general by his conception of the world as a creation of law, based upon certain unchanging values; and with the Renaissance interpretation of that tradition in his insistence on man as an active agent through whom those values are made effective, and as a spectator gifted with the power of discerning the truth behind the instability of phenomena. For him no less than for Petrarch life and philosophy were things inseparable, but the ideal of the true philosopher, superior to the changes of fortune and the cares of the multitude, is tempered in him by a sense of social solidarity that Petrarch sometimes lacked. Some of his contemporaries regarded him as a pagan, but whatever truth the charge may have had in the early stages of his development, it would be more accurate to think of him in his maturity as a Christian Stoic with a strong tincture of Platonic idealism. In later years at least he had a firm belief in the existence of a benevolent power in the universe. God abides apart from the world in His own simple perfection, and yet is present to the whole creation as an operative force. The world of which we form a part is continually changing. Nature moves by cyclic processes, birth, growth, and decay, and human history, too, has its cycles; but behind this uncertain world, untouched by it yet working through it and in it, is the divine nature which is alone the inner necessity of things. Our rebellions against that law are as if a foolish child should try to upset the household order established by a wise father.[1] On the contrary, it is possible to make the

[1] Plus ergo Deus quam nos ipsi nos diligit. Et tamen cum optimus sit et sapientissimus et tante nos dilectionis efficacia prosequatur nos stulti et salutis propriae desertores contra id quod efficit murmuramus. Sapientissimus enim et optimus Deus longe melius et sapientius de nobis consulit quam nos ipsi. Stultum equidem crede mihi et sacrilegium est Deus resistere voluntati (Salutati, *Epistolae*, ed. Novati, 5 vols., Rome, Vol. II, p. 451. Cf. III, 436.)

principles of reality our own and to live in the present as possessors of eternal verities.

Truth and love are God's two most glorious attributes, and it is by them that He is chiefly manifest in the world. They are eternal values that exist, whether man recognizes them or not, but they cannot be fully realized in earthly conditions without man's agency. Equally he cannot live without them. Truth may have an absolute existence independent of his knowledge of it, but it is also his spiritual bread of life, the necessary presupposition that underlies his every thought and action.[1] Moreover, truth, which has its common origin and fountain head in God, is latent in all created things and in the human intellect itself, so that a man by considering the world around him and his own heart may be drawn back to God.

"Omnis quidem creatura et creaturarum inventa si quis velis recte respicere possunt ad illam eternam patriam nos certis respectibus invitare."

The germ of the Ficinian conception of natural religion appears when Salutati says that even in the worship of idols men "semper tamen in eis aliquam essentiam divini numinis somniabant," and so were more ready to receive the true faith when it was disclosed to them.[2]

Perfect truth can only be revealed by grace, but there is a measure of reality that man can conquer by his own efforts. If all good in the world is a manifestation of eternal principles knowledge

---

[1] Veritas vero quae enunciatio est qua dicimus esse quod est vel non esse quod non est quaeque veraces sumus et dicimus si vitam speculativam elegerimus adeo necessario cadit in usum nostrum quod sine ea nec docere et nec doceri possumus nam et multi quibus a nativitate vocis usus non est nutu signis quae loquuntur interrogant et respondent et multarum rerum ac passionum voluntatumque suarum veritatem exprimunt et percipiunt aliarum. Activa vera vita quomodo transigi potest, si tollas usum et commertium veritatis si cum declarari velimus de quaecumque re, quam nesciamus, vel omnino non detur responsio vel contingat semper mendacim respondere? Crede mihi, tollatur humana societas necessarium est si sustuleris omnimodo veritatem (*Ep.*, III, 444. Cf. ibid., 441). ". . . nos usu panis ad vitam minus quam usu veritatis si cuncta perspexeris indigere."

[2] Ibid., I, 323.

of whatever kind may become a means of approach to the source of good. Truth is ultimately one, but the evidences of it are scattered through a multiplicity of things, and it requires the exercise of all our faculties to make it our own. The liberal arts are so called not only because they are becoming to free men, but because they liberate the mind by raising it above the accustomed desires and pleasures of the flesh (solitis carnalibus delinimentis et voluptatibus).[1] By mental activity we withdraw ourselves from the continual flux of things and live in the eternal world, so long as our efforts are directed towards virtue. Otherwise learning may degenerate into mere tedious mechanical repetition.

"Bona et admirabilis est scientia, si tamen ad virtutis exitium dirigatur alias verissimum est illud Sapientientis qui addit scientiam addit et laborem."[2] As the understanding is enlarged and illuminated the soul discovers its own true nature and finds within itself the secrets of its own nobility and happiness. Fortune is responsible for the outward vicissitudes of life, but the man who rules his inner world in righteousness has overcome fortune. The victory can, however, only be won by continual striving, by the ceaseless quest for true knowledge and inward purity and sincerity.[3] Without this labour virtue itself would decay "sine labore marcesceret." Salutati had a horror of any self-complacency that would abandon the quest through belief in the finality of its own knowledge.[4] The vein of scepticism implicit in all Platonic thought here joins with the free and inquiring spirit of the Renaissance in the desire to try and prove all things, including our own perceptions. The later disciples of the Academy had declared knowledge to be impossible of attainment.

[1] *Ep.*, III, 68, 600. The belief that divine truth may be sought not only in the creation but in the arts (especially poetry) which are creations of man's mind pervades all Salutati's polemical letters (in *Ep.*, IV, 170–204, 205–40; III, 225–541), and the enthusiastic defence of poetry, *De Hercule eiusque laboribus* (Urb. Lat., 201).   [2] Ibid., II, 274. Cf. I, 229–30; II, 390, 385.

[3] Ibid., I, 8; III, 139, et seq. This conception of the relation between fortune and free will is treated more elaborately in *De Fato et Fortuna*.

[4] Ibid., III, 604.

Salutati, quoting St. Augustine on this point, says that the statement, though not true, is not wholly ridiculous. . . . "Nam si rite diffinire voluerimus scire nostrum nichil aluid est quam rationabiliter dubitare."[1] He attempts no elaborate answer to the gnoseological problem he has raised, largely no doubt because it is not for him the most important. The gulf that divides us from reality must be bridged, according to him, not by intellectual apprehension but by love. Truth and charity, considered as divine attributes, are equal, since God cannot in anything be less than Himself; but humanly speaking truth has the wider range. We are bound to love God and our fellow men for His sake, but truth is present even in things that we are not called upon to love.[2]

Yet if Truth and the intellect that apprehends it are infinite in range they are far less in dignity than Love and the will of which Love is the most perfect expression.[3]

The intellectual pursuit of truth cannot of itself suffice for the good life; it is only by the double exertion of intellect and will that man comes to his full stature. Life demands the exercise of all his powers, for it is through his will that the will of God is actuated in the world. The passions themselves may be so controlled as to be brought "in regione regnoque virtutum," a naturalistic conception that other humanists like L. B. Alberti were quick to emphasize.[4] Activity is raised to a position of great importance in such a moral scheme, though Salutati does not go so far as to include bodily activity under this head, as some of his successors came to do. It is continual spiritual exertion that he desires, manifesting itself in virtuous living, in political wisdom, and in the creation of those intellectual treasures which are alone immortal.[5] The motive power of all such action is the will, and that, in its most perfect form, becomes love or charity. This is the bond that holds human society together, and creates all the civilizing institutions that redeem man from barbarism. It is the

[1] *Ep.*, III, 603. [2] Ibid., III, 444–5. [3] Ibid., III, 446.
[4] Ibid., III, 471. Cf. Alberti, *Della tranquillità dell'animo opp.*, I, p. 24.
[5] Ibid., III, 542. See also ibid., 600.

foundation of true morality and of friendship, which is the highest human relation because it is based on free choice. By participating in it man is made like God, and is in the end united to Him. In the intellectual contemplation of truth the thinking subject remains distinct from the object it contemplates, but love tends to make the lover identify himself with the beloved object, try to be like it, and finally transform himself into it.[1]

Love of country assumes a dominant importance as the sentiment in which all lesser personal feelings are included and transcended. The state, if it is not precisely "man writ large," is at least the sum of all the separate pieties of home and kindred and friendship. Moral perfection, though it is an individual conquest, explicates itself naturally in social virtue.[2]

Finally, it is only by the power of love that man can reach out towards God, who is incomprehensible to human thought but who may be loved though He cannot be known.

The question of fate and free will, which Salutati discussed on more than one occasion, was another favourite theme with the writers of the Renaissance.[3] The idea of fatalism or determinism was obviously repugnant to the humanistic belief in man as an autonomous being. The debate was taken up by Valla, Alberti, Bessarion, and others, who all arrived at very similar conclusions, namely that "things contingent" are established by fate, but that man has within himself the power to rise above them if he will.[4] The freedom of the will and man's superiority to the accidents of fortune are Platonic tenets, but it is probable that the humanists referred themselves mainly to favourite stoic authors like Seneca, and, of course, to Petrarch, from whom came also

[1] *Ep.*, I, 246. Cf. I, 212; II, 138.
[2] Ibid., Vol. I, 21. Nulla enim caritas est quae sit cum caritate patriae comparanda. Parentes, filii, fratres, amici, agnati, affines et cetere, necessitudines quedam singula sunt et simul omnia collata minus habent ipsa republica.
[3] Salutati, Ibid., II, 318. Valla, *De Libertate Arbitrii*, *Opera*, Basle, 1640, p. 1000. Bessarion, *In calumniatorem Platonis*, Venice, 1516.
[4] A curious exception is Pletho's *Libellus De Fato* [Leiden, Conrad Wischoff, 1721] in which there is a marked fatalistic bias, thinly veiled by ingenious casuistry. See, e.g., p. 11.

the first defence of Epicureanism. The prominence given to the function of pleasure as a motive force in moral conduct is common to both the Neoplatonists and the Neoepicureans of the age. Their interpretation of pleasure differed considerably, but it was in them all a part of the general reaction from mediaevalism and of the vigorous apology for natural instinct and sentiment that overflowed in more and more enthusiastic panegyrics of man and nature as the Renaissance advanced. Marsigli, commenting on Petrarch's phrase "Ben providé natura," is one of the first to champion the idea of a divinity inherent in the natural order.

"Qui pruova il proposito suo per ragione presa da esemplo naturale dicendo in effetto così; cosa che natura faccia sempre è buona e utile, e ciò che contra natura si fa riesce a mal fine; adunque alla natura si vuole obbedire e non contrastare però che natura secondo Platone è la divina volonta. Dice adunque NATURA, cioè Dio ordinatore delle cose naturali."[1]

This feeling takes forms that range from the frank naturalism of Lorenzo Valla and the hymns to Venus Genitrix of Filelfo and Pontano to the pantheistic tendencies of Pico della Mirandola and Leone Ebreo and the *Deus sive natura* of Bruno.[2] In the earlier humanists, however, the emphasis is laid not on universal nature, but on man; the cosmic vision is of far less worth than the human being with his varied and brilliant potentialities.

Giannozzo Manetti, in his famous treatise, *De excellentia et dignitate hominis*, writes with the express purpose of refuting the mediaeval view of man's helplessness and misery, and speaks of his upright carriage, of the beauty and harmony of his body, of

[1] Luigi Marsigli, *Commentary on Petrarch's Canzone "Italia Mia"* in Società di Curiosità Letteraria, Bologna, 1863.
[2] Cf. Valla, *De Voluptate*, *Opera*, p. 906. Principio igitur quod de natura dixisti, possem pie religiose et non aversis hominum auribus respondere. Quod natura finxit atque formavit id nisi sanctam laudabilemque esse non posse. Ut hoc caelum quod supra nos volvitur divinis noctisque luminibus distinctum, tantaque ratione pulchritudine, utilitate compositum. Quid commemorem maria, quid terras, quid aerem quid montes plate compositum? Quid pecudes, cicures, aves, pisces, arbores, segetes? Nihil invenies non summa ut dixi ratione vel specie vel utilitate perfectum instructum, ornatum.

the skill and genius by which he has created all the arts of civilization, of his capacity for virtuous living, and of his unique place in the creation as spectator and interpreter of the other works of God.[1] Man is before all the alert and conscious agent of the divine will. "Stare quidem," wrote Ambrogio Traversari to his brother, "pro castris Domini exspedit semper et in eius laborare militia qui nos de tenebris vocavit in admirabile lumen suum ut simus cooperatores gratiae Dei."[2] The perfection that Traversari had in mind was a contemplative and ascetic one, but the means of achieving it was by the deliberate return of the spirit to itself (In interiora tabernacula quantum licet nusquam egredere).[3] The divine, far from being immeasurably removed from man, is in fact his most intimate possession. "Alioquin non illum invenire poteritis quia verbum Dei non longe est ab unoquoque vestrum; sed in ore nostro et in corde nostro. Abs te itaque ad te occurre, ut eum invenias et per illum ad illum pervenire merearis. Praeparate illis sedem in corde vestro ivstitiam ac iudicium."[4] Few perhaps among the other humanists felt this alliance of God and man so sacramentally, but the sense that the human soul is in some manner divine, whether by reason of the indwelling spirit of God or simply as the loftiest form of being that our known universe can show, is a recurrent undertone in their works. Reverence for the individual soul and the tendency to regard it as a free and creative activity are sentiments common to them all.

They are implicit in the whole humanistic conception of education in which so much of the thought of the age is concentrated. If it were necessary to summarize in the fewest words the teaching of a long series of educational and moral treatises, one might call it a desire for the full and spontaneous development

---

[1] G. Manetti, *De excellentia et dignitate hominis*, Basle, 1532. See study by G. Gentile in *Giordano Bruno ed il pensiero del Rin*, Florence, 1925, 2nd ed., pp. 1 et seq.

[2] A. Traversari, *Epistolae*, ed Méhus, Florence, 1759, 2 vols., Vol. II, Bk. XI, Letter 393, p. 512.

[3] Ibid., Bk. XI, Letter 408, p. 526.

[4] Ibid., Bk. XIII, Letter 526, p. 639.

of the whole man considered as a harmony of body and soul. Freedom is essential for such development; virtue is but another name for liberty. Fear and superstition and vice are the chains of the soul and must at all costs be eliminated.[1] For this reason children should not be submitted to degrading punishments, but should, as far as possible, be won to obedience by love.[2]

The liberal life, which consists of action and thought, must be fed by culture.[3] Study builds up the mind for the worthiest things—honour, glory, and virtue—not by adorning it with extraneous ornament, but by stimulating its inward growth and helping it to discover its own true nature.[4] So one finds a continual recall to experience and an impatience with all merely abstract and wordy learning. An excessive preoccupation with literature in the narrowest sense of the term was at times the bane of humanism, but its best spirits rejected an ideal so limited. A man's education consists not in amassing ready-made knowledge, but in building himself up in virtue by the deliberate exercise of all his powers. The wise and diligent study of letters is necessary as a sure foundation for all culture, but it must be carried on with discernment.

---

[1] Pier Paolo Vergerio, *De ingenuis moribus*, ed. Gnesotto, Padua, 1918, pp. 15 et seq.

[2] Maffeo Vegio, *De Educatione Liberorum*, Magna Bibliotheca Veterum Patrum, 1622, t. XV, pp. 839 et seq., Ch. XVI, p. 849.

[3] The ideal was not merely a literary fabrication. It found a practical expression in the work of the best humanist educators. The harmonious development of body and mind by the alternation of physical activity and study; the careful training of the individual as a citizen capable of serving the community in peace and war by exercising for its benefit his own peculiar gifts; the importance of delight in education, and therefore of the freedom and dignity of the spirit are the underlying principles upon which the famous schools of Guarino Veronese and Vittorino da Feltre were conducted.

"Il motivo ispiratore che guidava tutta l'azione educativa di Vittorino era questo: che si plasmassero esseri umani i quali svolgessero la loro attività come realizzazione del divino" [Saitta, *Educazione dell'Umanesimo*, Ch. VII, p. 114].

[4] P. P. Vergerio, *Epistolario*. R. Deputazione Veneta di St. Patria. *Ep.* XLIII, 62, and throughout *De ingenuis moribus*. Filelfo, *Orationes*, Venice, 1496, pp. 74 et seq. Battista Guarino, "De ordine Docendi et Studendi" in Woodward, *Vittorino da Feltre*, Cambridge, 1897, p. 162. Maffeo Vezio, o.c., Bk. II, p. 856.

The mind must be fed on the best things and must at the same time submit all its studies to vigilant criticism. It is the arbiter of its own intellectual life and must think and select and create for itself, preserving always a close contact between theoretical knowledge and experience.

The principle of "doubting rationally" begins to make headway amongst all the uncritical enthusiasms of the age, preparing the way for the Reformation and for the growth of modern philosophy and of the physical sciences.

Not that science as it is now understood appealed to the humanists. Natural philosophy, the knowledge of phenomena, they regard generally as interesting, delightful, and laudable, but as extraneous to the one fundamental human science, the knowledge of the soul, and therefore not of the first importance. Man's one absolute need is to know the things that pertain to his peace. To use his only real possessions, body, soul, and time, so that he may attain the utmost perfection and at the same time the utmost felicity of which he is capable must be his goal; and the means by which to reach it are inherent in himself.[1]

A man's life is, in fact, as Petrarch had tried to demonstrate, a continual process of self-creation. Here the aesthetic bias of the age makes itself felt in the unceasing aspiration towards harmony and completeness. A noble human being is at once the most consummate artist and the most glorious of works of art. With much that is merely literary in their attitude the humanists are united in the sincerity of their belief that personality is the final miracle of beauty in a glorious universe.

Yet though virtue is pre-eminently an inward and individual thing, they almost with one voice insist on its social aspect. Their highest ideal is a fusion of the good Christian and the good

[1] "Ma questa altra parte di filosofia è tutta nostra, guida de gli huomini, maestra delle virtù, scacciatrice di vitii, amica del ben vivere, consigliatrice de buoni e ferma certezza di nostra vita, da la quale non a caso come le bestie, ma con ordine diritto nel vero fine s'impara a vivere."
Matteo Palmieri, *Libro della Vita Civile In Firenze per li heredi di Philippo di Giunta ne l'anno del Signore*, MDXXIX alli 5: di ottobre, p. 19 verso.

citizen.¹ Even Cristoforo Landino, in the Neoplatonic *Quaestiones Camaldulenses*, grows eloquent in praise of the active life, though he yields the palm to the contemplative. There is everywhere the feeling that the highest knowledge cannot be attained unless this realm of social and political virtue has been won. No man can penetrate into the mystery of things until he has achieved and practised the "political virtues," just as Aeneas had to pick the golden fruits before he was able to descend to the shades.²

Virtue, wisdom, and prowess, mental or physical, are precious contributions to the sacred whole of human history, besides being the gifts due from the individual to the State which begins now to assume the guise of a sovereign spiritual entity to which the citizen must subordinate and at need sacrifice himself.

"Putare perfecte (ut ait Plato) unusquisque debet omnia qua possidet eorum esse qui nos genuere quique educavere: secundo loco: eorum quibus cum geniti et educati sumus. Nam si contentio quidam et comparatio fiat quibus plurimum debeamus post deum et patria sequuntur parentes quorum beneficiis, et quidem gravissimis astricti sumus, sequuntur liberi, fratres, et bene convenientes propinqui."³

Side by side with this foreshadowing of the sovereign state rises the type of the ideal ruler, modelled on the philosopher-king of the *Republic*; the man who clearly understands himself and his duties and who, by careful self-discipline, has made himself capable of giving law to others.⁴

Certain other ideas that became of central importance with the

---

[1] P. P. Vergerio, *De Ing. Mor.*, ed. c., p. 34. M. Vegio, o.c., Bk. VI, Ch. 6, p. 888. See also Saitta, *Educazione dell'Umanesimo*, Venice, 1928. San Bernardino da siena, Ch. IX, p. 136.

[2] M. Palmieri, o.c., p. 21. The moral system of Palmieri's poem, *La Città di Vita*, is largely an elaboration of this idea.

[3] Platina, *De optimo cive*, in a volume containing the *Historia Pontificis* and other works, Leiden, 1512, p. K. IIII verso.

[4] See Francesco Patrizi, *De regno et regis institutione*, Paris, 1518. Filelfo, *Orationes*, Venice, 1496, Treatise on the prince, p. 74. Aeneas Sylvius Piccolomini [Pius II], *Opera*, Basle, 1551, p. 965. Vergerio, *Epistolario*, No. XCV, p. 140.

Florentine Neoplatonists receive comparatively little attention from their forerunners. The immortality of the soul, one of Ficino's dearest themes, they treat on the whole very scantily. They do not, naturally, deny the belief, but they have no intimate conviction of its truth. Man may be a god-like being, but something fails them when they try to picture him apart from the conditions in which they see him live and move. There are, of course, exceptions. Giannozzo Manetti, in his *De excellentia et dignitate hominis*, claims immortality as the natural and fitting consummation for a creature so glorious as man. One may, if one will, add Valla's picture of heaven as an endless prolongation of pleasure, physical and mental. Yet it is generally true that the shadow of death broods on the hopefulness and vigour of humanistic literature. The world and the varied life of man have become so vivid and so dear that to be taken from them is to pass into a state dim and uncertain as the world beyond the Styx. The humanist, in the very moment of exultation, is painfully conscious of the instability of the life on which he has fixed his hopes. Even to Salutati, one of the devoutest of the band, death appears as the greatest of all evils, a disruption of the human harmony. Eternal life apart from the present world is a thing but faintly realized. In its place rises the conception of an immortality of glory, survival in the minds of men by the record of great deeds or of intellectual excellence, since "extinctus est cuius pariter et vita finitur et fama."[1] Yet at times a doubt of the value or the permanence of this posthumous

---

[1] Salutati, *Ep.*, II, 106. Salutati in point of fact shows three distinct phases of thought on this question. In youth he affected a Stoic indifference to death; later he spoke of it as the worst of all evils; finally he came to regard it as a great evil in the natural order but as a happiness for the good man in the spiritual order. *Ep.*, I, p. 186, is interesting among his early letters for containing a reputed dying speech of Hermes Trismegistus that ends: ". . . Jam michi repleri videor suavitate mirifica, qui cogitem meo me auctori coniunctum, omnique mutabilitatis condicione fugata inviolabilis perfectique boni fore participem. Cavetote itaque ne cum hoc relicto corpusculo meliore mei parte visus fuerim de loco viventium evolasse me quasi mortuum lugeatis. Nunc enim vobiscum mortuus sum et tunc demum vitae redditus vos apud summum omnium rerum opificem expectabo."

renown strikes coldly on the humanists, and calls forth the most poignant note of all the Renaissance, the overwhelming melancholy that lingers in an elegy of Politian's, *Ah miseri somnus et levis umbra sumus*, or in the beautiful Landor-like passage where Lorenzo Valla shudders at the nescientness of death.[1]

Two other favourite motives—the idealization of Love and of Beauty—are latent rather than explicit in the literature of this period. Love is not the mystic rhythm of ascent and descent or the cosmic force that it becomes with the Neoplatonists; yet it has sovereign dignity as the true basis of morality, the creator of all civilizing influences, the power by which man may reach out of himself and draw near to God. The preoccupation with ideals of comeliness and aesthetic perfection is widespread, too, but there is as yet little attempt to analyse these ideals or find any philosophical implications in them.[2]

The sojourn of the Greeks in Italy for the Councils of Ferrara and Florence marked an epoch in the philosophical developments of the century.[3] By the prominence it gave to the Platonic-

---

[1] It is almost impossible to open any work of this period without being confronted with the idea of glory. For the mood of doubt see besides Politian [Elegy on Albiera] in *Opera*, Basle, 1553, p. 587. M. Vegio, o.c., Bk. VI, Ch. 6, p. 887. The passage of Valla is in *De Voluptate*, *Opera*, p. 935. I quote a fragment: "Nam enim recte sit de fama post mortem laborare. Nam quid ad defunctum pertinet id, cuius sensum non habet? Tu labores, tu industriam, tu obitum meum supra sepulchrum ad lyram aut ad citharam cantas et aures meae non audiunt. In ore sum omnis populi et membra mea assidue dissolvuntur. Non magis ad me ista perveniunt, quam illa liliorum rosarum florumque in busta conspersio. Non resupinum corpus erigunt, non delectant, non iuvant."

[2] These two points will require a little further elucidation, but it seems more appropriate to give it when it is time to discuss the problems of Art and the "Trattato d'amore."

[3] Council of Ferrara, January 1438 till January 1439. Council of Florence, February 1439 till April 1442. The assembly was then prorogued to Rome until 1445. The Greeks arrived in Italy in February 1438 and most of them returned home in October of the following year, though Bessarion, George of Trebizond, and others remained in Italy. Among those who came to Italy in 1438 were Pletho, Bessarion, Isidore of Salonika, and possibly Theodore Gaza. George of Trebizond may have been in Italy as early as 1418. See Sabbadini, *La Scoperta dei Codici*, Florence, 1914, Vol. II, p. 66.

Aristotelian controversy, and by bringing the Italians into direct contact with the Greek scholars at a time when they were themselves in a state of keen intellectual activity, it prepared the way for the triumph of Ficino and his followers. Greek philosophy had been decadent for many centuries, but at the period of the Councils it seemed to have broken into a last flare of life, as if to kindle the waiting minds in Italy before being itself extinguished. Aristotelianism found an important exponent in Georgius Scholarius [Gennadius] and Platonism in that strange personality George Gemisthus Pletho and in his pupil, Bessarion. Other scholars of varying merit—John Argyropoulos, Isidore of Salonika, George of Trebizond, Theodore Gaza, Michael Apostolius, the two Lascaris and Andronicus Callixtus—grouped themselves around these central figures and shared in their disputes. Pletho, who came to Italy already famous and far advanced in years, has been the subject of some controversy. The commonly accepted belief that he wished to found a new pagan religion has recently been challenged, and may be regarded as questionable; but it is certain that he hoped to find, in the past greatness of Greece, forces capable of raising his country from her present degradation and that he favoured Platonic idealism and some form of Spartan morality for the purpose. He may or may not have wished to give them a Christian interpretation.[1]

[1] The belief in Pletho's paganism is questioned by G. Ruggiero, *Storia della Filosofia: Rinascimento e Riforma*, Laterza Bari, 2 vols., 1930; Vol. I, p. 117. The evidence for it, as he points out, rests mainly on the untrustworthy witness of George of Trebizond; and it is certainly unlikely, on the face of it, that the Greek Church would have sent, on a most vital and delicate mission, a man not merely lax or sceptical in matters of faith, but actively hostile to Christianity. Pletho played a distinguished part in the negotiations between the two churches and contributed to the polemic *De Processione Spiritu Sancti*, and his Latin works contain little that is definitely unorthodox, beyond a general suggestion of fatalism. Still the fragments of the $N\acute{o}\mu o\iota$ strike one as at least suspicious. [See the edition of C. Alexander, *Traité des Lois*, Greek text and French translation with introduction and notes, Paris, 1858.] It is true that the gaps in the argument have to be filled in with the comments of Gennadius who records Pletho's championship of metempsychosis, polygamy, and other pagan beliefs and practices. Gennadius was one of Pletho's life-long opponents, but by all

He had an unbounded reverence for Plato, but regarded the Neoplatonists, especially Proclus and Porphyry, as the surest interpreters of Platonism, and Platonism itself as the culminating point in a philosophical tradition that had its origin in Zoroaster and Orpheus and Hermes Trismegistus and the obscure beginnings of human wisdom. He had evidently much of the taste for the arcane and the extravagant that appeared in some members of the Florentine group.[1]

At the time of the Councils his teaching had no widespread immediate effect. Perhaps he urged his opinions rather tactlessly on a society which was still mainly Aristotelian and which was passing enthusiastically through a great period of Latin humanism. His violent partisanship, too, may well have repelled many of the Italians with whom he associated, since they tended generally towards a large inclusiveness and often attempted to reconcile the most incompatible views.

Yet, if Pletho did not immediately gain many supporters, he made one friend of the first importance in Cosimo de' Medici. The two had many philosophical conversations which fired Cosimo with the determination to make Florence the centre of a new Platonic school. It was perhaps as a corollary to these talks that Pletho published his treatise *De Platonicae atque Aristotelicae Philosophiae Differentia*,[2] ostensibly a comparative study of the two systems, but in reality a sourly disapproving criticism of

accounts a reasonable and even respectful one; and the text as it stands suggests much more an infiltration of Christian ideas, moral and liturgical, into an essentially pagan scheme, than an attempt to absorb the best qualities of paganism into Christianity. There remains also the fact that Pletho would not allow the book to be known during his lifetime though it may have been written as early as 1428. [See Alexandre, o.c., Introduction, p. xiii.] Perhaps the question of whether he was or was not a consummate hypocrite must remain undecided.

[1] This tendency may be traced in the *Νόμοι* and in *Oracula Magica Zoroastris cum Scoliis Plethonis et Pselli nunc primum editi e Bibliotheca Regia Studio*, Johannis Opsopoei, Paris, 1607. A collection of moral and mystical *dicta* of no special originality. Cf. Pico della Mirandola, *De Arte Cabbalistica*, *Opera*, Basle, 1572, Vol. I.
[2] Basle, 1574.

Aristotle. Without being strikingly original the pamphlet is typical of the Platonic argument as it appeared in the polemics of the age.

It was the first important contribution to a quarrel that continued to smoulder, with sporadic outbursts of angry controversy, for about thirty years. The details of this long and often acrimonious dispute, complicated as it was by personal and religious differences, need not be considered here.[1] There is little originality in the ill-regulated enthusiasm of the Aristotelian, George of Trebizond, and the Platonist, Michael Apostolius, or in the milder polemics of Theodore Gaza and Bessarion that occupied the years before 1464. Moreover, the controversy remained, until its final phase, a domestic affair among the Greeks, and one in which the Italian scholars scarcely shared. Nicholas V played a certain part in it, through the translations of Greek works which he caused to be published in Rome during his pontificate. These were undertaken with the ostensible purpose of making Greek thought accessible to Western Europe, but a subtle latinity of interpretation made them in reality useful weapons in the hands of the Church, a fact which the Greeks were quick to see and to resent.

One of the most famous of these translations was the version of the *Laws* by George of Trebizond, whose innumerable errors and falsifications were unsparingly exposed by Bessarion. Largely as a revenge for these criticisms George published, in 1464, his *Comparatio Platonis et Aristotlis*, in which he vented the accumulated spite of years on his opponents, living and dead.[2] Pletho he described as a second Mahomet, intent on paganizing the world, while on Plato he heaps every imaginable calumny from ignorance and want of literary skill to the worst forms of immorality. The book had a considerable diffusion and may have provided Paul II

---

[1] The principal documents may be found in Migne, *Patrologie Grecque*, Vols. 159, 160, 161. See, for accounts of the quarrel; Fiorentino, *Il Risorgimento Filosofico del'* 400, Naples, 1888. H. Vast, *Le Cardinal Bessarion*, Paris, 1878.

[2] Printed at Basle, 1523.

with an additional excuse for his persecution of Pomponio Leto, who had formed at Rome an "Academy" modelled on Ficino's group in Florence, which professed a Neopagan Platonism more fanatical than profound. This persecution took place in 1468, and in the year following Bessarion, with really notable courage, published his *In Calumniatorem Platonis*, begun in 1465.[1]

Bessarion's part in the philosophic quarrel was throughout that of a mediator and reconciler of opposing claims. While controversy raged among his fellow countrymen he used his influence steadily on the side of moderation, and it was fitting that he should bring the question of Plato's pre-eminence out of the enclosed circle of the Greeks and proclaim it to the world. His advocacy was especially valuable to the Italians who held him in high honour. He had come to Italy for the Councils, and had there been reconciled to the Roman Church and raised to the cardinalate. He was well known as a man of integrity and as a sane, conscientious scholar; and, though a professing Platonist, he had translated the *Metaphysics* of Aristotle and had urged Theodore Gaza to defend the Aristotelian system against the attacks of Pletho and Argyropoulos. It has been said of him that he did as much for the cause of Plato in Italy as Ficino himself; and certainly it is doubtful if Ficino's major works would have met with such wide and eager acceptance if Bessarion's book had not been written. The *In Calumniatorem Platonis* is remarkable not so much for novelty of thought as for soberness of argument and solidity of culture. Bessarion shared in some errors common among his contemporaries, as when he read into Plato the conception of the Plotinian "Trinity," but he was deeply read in both Platonism and peripateticism and his words, sincerely pondered, came weighted with authority. He did, in fact, what Pletho had professed to do in the *De Platonica*, that is he attempted a comparative study of the two philosophies, but he pointed out

[1] *In Calumniatorem Platonis* was first printed in Rome, 1469, in fol. and again in *Bessarionis Opera*, Venice, Aldus, 1516 (cited here). This also contains Bessarion's translation of Aristotle's *Metaphysics*. For Pomponio Leto see Zabughin, G. *Pomponio Leto*, Rome, 1909.

that a preference for the one need not exclude a sound appreciation of the other. He appealed to the literary men of the age by his long defence of Plato's qualities as a writer and scholar. He conciliated the orthodox by demonstrating the affinities between Platonism and Christianity. There was nothing new in any of these lines of defence, but they had never before been treated so systematically by a churchman of such eminence. A more original point, and one that his successors seized upon with eagerness, was his endeavour to prove the substantial agreement of the two philosophers on many subjects.

In the opening chapter Bessarion says that he writes in order to defend Plato from three charges commonly put forward against him—the first, want of culture (imperitia), the second, incompatibility with the Christian revelation, and the third, immorality of life and doctrine. He believes that these accusations proceed from ignorance, for Plato, though well known and often quoted by the early Church, is imperfectly known by the present generation.

Taking the question of Plato's "imperitia" first, he points out that this cannot be proved by the fact that he wrote little. This was only in accordance with the example of Pythagoras and others and was in harmony with the precepts of the Gospel. Plato was in reality accomplished in the arts of rhetoric and far more eloquent than Aristotle; he had great skill in logic, by which he was able to prove such weighty postulates as the immortality of the soul and the generation of the heavens; and he was great as a mathematician and a natural philosopher, forestalling and excelling many of Aristotle's conclusions. Above all, he penetrated as no other pagan had done into the mysteries of true religion.[1]

This introduces the further question of Plato's affinities with Christianity.[2] The argument leads Bessarion into some rather

[1] *In Calumniatorem Platonis*, Bk. I, Chs. 1–9.
[2] Ibid., Bk. II. The idea of the Trinity discussed in Ch. IV. Plato's affinity with Christianity was one of the central arguments of all his Renaissance apologists. The belief that he had learned from the Hebrews is mentioned by Leonardo Bruni in the preface to his translation of the *Phaedo*; both Ficino and Pico speak of him as an "Attic Moses." Three little-known judgments may have the

perilous analogies between the theories of Plato and the Neoplatonists and the doctrine of the Trinity; and involves him in by-paths of Pythagorean number mysticism. In the third book he attempts an elaborate apology for Plato's ignorance of the true doctrine of the Trinity, of which he had none the less a shadowy apprehension.

This appears to Bessarion as the most serious flaw in a prointerest of curiosities. Matteo Palmieri not only calls Plato the most Christian of the ancient philosophers but places the Sybils and Hermes Trismegistus beside Moses and the Hebrew prophets as inspired teachers of mankind. On the other hand, he consigns Apuleius and Zoroaster to Hell as magicians [II, 32, 17].

> Platone innanzi agli altri il più sovrano
> Pensò molto alto, e suo fin esse volle
> Quanto men può farsi da Dio strano.
> Ad questo disse la virtu estolle
> Con gli strumenti aggiunta che la fanno
> Venire allacto el fructo d'essa colle.
> Ell secondo di que che pur ne fanno
> Aristotile fu, che volle l'uso
> Delle virtù con vostra vita vanno.

Magl., II, 11, 41. *Città di Vita*, III, 4, 30. Cf. Ugolino di V. Verino, *Paradisus*, MS. Laur., XXXIX, 40, p. 97.

> ... est Plato similem cui nulla tulerunt
> Saecula cui rerum sensum natura reclusit
> Ut quod mortali licitum est, cognoscere novit
> His animus miro dictis ardebat amore
> Compellare virum, e dextram congiúngere dextra
> Sed pudor, et tantj tenuit reverentia vatis
> At prior ille inquit nate o melioribus annis
> Cum verbum christique fides totum occupet orbem
> Christicolis nunc lux ablatis clara tenebris
> Fulget et aeterni portam referavit olimpi.

Also Giovanni Nesi, *Poema Visione*, Cod. Ricc. 2750 [O, IV, 32]. Canto VII, v. 24 et seq., in which the Platonic account of the Creation is described as most akin to the Biblical one.

> Hor se la tua lyra havessi Orpheo
> Canterei come et gli elementi et il mondo
> Diterminò et infinito il signor feo
> In numero creò misura et pondo
> Tempio si bel che tre persone sembra
> Nume divino mirabile et profondo.

foundly Christian conception of truth. Plato believed that mind was the creator and ruler of all things, whereas Aristotle merely says of natural things that God and nature do nothing in vain and that the world is eternal. Plato, in closer conformity with Christian belief, held that the causes of the universal order were the will and goodness of God. The world reflects the eternal reality, but has not itself existed eternally, since the first matter, the primal formless stuff that is capable of receiving all forms, was created out of nothing. All creatures are preserved from age to age by the processes of generation, and Plato did not think it consistent with the goodness of God for Him to destroy what he had made. The world, though it began at a definite point of time, will not at another point be annihilated.

Plato, moreover, believed in Providence. He prayed and sacrificed, believed in a future life, and insisted on the need of faith for the attainment of righteousness, points upon which Aristotle's views are difficult to define. At the same time, he declares that man's will is entirely free and not subject to fate. The divine nature is the cause of all good, but evil deeds are man's responsibility and not God's. The mind of man is incorruptible and exists before the body. Between mind and body is the intermediate essences, Soul, immortal in itself, but capable of being imbruted by the vices of the flesh. In the cosmos, as in the individual, Soul, which is diffused through the whole creation, is the link between the sensible or material and the intelligible or spiritual. The first principles of things are known only to God and to those men who are most dear to Him.[1]

In the third book Bessarion's argument becomes a maze of theological subtleties into which it is not necessary to follow him here. In the fourth he sets out to defend Plato's moral character from the charges brought against it. Views such as those on the relation of the sexes in the *Republic* are explained as familiar to the age and country of the writer, and are confronted with examples from actual life. Finally, the criticism of George of Trebizond's

[1] Bessarion, o.c., Bk. II, Chs. 3, 4, 5, 6, 7, 8, 9, 10.

inaccurate translation of the *Laws* is printed as a decisive blow at the calumniator.

Bessarion's work was enthusiastically received.[1] The cult of Plato seemed at last to be settled upon a reasoned, scholarly, and acceptable basis; and Aristotle, for the time being, passed to the second rank in the philosophic hierarchy. He became a pagan sage of great but by no means infallible wisdom, while Plato was exalted as one scarcely less inspired than the Hebrew prophets. It was not far from the apology of Bessarion to the full ardours of the Platonic Academy of Florence. The tradition that Ficino kept a lamp continually burning before the bust of Plato may be a legend but conveys a truth.[2]

[1] See, for an instance, Platina's Panegyric on Bessarion in *Historia pontificis*, etc., Leiden, 1512. Ficino, *Opera*, Basle, 1573, Vol. I, p. 616.

[2] Nothing in the last paragraph should be taken to mean that the enthusiasm for Plato broke the continuity of the Aristotelian tradition in Italy. Peripateticism was still the philosophy of the Church and in great measure the philosophy of the schools. Nor should it be forgotten that Neoplatonism itself was largely interpenetrated with Aristotelian elements.

Even in the great days of the Florentine Academy there were scholars like Ermolao Barbaro who wrote to Politian:

"Omnes enim philosophi discipulorum suorum ingenio probabant. Pythagoras ex insomniis quae per quietem vidissent, Plato in conviviis atque potu, Aristoteles utroque melius ex ipsa sermonis obscuritate, ad quam non praesentes adeo, sed et posteros exploravit quasi aquila infantes suos ut quorum oculos connivere senserit, praecipitet e schola tanquam adulterinos; quorum vero acies firma contra steterit educet et recipiat ut legitimos atque suos. [Angeli Politiani et Aliorum Virorum illustrium Epistolarum Libri XII. Hanoviae Apud Heredes Guillielmi Antonii, 1612, p. 566. The letter dates from *c.* 1480.]

With the Counter-Reformation Aristotelianism was reinstated officially in something like the pre-eminence it had held during the Middle Ages; but even in the early part of the sixteenth century its professors were by no means inactive —witness the controversy on the immortality of the soul that centred round Pomponazzi. All through the century, moreover, the influence of Aristotle on the physical sciences and on critical historical and political theories was predominant.

Though the Aristotelians preserved the traditional language, and the traditional methods of the school, it would be a mistake to think of their activities, even during the Counter-Reformation, as purely reactionary. Within the ancient forms and under the tortuous casuistries with which the later writers try to protect themselves from the imputation of heresy the force of humanistic thought makes itself felt principally in sceptical and naturalistic tendencies. [See Ruggiero, o.c., Vol. II, pp. 1 et seq.]

TRANSLATIONS

Page 36. *Omnis quidem* . . .
Every creature and invention of the creatures, if thou wilt rightly consider it, can, by certain recollections, call us back to that eternal fatherland.

Page 36. *semper tamen* . . .
did ever dream that there was in them some essence of the divine spirit.

Page 37. *Bona et admirabilis* . . .
Good and admirable is knowledge if it be directed to virtuous ends, but otherwise it is most true, as, says the Ecclesiast, that whoso increaseth knowledge increaseth labour.

Page 38. *Nam si rite* . . .
For if we would define it rightly our knowledge is no more than rational doubt.

Page 38. *in regione regnoque virtutum.*
within the sphere and dominion of the virtues.

Page 40. *Qui pruova* . . .
Here he proveth his contention by an argument taken from a natural example saying, in effect, thus: what nature doth is ever good and useful, and whatever is done contrary to nature cometh ever to ill; therefore must nature ever be obeyed and not thwarted, since nature, according to Plato, is the divine will. Therefore he saith NATURE, that is to say God, the ordainer of natural things.

Page 41. *Stare quidem* . . .
It is expedient truly [wrote Ambrogio Traversari to his brother] ever to be stationed in the courts of the Lord and to strive in the service of Him who has called us out of darkness into His marvellous light whereby we are made fellow-workers with the grace of God.

Page 41. *Alioquin non illum* . . .
Ye can in no otherwise find Him, because the word of God is not far from each one of you, but on our lips and in our hearts. From thyself flee therefore unto thyself that thou mayest find Him and be worthy through Him to come to Him. Prepare for Him in your heart a dwelling and justice and judgment.

Page 44. *Putare perfecte (ut ait Plato)* . . .
Every man (as Plato saith) ought to hold all that he possesses as belonging wholly to those who begot us and reared us, and, in the second place, to

those with whom we were born and bred. For if any dispute or comparison should arise concerning those to whom we are most indebted, there follow, after God and our country, our parents to whom we are bound by their most weighty benefits and then our children, our brethren, and our kinsfolk in due order.

Page 45. Extinctus est . . .
He is dead indeed whose life and fame end together.

CHAPTER III

MARSILIO FICINO AND THE PLATONIC ACADEMY OF FLORENCE

WHEN Bessarion's book appeared the literary circle commonly known as the Platonic Academy of Florence was already well established. The name is time-honoured and convenient and may stand if one remembers that it does not represent an organized society with rules, officers, and a settled programme of study, but the group of friends and disciples who gathered round Marsilio Ficino and who were bound together by a common interest in his teaching and by the friendship and patronage of the Medici. They were artists, poets, men of letters, and professional and civic dignitaries rather than philosophers; and if they called Ficino "alter Plato" and held banquets on the seventh of November it was more because such practices pleased their imagination and liberal sense of pageantry than because they had exalted them into ordinances.[1]

[1] Della Torre in his *Storia dell'Academia Platonica di Firenze*, Florence, 1902, discusses the title of the Academy at great length and with his usual massive erudition. According to him the first to call Ficino's circle the Academy was Stephanus Joanninensis, writing in 1524 [*Della T.*, p. 9]. Ficino himself, however, seems to have used the title. [See *Opera*, Basle, 1573, 2 vols., Vol. I, *Epistolae*, Bk. III, p. 730. To Bernardo Bembo. "Rogas quid nam agat Academia? Amat Bembum. Quid rursus? Veneratur Academia Bembum."] The fact does not, of course, prove that the Academy possessed any rigid organization. The impression one gathers from contemporary literature is almost that of an amazing game of make-believe. The inner intention of the Academy was solemn, but its outward celebrations seem to have been carried on in the friendly and easy spirit of the "Platonica familia" that its members claimed to be. The reunions that took place in the Orti Oricellari after Ficino's death, though ostensibly a continuation of the "Platonic Academy," were actually more concerned with linguistic and political questions and even with political conspiracy, than with philosophy, although Ficino's faithful disciple, Francesco di Diacceto, was a prominent figure in the discussions.

Ficino, in a letter to Martino-Uranio [*Opera*, Vol. I, p. 936, *c*. 1492] gives a list of all those who had at any time frequented his discourses. Few laid claim

Ficino himself, who was born in 1433, was the son of Cosimo de' Medici's physician.[1] While he was still a youth Cosimo detected his promise and supplied him with the means and opportunities of study, hoping that he would become in course of time the restorer of Platonism in Italy. Marsilio accepted his patron's plans with the fervour of an apostle. His uneventful life was spent almost exclusively in Florence and its environs, and wholly dedicated to the work he loved and to the service of his many friends. He was first the tutor and afterwards the trusted adviser of Lorenzo, and besides enjoying great popularity in Florence he had a wide circle of correspondents in Italy and beyond. At some time between the ages of twenty-five and forty he passed through a long period of religious depression due to his inability to reconcile his first philosophical enthusiasms with his faith.[2] Little is known of this episode,

to being philosophers; only Pico della Mirandola, Diacceto, and Peregrino Aglio being accorded the title. Among the poets Lorenzo and Politian are pre-eminent, but the group included Girolamo Benivieni, Matteo Palmieri, Ugolino, and Michele di V. Verino, Giovanni di Francesco Nesi, Lorenzo di Giovanni Buonincontri, Giovanni Cavalcanti, Naldo Naldi, Antonio Pelotti, Francesco di G. Berlinghieri, and Alessandro Braccesi. Other men of letters were Cristoforo Landino, L. B. Alberti, Bernardo del Nero, Antonio Manetti, Filippo Valori, Tommaso Benci, Alamanno Rinuccini, Antonio Canegiano, etc.

[1] The principal sources for the biography of Ficino are the *Vita*, by Giovanni Corsi, 1506, ed. A. M. Bandini, Pisa apud Augustinum Pizzorno, 1771, and L. Galeotti, *Saggio intorno alla vita ed agli scritti di M. F.*, Arch. St. It., N. Serie, 1859, Vol. IX, Pt. II, p. 29; Vol. X, Pt. I, p. 1. Also Della Torre, o.c., and the letters of Ficino, Pico, Politian, and Lorenzo. Much the best study of F.'s philosophy is G. Saitta's *La Filosofia di M. F.*, Messina, 1923, to which I am deeply indebted, though I cannot help feeling that the author has perhaps pushed his philosopher a little further along the road of subjectivism than Ficino himself would have consented to go. The edition of F.'s works used throughout is that of 1573, cited in note 1, p. 57.

[2] The date and the exact nature of this crisis have been much discussed by students of Ficino. The point is an obscure one, as there is scarcely any definite information to be had, but on the whole I should be inclined to agree with A. Conti [Arch. St. It., t. II, Pt. II, p. 172, 1865], who places the period of doubt rather early in F.'s life, i.e. roughly between 1458 and 1468, and before the composition, or anyhow before the completion of the *Theologia Platonica*. This view is supported by the fact that the *T.P.* seems to contain F.'s considered

but the works of his maturity definitely bring his massive classical and philosophical culture into the service of Christianity. In 1475 he entered the Church and scrupulously performed his duties as a parish priest until his death in 1499.[1] He has some claim to be regarded as one of the saints of humanism. He stands out from the other men of letters of the age by his singular disinterestedness. His work, which he looked upon as a sacred charge, was carried on unflinchingly throughout a lifetime of ill-health. In his personal life he was almost an ascetic, but his gentle and affectionate nature won him the love and veneration of the most divergent types of his fellow citizens.

The mass of his extant writings is very large, but does not represent by any means the whole of his output. Until 1463 he was engaged on a number of short philosophical essays and some translations of minor importance, and many of these youthful works have disappeared. In 1463 he began his great translation of Plato on which he worked for twenty years. During the same period he undertook an intensive study of Christian authors, especially of St. Augustine, and produced his two most important original works, the *Theologia Platonica De Immortalitate Animae* and the *De Christiana Religione*.

The visit of Pico della Mirandola to Florence in 1484 inspired him to begin the translation and exposition of Plotinus, and of the principal works of the lesser Neoplatonists. He completed the commentary on the *Enneads* in 1491, and after that wrote but little more. His letters, many of which were published in his lifetime, seem to have acted throughout as a sort of clearing-house for his

opinions. He quotes it in the *De Christiana Religione* and never in any subsequent work refuted it; but it is fairly established that the *T.P.* as we know it is the work of the years 1468-74 [see Saitta, o.c., Ch. II, pp. 28, 29], and it seems improbable that this massive expression of faith should coincide with a serious state of uncertainty in the author's mind. The only work definitely known to belong to the period of doubt is the *Symposium*, begun about 1463. It was undertaken by F. at the suggestion of Cavalcanti, who thought it might relieve the depression from which his friend was suffering "Sed frustra omnia" says Corsi.

[1] "Ex Pagano Christi miles factus," Corsi, o.c., p. 34.

ideas, and contain the germs and occasionally the summaries of his major works. His oral teaching may sometimes have been delivered in church, but the greater part of it must have taken the form of casual friendly talk with his associates. He never held any position in the Studio Fiorentino and it is unlikely that he ever taught there even informally, though it has sometimes been suggested that he did.

The most notable of his disciples was Pico della Mirandola, one of the few to be honoured with the title of "conphilosophus."[1] There are writers who live though their works die, and Pico is one of them. His books are given over to the specialist. After being immoderately praised by his contemporaries they have often been immoderately decried. One need not read far to find in them inconsistencies, prolixities, and masses of tormented symbolism, borrowed largely from Oriental sources such as the Talmud and the Cabbala and Persian and Chaldee writings. It is not always

[1] Giovanni Pico della Mirandola, b. 1463. Showed extraordinary precocity and prodigious memory from very early youth. In 1486 published his famous 900 Theses or "Conclusiones" and invited all who wished to do so to come and discuss them with him in Rome. Thirteen of the "Conclusiones" fell under the ban of the Church and Pico was obliged to take refuge in France. The ban was not removed until 1493, in spite of his own *Apologia* and the efforts of his friend, Lorenzo. He first visited Florence in 1484 and returned in 1488, when he settled at Querceto and gave himself up to writing and study and especially to the study of Oriental languages and philosophies. In his last years he became an ardent disciple of Savonarola and intended to write a great work of Christian apologetics and then to forsake the world and become a missionary friar. His commentaries on the Psalms and the Lord's Prayer and his letters to his nephew, Giovan Francesco Pico, show the development of the ascetic strain in his nature. He died in 1494 on the day that Charles VIII entered Florence, and was buried in the habit of a Dominican monk. For his life see the *Vita* by his nephew in *Pici Opera*, Vol. II, Basle, 1572. The best modern biography is that by Giovanni Semprini, Todi, 1921.

A really penetrating study of Pico as a writer does not, to my knowledge, exist. Ruggiero, o.c., Vol. I, has a few interesting remarks especially on the cabbalistic and magical aspects of his work and their relation to the work of the early natural scientists. The *De Hominis Dignitate* was written in 1486 as a preface to the "Conclusiones" and contains in germ the ideas elaborated in the *Heptaplus* (1489). The commentary on Benivieni is closely modelled on Ficino's *In Conivivium Platonis Commentarius* and belongs probably to 1484-6.

easy to disentangle the essential from the fantastic. Yet in a profound sense the popular imagination is right; it is Pico himself rather than his work that is still vital. He was the raw material of a poet, lacking in literary gift yet possessed of an inherent poetry of mind and character that illumines his life and breaks in veiled flashes through the inchoate clouds of his learning. More perhaps than any other individual he is a living symbol of his age, embodying its diffuse intellectual curiosity, its generous warmth and eagerness of spirit, its belief that nothing on which men have lavished love or interest or endeavour can be wholly without value. By his ardent faith in humanity, and his piercing consciousness of a single being that permeates and embraces all forms of existence, he reminds one of Shelley.

He derived largely, though not slavishly, from Ficino, and possessed wide but unsystematic learning. His most important works for the present argument are the short treatise *De Hominis Dignitate*; the *Heptaplus*, a sevenfold commentary on the first chapter of Genesis; and *In Platonis Convivium*, a commentary in three books on the *Canzone del Amor Divino* of Girolamo Benivieni.

The few remaining members of the Academy who were generally considered as philosophers may be mentioned briefly.[1] They were Leon Battista Alberti; Christoforo Landino, the great Latinist and commentator of Dante, author of the attractive *Quaestiones Camaldulenses*; Peregrino Aglio, who died too young to have given much proof of the great powers Ficino discerned in him; and Francesco Cattani di Diacceto, Ficino's philosophical shadow, of whom Corsi wrote: "Ac Picus a Marsilio aperte quandoque dissentire; Diaccetus praeceptorem suum ubique laudare ac defendere."[2] To avoid overloading the present chapter

[1] For Landino and Aglio see Chapter IV of the present study, "The Medici Circle" (1); for Diacetto see Chapter VI, "The Trattato d'Amore," and for L. B. Alberti see also Chapter VI and especially Chapter VII, "Neoplatonism and the Arts."

[2] Corsi, *Vita Marsilii Ficini*, ed. Bandini, p. 63.
This chapter is concerned with the broad lines of Neoplatonism on which

it has seemed better to discuss their works elsewhere. All the essentials of Florentine Neoplatonism may be found in Ficino and Pico; and were derived from them by the other writers of their circle.

The philosophy of the school can no longer be dismissed, as it has sometimes been in the past, as a revival of more or less literary paganism like that of Pomponio Leto's Academy. The central inspiration of Ficino and Pico was, in fact, religious and in intention definitely Christian. It aimed at giving reason its full function in matters of belief and, at the same time, emphasized the value of religious experience as distinct from the acceptance of any particular creed or system. It was also an attempt to bring every manifestation of being within the compass of the divine life, and to conciliate the age-old opposition between the Creator and the created. The Reformation on the one hand and the scientific pantheistic and subjectivist schools of modern philosophy on the other, owe it a large and often unacknowledged debt. In the light of these developments there is perhaps some danger of ascribing to the Florentine philosophers views more extreme than any that they in fact professed. They remained faithful and devout members of the Roman Church and would have been the first to be horrified at some of the uses to which their work was turned.

The humanists as a whole inclined towards a monistic view of the universe; and with the belief in a divine presence in nature and man there arose the conviction that some trace of universal truth must be discoverable in the recorded speculations of man's

Marsilio and Pico showed substantial agreement, most of their differences being upon minor points. Three of more importance may, however, be noted here.

Pico shows more traces of mysticism, in the strict sense of the word, than Ficino does; and it is probable that the ecstatic and contemplative faculties in his nature would have been still further strengthened, had he lived, by the influence of Savonarola. [See *De Hom. Dig.*, p. 319; *Heptaplus*, Bk. VIII, p. 45; *De Ente et Uno*, pp. 250, 261.] Unlike Ficino, he ruled all consideration of profane love out of his *Commentarius in Symposium*, and he differed profoundly from the older man in his attitude towards astrology. [See Chapter V of this study, page 148, note 2.]

mind. The syncretism for which the Florentines have often been blamed was an attempt to apply this principle and so reveal a single core of truth under the external differences of the various systems of thought. They tried, in the midst of a very real and widespread relaxation of faith and morals, to establish rational bases for religion by showing how the witness of all philosophies pointed to the truth of the Christian revelation. Hence the strange and often extravagant parallels that they drew between the Hebrew prophets and the Greek philosophers and the sages of Persia and Chaldea. Pico, in whom this tendency is most marked, did not live to execute the great work of Christian apologetics which he had planned to write before finally renouncing the world; but Ficino, in the *Theologia Platonica* and the *De Christiana Religione*, did his utmost to build up a positive "docta religio."

Rational or religious activity (for him there is no rigid distinction between the two) is the distinguishing mark of man. It is the eternal element in his being and must, therefore, at all costs be kept free from error and ignorance and enriched with all the treasures of wisdom and experience.

"Liberamus obsecro quandoque philosophiam sacrum Dei munus ab impietate si possumus, possumus autem si volumus; religionem sanctam pro viribus ab excrabile inscitia redimamus."[1]

Like Nicholas of Cusa he aspired towards a vision of truth in which all contradictions are reconciled. Unity, truth, and goodness form a single stable reality that underlies this unstable and inconsistent world, and all knowledge is a return towards a single source. God is everywhere "secundum praesentiam." He is in all forms by "virtue," since there is in everything the effective virtue of the deity; in rational creatures He is "secundum unitatem personae," while within the Divine Mind only He is "secundum unitatem essentiae."[2] Grace is the pervading expression of the divine in

---

[1] Ficino, *Opera*, Basle, 1573, Vol. I, *De Christiana Religione*, p. 1. For the kinship of philosophy and religion see Vol. I, p. 854. [*Epistolae*, Lib. VII.] See Saitta, o.c., p. 76.

[2] *De C.R.*, Ch. XVI, pp. 20–21.

the world; therefore, all religions contain some good, though the Christian faith which alone is founded on the sole virtue of God is supreme among them. In Christ the union of God and man, infinite and finite, is accomplished; in Him may be sought the unity and harmony that the world of appearance seems to deny. He is "idea et exemplar virtutum." "Quid aliud Christus fuit nisi liber quidam moralis imo divinae Philosophiae vivens de caelo missus et divina ipsa idea virtutum humanis oculis manifesta."[1]

In spite of this, and in spite of Ficino's personal devotion towards the historical Christian revelation, a good many of his followers, fascinated by his doctrine of natural religion, inclined towards a theistic form of belief that treated the historical and traditional aspects of Christianity somewhat perfunctorily.

Florentine Neoplatonism retained, naturally enough, much of the cosmogony and the vocabulary of its predecessors; and as it was on these traditional features, rather than on its more intimate spirit, that many of its disciples fastened, a rapid summary of them may be of value. The same cosmic vision is implicit in all the work of the school, but receives its fullest and clearest exposition in Pico's *Heptaplus*. Here one is confronted at first sight with the familiar Neoplatonic hierarchy of being. At the head of it is the One, the ineffable Godhead, perfect in simplicity, unity, and stability, exalted above all being and all knowledge. From the One there proceed the three degrees of "emanation" that form the three worlds of the cosmos. The first hypostasis, mind or spirit, becomes, in Pico's phraseology, the angelic or intellectual world, which is imperfect in so far as it is created and therefore exists not of itself, but by participation in the first being. Neither

---

[1] *De C.R.*, Ch. XXIII, p. 25. Cf. Pico, *Heptaplus*, Bk. I, Ch. VII, p. 15. "Quemadmodum autem inferiorum omnium absoluta consummatio est homo, ita omnium hominum absoluta est consummatio Christus. Quo si, ut dicunt philosophi ab eo quod unoquoque in genere est perfectissimum ad caeteros eiusdem ordinis quasi a forte omnis perfectio derivatur. Dubium nemini est a Christo homine in omnes homines totius bonitatis perfectionem derivari. Illi scilicet uni datus spiritus non ad mensuram ut de plenitudine eius omnes acciperemus."

is it perfect unity nor pure intelligence; perception and its object are not one thing in it as they are in God. The angelic world is a stable and unmoving multiplicity, and its distinctive activity is that of continually contemplating, beholding, and loving God. The eye cannot be filled with light, except by the sun; so the angel cannot receive virtue without being turned to God and the movement by which it returns is love. Besides carrying on their functions of contemplation and worship the ranks of the heavenly hierarchy govern and care for the celestial and sublunar worlds.

The first of these is incorruptible, but inferior to the "intelligible" world because it is continually in movement and because it is a world of mingled light and darkness.[1] It is divided into nine spheres or heavens, each ruled by one of the nine angelic orders, and its two great operations are movement and illumination. The movement is twofold, and consists first in the circular motion of the heavens round the earth and, second, of the movements of the stars among themselves. The light of the empyrean derives immediately from the Spirit of God and is diffused through all the spheres.

The material or sublunar world is the region of darkness and corruption. It contains nine orders of sublunar life, corresponding to the souls of the spheres. Matter is simply void and formlessness "omnibus formis suscipiendis, sua tamen natura omnibus privatam."[2] Forms are given to it by an "efficient cause" and are imperfect images of things that exist in the higher worlds after a more real and perfect fashion. There is indeed the most intimate connection between the three worlds, as the ancients taught obscurely by signs and figures "totius naturae et amicitias et affinitates edocti."[3] Each created essence looks for guidance to the one immediately above it in the scale of being, and endeavours to reproduce what

---

[1] "Hic vitae et mortis vicissitudo, illic vita perpetua et stabilis operatio in caelo vitae stabilitas operationum locumque vicissitudo. Hic ex caduca corporum substantia, ille ex divinae mentis natura caelum ex corpore sed incorrupto, ex mente, sed mancipata corpori constituitur." *Heptaplus, Pici Opera*, Basle, 1572, Vol. I, Bk. I, Ch. I, p. 5.
[2] Ibid., Bk. I, Ch. I, p. 11.   [3] Ibid., Bk. I, Ch. I, p. 7.

it sees there in the one immediately below it. The angelic intelligence receives the ideas or types of all things from God and infuses them into the celestial world where they exist as virtues; and the soul of the celestial world contemplates the perfection of the angels and endeavours to transmit something of that perfection to the sublunar world by endowing matter with "forms" or "qualities." All things that exist in the material world are dim shadows of the eternal realities. "Est apud nos calor qualitas elementaris, est in caelestibus virtus excalfactoria, est in angelicis mentibus idea caloris. Dicam aliquid expressius. Est apud nos ignis quod est elementum. Sol ignis in caelo est, est in regione ultramondana ignis seraphicus intellectus. Sed vide quid differant. Elementaris urit, caelestis vivificat, supercaelestis amat."[1] The Neoplatonists stood here in obvious danger of seeing "loose types of things through all creation," a danger into which their more unwary and unimaginative followers in all ages have fallen heavily; but they also shared, with the great Romantics, in a genuinely poetic feeling for the presence of the spiritual in the material.

The visible world is a shadow, but a shadow of truth, or in a favourite simile, a house built in a material medium after the pattern already existing in the mind of the architect. It would be untrue to speak of Pico or Ficino as pantheists in the full sense of the word. God for them is manifest and active in the universe, but not identical with it; He may be apprehended through His creation, but it is dependent on Him while He is independent of it.[2] He is in all things because all things are in Him; or, as the Platonists have it, the divine goodness so overflowed that it left no particle destitute of itself. "Si ergo in uno mundi corpore vivente una quodam vita unique est quod alias ostendimus multo magis unum ipsum bonum est ubique etiam extra mundum."[3]

[1] *Heptaplus*, Bk. I, Ch. I, p. 7.
[2] Minus enim est mundus ad Deum quam corpus ad animam magisque eget Deo mundus quam corpus anima. Ficino, *Opera*, Vol. I., *Theologia Platonica*, Bk. I, Ch. VI, p. 91. But see Saitta's remarks on Ficino's "energico pamsichismo," o.c., p. 196.
[3] *T.P.*, loc. cit.

This divine goodness, which is for ever fulfilling itself in the care and government of the world, so penetrates the whole creation that "Tum Musarum dux Bacchus in suis mysteriis, id est visibilibus naturae signis, invisibilia Dei philosophantibus nobis ostendens, inebriabit nos ab ubertate domus Dei in qua tota sicuti Moses erimus fideles."[1]

The mind of man, by an innate instinct (instinctus essentialis), seeks God always and in everything, and cannot be satisfied till it finds Him. There is in us all the desire [conatus] to deify ourselves, by an exaltation of the spirit which takes on the form of God as a burning object takes on the form of fire. It is natural and inevitable for man to desire perfect goodness and felicity, or, in other words, a god-like life; he has, moreover, not merely the desire but the capacity to know and possess the forms of all things including, therefore, even the "Summum Bonum."[2] His mind cannot be satisfied with the finite because it contains a ray of the divine light. God transcends our faculties, but He is none the less a part of them, the part by which the identification of the human mind with the divine is accomplished. In other words, the Absolute is within us, and God became man in order that man might become God.[3]

Where ancient Neoplatonism had tried to fill the chasm between God and the world with a succession of emanations, Ficino, without discarding the old framework, tries to reconcile all opposing terms in the soul of man, the "essentiam tertiam ac mediam," which by a natural impulse allies itself both with those things which are eternal only and those which are temporal only. The

---

[1] Pico, *Opera*, Vol. I, *De Hominis Dignitate*, p. 320.

[2] Ficino, *Opera*, Vol. I, T.P., Bk. XIII, Ch. I, p. 305. Cf. p. 91. Finis ignis est ultimi caeli concavum. Ideo flammula quaelibet si nihil prohiberet, illuc usque evolaret et quando concavum illud attingeret si dimensionem haberet sufficientem se per totum illud amplificaret ut toto eo quod sibi naturale est frueretur.... Scopus finisque mentis est ipsum verum bonum id est Deus." See Saitta, o.c., p. 78.

[3] T.P., XIV, Ch. VII, p. 317. Deus agitat mens humana quotidie, Deo ardet cor, Deum suspirat pectus.

former it bends to its own capacity while it spiritualizes and ennobles the latter. "Quapropter naturale instinctu ascendit ad supera, descendit ad infera. Et dum ascendit inferiora non deferit et dum descendit sublimia non relinquit. Nam si alterutrum deferit ad extremum alterum declinabit neque vera erit ulterius mundi copula. Profecto idem facit, quod aer inter ignem et aquam medius qui cum igne in calore cum aqua convertit in humore."[1]

Ficino differs from his predecessors in making this deification a spontaneous act of the divine principle in man, or at least its natural reaction to the divine principle in the universe.

"Proinde quia Deus homini absque medio se coniunxit meminisse oportet nostram felicitatem in eo versari ut Deo absque medio haereamus."[2]

He is divided between the idea of the Absolute as utterly superessential and unknowable, and that of the Absolute latent in every soul and created in it anew with each increase of spirituality and true knowledge. The uncertainty has given rise to most of the contradictions that have been noted in his work; and it was mainly in an attempt to resolve it that he elaborated his theory of love. This is of fundamental importance in his thought.[3] Beatitude for him consists in a supreme act of love by which the human soul gives itself to God and so becomes assimilated to Him. Such an act is a voluntary death; it entails the rejection of the life of passion and opinion in which the soul is immersed while it is subject to earthly conditions. Yet the lover lives again in God and there finds his true self, and knows himself as he is known. He becomes at once a complete personality and a sharer of the divine life, since the inmost truth of his being is the divine activity that dwells in him. The two lives, God's and man's, are made one while yet remaining two. Since man is made in the image of God he carries on like though not identical activities. He can give himself in love to God, because God out of love created him.

---

[1] Ficino, *Opera*, Vol. I, *T.P.*, Bk. III, Ch. II, p. 119.
[2] *De C.R.*, Ch. XXI, p. 22.
[3] See end of chapter for analysis of the theory of love.

There is a reciprocal affection like that of parent and child, but it has its origin in the parent, "We love Him because He first loved us."[1] Man's love is a spontaneous act which he is free to make or not as he wills, yet at the same time a response to something that is at once the utmost goal of his desire and a presence at the root of his being deeper than all conscious life.

He is further endowed with the god-like faculties of understanding and creative power. He is continually endeavouring to understand himself and the universe, but he cannot be satisfied unless that understanding brings him to knowledge of the good.[2]

Each increase of true knowledge must be a participation in God's knowledge, since that alone is truth; but we do not simply acquire something external to the mind; we re-create truth for ourselves as we apprehend it. Man's thought is a shadow or image of the divine thought. It is "a repetition in the finite mind of the eternal act of creation in the mind of the Infinite I AM."[3] Human art, science, and speculation are the means whereby we lay hold upon reality and bring it within the sphere of our consciousness. The peculiar character of Florentine Neoplatonism appears in nothing more than in its insistence on man's power to seize reality by his own efforts; in its endeavour, one might almost say, to take the kingdom of heaven by force. Even when he writes of the superiority of the contemplative over the active life Ficino is not really contradicting the fundamentally dynamic tendency of his thought. Contemplation for him is not a static condition; it is the soul's grasp on essential truth brought about by the full and harmonious exertion of reason and love. As he says, it is the only form

[1] Diligit faber opera sua, quae ex materia fecit externa. Amat multo magis filium genitor quem ex materia intrinseca generavit, quamvis eam priusque restit nihil (*T.P.*, Bk. II, Ch. IX, p. 111).
[2] *T.P.*, Bk. I, Ch. VI, p. 91.
[3] S. T. Coleridge, *Poems*, Nelson, Preface, p. xii. In *T.P.*, Bk. XII, Ch. IV, p. 272, Ficino speaks of God as "agens primum et commune" who continually infuses truth into the mind of man "agens proprium et secundum." Reality is objective and eternal but "immortalis est veritas atque est continuus animi cibus, ut certe est sive ipsa convertatur in animum sive animum in seipsum convertat" (*T.P.*, Bk. XI, Ch. VI, p. 261).

of pure activity; action that spends itself on material objects dissipates itself and falls away, but the activity of the mind is self-sufficient. It is the life of the spiritual man; a return to our own true being which dwells in God and is already a part of eternity, though we ourselves are ignorant of it.

"Cognosce te ipsum, divinum genus mortali veste indutum, nuda quaeso teipsum segrega quantum potes autem quantum conaris, segrega inquam a corpore animam, a sensum affectibus rationem. Videbis protinus purum segregatis terrae sordibus aurum, videbis lucidum disiectis nubibus aerem reverberis tunc, crede mihi teipsum tamque divini Solis radium sempiternum. Neque audebis coram te ulterius turpe quicquam aut vile vel aggredi vel cogitare. . . . Es enim extra dum mundum ipsa complecteris. Sed esse te putas in infimo loco mundi, quia te ipsum quidem non cernis super aethera pervolantem sed umbram tuam corpus vides in infimo. Perinde ac si puer aliquis super puteum constitutus esse se in fondo putei arbitretur dum in se ipsum aciem convertit, sed suam quasi in fondo prospicit umbram. Aut si avis in aere volans, credat se in terra volare, dum umbram suam videt in terra. Ergo relictis umbrae revertere in teipsum, sic enim revertaris in amplum.[1]

The kind of consciousness that Ficino has in mind is evidently something more than the insight into one's own psychological peculiarities that is generally called self-knowledge. It is a direct awareness of a life that transcends all our purely empiric experience; and one may question how far such a state may be attained by any ordinary process of reasoning. Ficino himself, though he makes of inner dialectic a necessary discipline for the soul, speaks of the actual passing to that deeper consciousness as "una certa illustrazione" of the rational soul by the divine "furores" of poetry, prophecy, or love. He attains the crown of his reasoning by an irrational or supra-rational act. Where he uses the language of the mystics he seems to do so because it comes nearer than any other to expressing a state of insight that he himself had known.

[1] Ficino, *Epistolae* [*Opera*, Vol. I], Bk. I, p. 659.

In a sense all experience is mystic, since there is in it something immediate and final that cannot really be reasoned about, but only apprehended through analogous experience; and there can be no experience more absolute than that by which a man is made aware of a harmony in himself that corresponds to a like harmony in the universe. That some such "simultaneous knowledge of the soul and of God" possessed Ficino in his moments of fullest conviction seems evident, but he was perhaps involved in an impossibility when he tried to turn the paradox of this direct apprehension into a strictly rational form. It is certain that he fell into many difficulties and inconsistencies in trying to explain exactly how the two harmonies were related. Over these metaphysical complexities there is no need to linger; what is, however, worthy of emphasis here is the characteristic quality of Ficino's mysticism, which is not an annulment but an intensification of human personality, implying the presence of the divine within the soul, and a free participation in the divine life, that is to say in love, knowledge, and creative activity.

Ficino's real weakness, easy to understand in one writing in an age so full of hope and so glorious in achievement, is that he makes the process of perfection appear too easy and inevitable. In the twentieth century one may, without cynicism, think he exaggerated. Still, in the members of the Academy the idea of human dignity takes on a freshness of enthusiasm that makes it curiously winning.

Man the microcosm, the "fourth world" of the *Heptaplus*, is the mirror in which the other three worlds are reflected, or still more he is ". . . creaturarum internuntium, superis familiarem regem inferiorem sensum perspicacia ratione indagine, intelligentiae lumine naturae interpretem, stabilis aevi et fluxi temporis interstitium et (quod Persae dicunt) mundi copulam imo hymenaeum, ab angelis teste Davide paulo diminutum."[1] At his birth he is endowed with the seeds and germs of every form of life, material and spiritual. He is potentially all things and, at the same time, entirely free to choose those in which he desires to participate.

[1] Pico, *De Hominis Dignitate* [1486], *Opera*, I, p. 313.

He can live the vegetative life of plants, the sensual life of the brutes, or the life of a rational soul. Aspiring higher, he may give himself to intelligible truth and become as one of the angels; and if he cannot find contentment in any creature he may withdraw into the solitude of his own soul, and there be made one spirit with God "in solitaria patris caligine qui est super omnia constitutus omnibus antestabit."[1] He is, above all, utterly unrestricted, neither good nor evil, mortal nor immortal, but a being formed by God to contemplate and understand the rest of creation and to unify and recreate the universe in himself.

"Jam summus architectus Deus hanc quam videmus mundanum domum divinitatis, templum augustissimum, arcanae legibus sapientiae fabrefecerat. Supercaelestem regionem mentibus decorarat, aethereos globos aeternis animis vegetarat, excrementarias ac faeculentas inferioris mundi partes omnigena animalia turba complerat. Sed opere consummato, desiderabat artifex esse aliquem qui tanti operis rationem perpenderet, pulchritudinem amaret, magnitudinem admiraretur. Idcirco iam rebus omnibus (ut Moses Timaeusque testantur) absolutis de producendo homine postremo cogitavit. . . . Nec certam sedem nec propriam faciem, nec munus ullus peculiare tibi dedimus ô Adam ut quam sedem, quam faciem, quae munera tute optaveris ea pro voto, pro tua sententia, habeas et possideas. Definita caeteris natura intra praescriptas a nobis leges coercetur. Tu nullis angustiis coercitus, pro tuo arbitrio, in cuius manu te posui, ut circumspiceres inde commodius quicquid est in mundo. Nec te caelestem nec terrenum, neque mortalem neque immortalem fecimus ut tuiipsius quasique plastes et fictor in quam malueris tute formam effingas. Poteris in inferiora quae sunt bruta degenerare. Poteris in superiora quae sunt divina ex tui animi sententia regenerari. O summam Dei patris liberalitatem, summam et admirandam hominis felicitatem. . . ."[2]

Nothing can or ought to limit the infinite ventures of man's mind, which endeavours to be all things, and is, therefore, an

[1] Pico, *De Hominis Dignitate* [1486], *Opera*, I, p. 315.
[2] Ibid., I, p. 314.

eternal progress. It may approach reality along many paths; by self-knowledge, since the mind is infinite potentiality (medium rerum) and by the study of history which confers a kind of universality on the individual by putting into his possession the collective wisdom and experience of the race. Every form of knowledge can indeed contribute something to the perfecting of the human spirit, since each contains an element of divinity and is transmuted into the spirit's substance as different kinds of food are transmuted into the substance of the body.[1] Man is alone among animals in inventing and practising many arts. Other animals have at most one art which they follow of necessity, but man aspires to be like God who is in all places and who endures for ever. Therefore he cultivates the earth and scrutinizes the height of heaven and the depths of the sea. His mind leaps huge intervals of time and space and pierces into all manner of secrets. No bounds can restrain him and he seeks always to bear rule and to be honoured. "Atque ita conatur esse Deus ubique. Conatur quoque esse et semper ut Deus."[2] His dignity is confirmed by his resentment of any form of servitude or degradation; by his impatience at being beaten even in trifles; and by every manifestation of natural shame.[3] His desires are so limitless that he cannot be satisfied with the world he knows but must needs, like Alexander and Anaxagoras, demand others. He is undisputed lord of the earth (Est utique Deus in terra) linking it to heaven by his activities and so rendering the very soil he cultivates almost divine.[4] The soul is the "form" of the body which it moulds in its own likeness. Bodily strength, beauty, and temperance are shadows of similar mental qualities,

[1] Ficino, T.P., Bk. XIV, Ch. III, p. 310. For the universality conferred on the mind by historical study see Ep., I, p. 658. "Ei quidem quae per se mortalia sunt immortalitatem ab historia consequuntur, quae absentia sunt per eam praesentia fiunt vetera iuvenescunt. Iuvenes cito maturitatem senis adaequant. Ac si senex septuaginta annorum ob ipsarum rerum experientiam prudens habetur, quanto prudentior qui annorum mille et trium millum implet aetatem."
[2] Ibid., T.P., Bk. XIV, Ch. V, p. 311.
[3] Ibid., T.P., Bk. XIV, Ch. IV, p. 311. "Esse servitutis omnis impatientem. Qui etiam servire cogatur, odit Dominum, utpote qui serviat contra naturam."
[4] Ibid., Bk. XVI, p. 378.

just as the beauty of things visible is the shadow of beauty in the intelligible world. Not only is each individual a cosmos of infinite value and wonder, but humanity as a whole is a lovely nymph "praestanti corpore nympha," an Idea in which all the component units become as one man (Singuli namque homines sub una idea et in eadem specie sunt unus homo).[1] The wise man first learns to know his own soul and then studies, loves, and cares for humanity as for a brotherhood descended from one father (ex uno quodam patre longo ordine natos). To love and understand his kind is a crown of wisdom and power to the philosopher, who stands as a medium between God and man; a man in the presence of God, a god among his fellows.[2]

Only the philosopher, that is the man who lives most perfectly in harmony with the law of the mind, is fitted to bear rule over this collective soul of humanity. It is he who ought to guide the fortunes of the state. Here again Ficino emphasizes the humanistic tradition; man is the heir of heaven, but he is also an "anima socialis" who carries on the divine activity under human conditions; and he who is inwardly perfect must offer his vision and counsel freely to the community. Ficino's own letters abound in advice on practical questions which shows how sincerely he endeavoured to carry out his own theories.[3]

His doctrine of love, which was destined to enjoy such astonishing popularity, is contained principally in his *In Convivium Platonis De Amore Commentarius*.[4] The fundamental importance of this

[1] *Ep.*, Bk. I, 635. Cf. *Ep.*, I, 658; IV, 762.
[2] Ibid., Bk. V, p. 805. To Lorenzo.
[3] See E. Galli, *La morale nelle lettere di M. F.*, Pavia, 1897, and *Lo stato la famiglia e l'educazione secondo le teorie di M. F.*, Pavia, 1899. Also Saitta, *L'educazione dell' Umanesimo*, Venice, 1928, Ch. XIV, p. 235, "Marsilio Ficino."
[4] In *Opera*, Vol. II, pp. 1320 et seq. Ficino himself translated it into "volgare" and dedicated the translation to Bernardo del Nero. The final version was not completed till 1474 or 1475. It is mentioned in a letter to Alamanno Donati and Lorenzo [*Ep.*, VII, p. 848], but remained in MS. until 1544 when it was published by Cosimo Bartoli. The edition is entitled *Marsilio Ficino sopra lo amore o ver convito di Platone*, In Firenze per Neri Dortelata Con Privilegio di N.S. di Novembre MDXXXXIIII.

theory has already been touched upon, but a somewhat lengthy analysis of the Commentary may be excused since it is the fountainhead from which all the writers of Neoplatonic lyrics and treatises derived. It contained not only philosophical suggestions that inspired Leone Ebreo and Bruno and Spinoza, but numbers of the legends, questions, and paradoxes that passed into the stock-in-trade of polite society in the sixteenth century.

The scene is set at Careggi, at a banquet held on November 7th to commemorate the legendary date of Plato's birth and death. After dinner the *Symposium* is read aloud and the orations are allotted among seven of the guests who proceed to expound them in turn.

The first treats of the origin of Love, the most ancient of the gods, who existed in the heart of Chaos before the world or Saturn or Jove had come into being.[1] It is most perfect in itself and of great wisdom, and has its origin in the relation of the universe to its creator. Each one of the three worlds, intelligible, celestial, or material, is at the moment of its first creation in some sense a chaos. In order to receive form and adornment it must turn to the essence immediately above it in the hierarchy of being.

"Principio Deus mentis illius creat substantiam quam etiam essentiam nominamus. Haec in primo illo creationis suae momento informis est et obscura. Quoniam vero a Deo nata est Deum sui principium ingenito quodam appetitu convertitur. Conversa in Deum ipsius radio illustratur. Radij illius fulgore ille suus appetitus accenditur. Accensus appetitus Deo totus inhaeret: inhaerendo formatur. Nam Deus qui potest omnia in mente sibi inhaerente creandarum rerum naturas effingit. In ea igitur spiritali quodammodo pinguntur, ut ita loquar, omnia quae in corporibus istis sentimus. Illis caelorum elementorum quae globi sydera vaporum

---

[1] "Orpheus. . . . Chaos ante mundum posuit et ante Saturnum, Jovem caeterosque deos. Amorem in ipsius Chaos sinu locavit, laudavitque his verbis," Oration I, Ch. I, p. 1321. Other authorities cited in the commentary are Hesiod, Hermes Trismegistus, Parmenides, and the Neoplatonists. Among the moderns Guido Cavalcanti is singled out for special praise.

naturae, lapidum, metallorum, plantarum, animalium forma gignuntur."[1]

These species of created things are the Platonic Ideas. Mythology is a personification of these Ideas; the Idea of heaven becomes Zeus, that of fire Vulcan, that of air Juno, and so forth.

Before receiving the Ideas the angelic intelligence had to draw near to God, and in order that it should do so its desire had to be awakened. A longing for the divine goodness is kindled in it by the infusion of a ray of the divine light without which it would remain dark and void. Yet even without such illumination it has a natural tendency to turn back to its Creator. This tendency is Love; the illumination that follows and perfects it results in the congregating and ordering of all Ideas or forms so that the chaos of the unillumined mind becomes a world or cosmos. The grace of the cosmos is Beauty, which draws the angelic mind to desire its own perfection and so turn back in love to God who can supply its need.

Love is worthily called most ancient of the gods, and said to be perfect in himself (since he perfects himself by his own activity) and of great wisdom, since he is enlightened from the source of truth. The Angelic mind turns to God as the eye to the sun. The eye first gazes; then it sees the light of the sun; and then by that light it comprehends all colours and all forms. As it cannot see without light so the mind cannot see without God. Similarly the World Soul turns for illumination to God and the Angelic Intelligence, and even the material world is drawn towards Soul and allows itself to be formed and adorned by it. Love, therefore, is the one universal activity, the force that circulates through every stage of being and brings the highest region of spirit and the lowliest atom of the material universe within the compass of a single harmonious life.[2]

[1] *Opera*, Vol. II, Com. in *Symposium*, Or. I, Ch. II, p. 1322.
[2] "Tres igitur mundi, tria et chaos. In omnibus denique amor chaos comitatur praecedit mundum, torpentia suscitat, obscura illuminat, vivificat mortuos, format informia, perficit imperfecta" (Or. I, Ch. II, p. 1322).

The utility of love is next discussed. It is, as the Christian humanistic tradition had often insisted, the true basis of morality. Where laws and philosophies can only win men slowly and with much difficulty to follow the Good, love impels them urgently to seek it. Also it is, as has already been decided, the desire for Beauty, which is defined as threefold in character.[1]

It may pertain to the soul, to bodies, or to voices, and it is apprehended by the mind, the eye, and the ear, respectively. If love, therefore, is the desire for beauty, and beauty is only perceived by the mind and the senses of sight and hearing, it must follow that love will be content with such perception and that the other senses can have no part in it. Sensual appetites are not love, but a madness that drags the mind towards deformity and deflects it from its proper state. They will consequently be hated and shunned by the true lover, who will scorn to profane the name of love by applying it to the disorders of passion.

Love inspires the desire for good and laudable things and a great hatred for all evil; since the lover wishes to stand well in the opinion of the beloved and to be in every respect worthy of him. Where the body alone is beautiful it inspires a shadowy and passing love; where beauty is in the soul alone love becomes lasting and ardent; where both body and soul are beautiful there arises also a vehement wonder and joy.[2] Beauty itself is the central term of the threefold nature of God who is Good in creating the universe, Beautiful in winning created things back to Himself, and Just in perfecting them to the utmost of their capacity when they once turn towards Him. For these same reasons He is the beginning, middle, and end of all things since He both makes them and wins them back to Himself.

[1] Or. I, Ch. III, p. 1322.
[2] "Et ubi corpus pulchrum, animus minime, tanquam umbratilem et fluxam imaginem pulchritudinis vix et leviter diligamus. Ubi solus animus pulcher, stabilem hunc decorem animi ardenter amemus. Ubi vero utraque pulchritudo concurrit, vehementius admiremur: atque ita ex Platonica familia se vera nos esse testabimur: ea quippe nihil novit nisi festum laetum, caelestem, supernum" (Or. I, Ch. III, p. 1323). Cf. Vol. I, *Ep.*, Bk. V, p. 795.

Love must be good because its origin and end is the Good; but to speak of an end means here not a conclusion but a fulfilment. It is a movement from an intuition of the divine perfection in things to a full consciousness of it as it is in itself. God (Bonitas) is the centre of four concentric circles—Mind, Soul, Nature, and Matter—in all of which Beauty is diffused. God alone is stable, simple, and immovable, yet there is in all creatures some inmost essence, stable, simple, and immovable, by which they touch God. ("... ita Deus omnium centrum qui unitas simplicissima est, actusque purissimus, sese inserit universis: non ob id solum quia cunctis est praesens, verumetiam quia omnibus a se creatis partem aliquam vel potentiam intimam simplicissimam praestantissimam indidit: quae rerum unitas nominatur: a qua et ad quam tanquam e centro et ad centrum suum rei cuiusque partes et potentiae reliquae pendent."[1])

The angelic mind or invisible world is continually aspiring towards God and so the lower orders of being do their utmost to ascend to the nature above them and to order themselves in the likeness of the superior existences. The things of sense are only the shadows of reality. The Good is like the sun; beauty, like the sun's ray, penetrates through the four circles of being, and paints upon them the types of all things which are Ideas in the Angelic mind, reasons (rationes) in the soul; seeds (semina) in nature, which is the generative virtue of the soul, and "forms" in matter. God, being the principle of Beauty, is the cause of all beautiful objects. So, as human knowledge must begin with the impressions of the senses, men at first dimly discern the qualities of divine things in natural objects, and surmise the power of God from the force of nature, His wisdom from its order, and so on. But no corporal beauty can content man, because it has only a shadowy existence.[2] The lover's ardour cannot be quenched by bodily sight or contact because what he desires is not this or that body, but the

---

[1] Or. II, Ch. III, p. 1324.
[2] "Corpora enim animarum mentiumque umbrae et vestigiae sunt" (Or. II, Ch. III, p. 1324).

divine splendour infused in the beloved object.[1] From this proceeds the fact that lovers do not know what they want or what they seek because they do not know God. The divine presence is like a delicious perfume in the world that fills men with eagerness to taste the unknown sweetness it suggests. Similarly the fear and reverence shown by the lover in presence of the beloved is really an unconscious awe in face of the divine; and the contempt with which the lover will treat riches and honours for his beloved's sake is symbolic of spurning earthly things for heavenly. Finally, the longing of the lover to transform himself into the beloved is really the fundamental longing of man to become a god.[2]

In spite of this it must be admitted that love is of two sorts. Pausanias, following Plato, says that love is the companion of Venus and that there are as many loves as there are Venuses. By ancient tradition there are two Venuses, the one celestial, the other terrestrial. The first is the daughter of Celios or heaven and has no mother, while the second is the child of Zeus and Dione. The celestial Venus is said to have no mother because she is in no way associated with matter, which is often called by the physicists the mother of all. The terrestrial Venus is the offspring of Zeus, the generative virtue of the World Soul; and since she is infused into the material universe and is therefore in continual contact with matter, she is reputed to have a mother. In other terms, Venus Urania is the intelligence of the Angelic mind; and Venus Dione the generative power of the World Soul.

The one is drawn by innate love to contemplate the Supreme

[1] Or. II, Ch. IV, p. 1325.
[2] "Deus namque pro homine fieri cupet atque conatur. Quis autem pro Deo hominem non commutat?" (Or. II, Ch. VI, p. 1326).
The other characteristics of lovers are explained in the same way. They sigh because they leave themselves and destroy themselves; they rejoice because they become more worthy by transferring themselves into a nobler being. They grow cold because they lose their natural heat, warm because they are warmed by the divine ray. From alternate heat and cold they are by turns bold and timid. Slow wits are sharpened by love, for what eye would not see by the aid of the Divine light? Cf. Vol. I, *Ep.*, Bk. VII, p. 861. "Qui humanum amorem in divinum transfert ex homine transfertur in Deum."

Beauty; the other, by a kindred impulse, is moved to create a likeness of that beauty in material form. The first embraces the divine splendour and diffuses it into the terrestrial Venus, who imparts it to the world of matter. Consequently, every created thing shares, in so far as it is capable, in a single divine glory. The beauty of material bodies is made known to the soul by the power of sight; and the soul has two powers, equivalent to the two Venuses; in other words, the powers of contemplation and of generation. The mind reverences and loves beauty as an image of the divine and at the same time the soul, dwelling in matter, desires to create a form resembling the beautiful object. Here Ficino makes a characteristic observation by insisting that both loves are honest and have the divine image for their object; it is only when "Venere volgare" usurps the place of her sister that evil ensues.[1] Elsewhere he emphasizes the division and even the enmity between body and soul, human and divine love, but here he makes of the two loves two moments of one activity.

He gives some further definitions of love according to Plato and Orpheus. It is a voluntary death, bitter because it is death, sweet because it is voluntary. The lover dies by forgetting and abandoning himself, and lives again in the beloved. In the case of "simple" love, where the lover's passion is not returned, he is dead utterly, as he lives neither in himself nor in his beloved; in the case of mutual love each of the lovers dies to himself and lives again in the other and possesses himself in the other's mind.[2] In reciprocal love there is a death when the lover dies to himself, but there are two resurrections—the first when his love is returned and the second when he finds himself again in the object of his love. So the one possesses the other and yet does not lose himself. Love comes of similitude or Affinity, the existence of some like quality

[1] "Utrobique igitur amor est. Ibi contemplandae hic generandae pulchritudinis desiderium. Amor uterque honestus improbadus? Uterque enim divinam imaginem sequitur" (Or. II, Ch. VI, p. 1327).

[2] "Equidem dum te amo me amantem, in te de me cogitante ne me reperio et me a me negligentia mea perditum in te conservantem recupero. Idem in me tu facis" (Or. II, Ch. VIII, p. 1327).

in each of the two lovers. Each gives himself to the other and is in turn loved and cared for by the other, since it is natural for human beings to care for the things that belong to them. Again, each carves the image of the beloved in his own soul, and becomes in a sense the mirror in which the other sees his own likeness. According to the Astrologers, love springs up naturally between people born under the same star, since they participate in the same idea. So when one friend is old and the other young (since love is the desire of and enjoyment of beauty) the eyes of the elder rejoice in the bodily beauty of the younger, and the mind of the younger is delighted by the elder's mental splendour.[1]

From the thought of love as a personal relation Ficino turns to consider it as a universal power. It is, he says, present in all things, the maker and preserver of all, and the master of all arts. God by love rules the Angels; they, together with Him, rule over the realm of Soul, and souls, under God and the angels, sustain all corporal forms. These in turn love their souls and are unwilling to part from them. Our souls desire the felicity of the angels, and the angels love and revere the divine majesty. Love is, therefore, as the life-blood of creation, circulating in unfailing rhythm through every grade of being, from the Deity to the humblest form of life.

Among equal things there is the same love as between the various hierarchies; the elements tend to congregate together, and beasts of the same species show a certain friendliness or benevolence among themselves. Love moves superior beings to care for the inferior, and the lower to aspire towards the perfection of the higher, and knits together those beings that are equal and alike. In this way love is the "creator and preserver" of the universe, for it was through love, "Cupiditatis perfectionis propagandae," that God first created all things and infused into them the desire to make others participate in their being.[2] Every part of the world is drawn to every other part by reciprocal love, and it is not possible for hate to exist between them. Fire flies from water not because

[1] Or. II, Ch. IX, p. 1328.
[2] Or. III, Ch. II, p. 1329.

it hates the water, but because it loves itself; and water does not try to quench fire through hatred, but from a desire to increase its own coldness by extending it to the fire.[1] So man cannot bear hatred to man, but only to the vices in man; and envy toward those greater or wiser than ourselves comes not of hate to them but of the love of self which cannot endure to see itself excelled. Evil is in effect only an aspect of love, and by implication a necessary and even desirable part of the universal order. "Qua propter nihil obstat, quin amor in omnibus sit perquam omnia penetret."[2]

The positive value of love in human affairs appears still further in its function as inspirer of all the arts. No man can set himself to learn any art unless he feels a vehement desire to seek for Truth; nor can learning be pursued successfully unless there is affection between master and pupil and unless the learner is possessed with love for his work. Every art is an expression of love, since it is an endeavour to impose order upon formlessness.

Medicine reconciles and harmonizes the disorders of the body. Agriculture brings about harmony between the earth and the seeds and plants that grow in it. Music seeks out the hidden affinities that exist between sounds, and combines them into beautiful cadences. Astrology deals with the "certain friendliness" (amicitia quaedam) by which the elements and the heavenly bodies are linked. Finally, it is the office of prophets and priests to expound the works of God and man, and to show men how to become the friends of God by loving Him and their fellow creatures. When he comes to interpret Aristophanes' famous myth of the double human beings, Ficino treats the slightly burlesque legend with his usual careful seriousness. The most interesting point in his argument is his attempt to show that when Aristophanes spoke of man he must have meant the soul and that all that is truly

[1] Or. III, Ch. IV, p. 1330. Cf. for Ficino's treatment of the problem of evil, *Ep.*, Bk. V, p. 800. To. F. Sassetti. The divine is, like the light of the sun, ubiquitous, and darkness cannot co-exist with it. Evil, therefore, has no real existence. "Ubi nam igitur malum habitat si non potest esse cum bono, ac bonum ipsum occupat universam?"

[2] Or. III, Ch. IV, p. 1330.

significant in the body is the work of the soul. The body consists of matter and quantity, or the potentialities of receiving forms and of being extended and divided; it is pure passivity and it acts not in so far as it is a body, but because it has in it "a certain force or quality almost incorporeal." The quality of fire is not its height or extension but its heat; the quality of the body is this incorporeal force which is finally identified with the soul, since the qualities of things, being inherent in matter and therefore not self-moving, are not capable of such activities as the human body carries out.

The body is, in fact, almost subsumed into the soul as an integral part of the complete man.

Man was created double or, in other words, perfect; endowed with two "lights," one innate and the other infused. By the first he perceives things equal to and inferior to himself; by the second things superior. Men think in their pride to equal God by their own endeavours, and in consequence they abandon the heavenly light and become immersed in the body so that their being is divided and they wander unhappily through life desiring their lost perfection. When the mind comes to years of discretion it tries by its natural light to regain the supernatural, and when that is attained it is made whole again. The soul is subject to the passions of the body, but by discipline and the exercise of the cardinal virtues it begins to understand itself and the world around it, and to apprehend the existence of an Architect of the universe whom it desires to know. He can be known only by supernatural light, but the desire for truth is kindled in the mind by considering its own nature. "Cognoscere illum vere omnino praesenti in tempore possibile est. Vere autem amare quoquomodo cognitum et possibile est et facile. Qui Deus cognoscunt nondum illi placent, nisi cognitum diligant qui cognoscunt, diligunt, non quia cognoscunt sed quia qui diligunt amantur a Deo."[1] Love is eternal, and is eternally renewed and contented by its divine object. It is the best and most beautiful of all things; its desire is beauty and its gifts are wisdom, strength, foresight, mutual contentment, peace,

[1] Or. IV, Ch. III, p. 1332.

and happiness. It is oldest and youngest of the gods, since it first moved God to create and is the natural movement of the creatures back to their author. It is older than necessity, for created beings by necessity tend to degenerate, but their first act is love. Love begins in God and necessity in the creatures; and so the legends of the gods binding or mutilating their fathers are explained by the dividing and limiting of the divine power as it participates itself to inferior beings.

According to Diotima and Socrates love is not so much a god as a daemon, "quia sicut daemones inter caelestia et terrena sunt medii," who is poised between beauty and ugliness, good and evil, joy and misery, God and man. It is the child of Porus (abundance) and Penia (poverty) and is rich because it possesses something of what it loves, and poor because it does not possess it completely. It is said to have been born on the birthday of Venus, that is at the moment of the creation of the Angelic Intelligence and the World Soul, and in the Garden of Jove, which is the fecundity of the Angelic life. Here Porus, the ray of the divine light (summi Dei scintilla) and Penia, innate desire, create love.[1] Love in so far as he is the son of Penia is depicted as thin, squalid, barefoot, humble, homeless, and needy. As the son of Porus he is audacious, fierce, vehement, warm, sagacious, a weaver of webs, and a being prudent and well spoken. He is a philosopher, an enchanter, and a powerful wizard and sophist. Under these guises he embodies all the qualities and passions of the lover.[2] Of the loves inherent in man, two—the supernatural love of God and the love of philosophy and virtue—are immortal; the other natural loves, pleasure in visual or auditory impressions and in the baser senses are mortal. The object of love changes, though love itself does not.[3] The same object may be loved as a mirror of divine beauty and hated as a

[1] Or. VI, Ch. VI, p. 1344. [2] Or. VI, Ch. IX, p. 1346; Ch. X, p. 1348.
[3] Or. VI, Ch. X, p. 1349. Idem itaque, feror et immortalis dicitur et mortalis. Immortalis quia nunquam extinguitur mutatque materiam potius quam evanescat; mortalis quia non ad idem semper incumbit; sed aut ex naturae mutatione aut ex diuturna rei eiusdem frequentatione orta satietate nova requirit oblectamenta: et qui in se una fermè defecit in alia quo dammodo reviviscit.

thief of the lover's self. Love longs to possess beautiful things and to possess them always, but since mortal things are for ever changing, it endeavours continually to replace the old by the new. This it does in the material order by generation and in the mind by memory. Divine things are always the same; mortal things at their passing leave kindred beings to replace them. The body restores itself with food and drink, and desires to perpetuate itself in its offspring. The mind seeks truth as its natural food and then tries to perpetuate itself by writing or teaching and so leaving a fair image of itself in the minds of others.[1]

Profane love is a kind of madness and various means of combating it are suggested, including the time-honoured one of getting thoroughly drunk.[2] Divine love is the highest of the four "furores" or grades of divine intuition, "a certain illumination of the rational soul." The highest faculties of the soul are normally asleep, and the lower are in consequence full of perturbations. The "furores" waken and harmonize the soul; first through the incantation of poetry and then through the purification of prayer and sacrifice. The soul so purified is assimilated to the mind, and by divination or illumination the two become a perfect unity. Finally, by love, this unity returns to God. Love is the noblest of the "furores" since all the others have need of him. All four are aped by counterfeits in the form of degenerate music, superstition, "fortune-telling," and lust.[3]

The book closes with a panegyric on Socratic love, the purest of human affections and the highway to paradise.[4]

The tentative speculations of the fifteenth century culminated triumphantly in the Neoplatonism of the Academy. It is small wonder that it bewitched the Renaissance; it gave form and authority to its dearest enthusiasms, adorning them with fanciful ornament and strange lore, yet stating them with the full force of

---

[1] Or. VI, Ch. XI, p. 1349.
[2] Or. VII, Ch. III, p. 1357; Ch. XI, p. 1360.
[3] Or. VII, Ch. XIII, p. 1361; Ch. XIV, p. 1362; Ch. XV, p. 1362.
[4] Or. VII, Ch. XVI, p. 1362.

belief. Its influence spread rapidly beyond Florence, through Italy, and through Europe. The works of Ficino and Pico were reprinted, copied, and translated into many of the vernacular tongues; and before the sixteenth century was far advanced Neoplatonism was not only a learned topic and an artistic inspiration but a fashionable accomplishment.

TRANSLATIONS

Page 61. Ac Picus a Marsilio . . .
Pico sometimes openly differed from Marsilio. Diacceto in all things praised and defended his master.

Page 63. Liberamus obsecro . . .
Let us, I pray, whensoever we are able, deliver God's sacred gift, Philosophy, from ungodliness, for indeed we can do so if we will; let us redeem our holy religion from accursed ignorance.

Page 64. Quid aljud . . .
What was Christ but, as it were, a living book of moral, nay of divine, Philosophy, and the very divine idea of virtue made manifest to human eyes.

Page 65. omnibus formis . . .
receiving all forms, but in its own nature void of all.

Page 65. totius naturae . . .
being instructed in the friendships and affinities of universal nature.

Page 66. Est apud nos . . .
With us heat is an elemental quality, in the celestial regions it is a heat-diffusing power, in the angelic minds it is the idea of heat. Let me expound this somewhat more clearly. There is among us a fire which is an element. The sun is a fire in heaven, the seraphic intellect is a fire in the supernal region. But behold how they differ. The elemental burns, the celestial gives life, the super-celestial loves.

Page 66. Si ergo in uno mundi . . .
If therefore in the one living body of the world there is everywhere a single life, as we have elsewhere declared, much more is there a single good which is present everywhere, even beyond the world.

Page 67. Tum Musarum dux Bacchus . . .
 Then Bacchus, leader of the Muses, showing forth to us philosophers in his mysteries, that is in the visible symbols of nature, the invisible things of God, shall satisfy us from the abundance of the house of God, in all of which we shall, like Moses, be found faithful.

Page 68. Quapropter naturale instinctu . . .
 Wherefore by a natural instinct he ascends to things above and descends to those beneath. And while he ascends he discards not the lower, and while he descends he forsakes not the higher. For if he relinquish either he will lapse to the opposite extreme, neither will he be the true bond of the external world. Indeed, he is like unto the air which, being intermediate between fire and water, turns with fire into heat and with water into moisture.

Page 68. Proinde quia Deus . . .
 Therefore, because God has joined Himself unto man without intermediary, it behoves us to remember that our felicity consists in being turned to Him, so that without intermediary we may cleave unto God.

Page 70. Cognosce te ipsum . . .
 Know thyself, O divine race clothed in mortal raiment; strip thyself, I beseech thee, in so far as thou canst; nay more, I say, with thine utmost endeavour separate the soul from the body, and reason from the affections of the senses. Then straightway thou shalt see the pure gold freed from the defilements of earth, thou shalt see the clear air when the clouds are dispersed; then, believe me, thou shalt reflect thyself as a sempiternal ray of the divine sun. Neither shalt thou henceforward dare either to think or to attempt any base or evil thing in thine own presence. . . . Yet thou believest thyself to be in the lowest part of the world, because thou seest not thyself soaring above the heavens, but only thy shadow, the body, in a lowly place. It is as if a boy, standing by a well, should think himself to be at the bottom, while he gazes at himself, but sees afar off his own shadow as it were in the depths. Or as if a bird, flying through the air, should think itself on earth while it sees its shadow flying on the ground Therefore, forsaking these shadows, return unto thyself, for thus shalt thou return unto greatness.

Page 71. . . . creaturarum internuntium . . .
 . . . the intermediary of the creatures, a friend to the gods above, king by clear-sighted reason of the baser senses, interpreter of nature by the inborn light of intelligence, a passage between stable eternity and the flux of time and (as the Persians say) the bond, nay rather, the marriage tie of the world; and but little lower than the angels, as David testifieth.

Page 72. in solitaria patris caligine . . .
in the solitary darkness of the Father who is established above all things, he shall pass beyond all things.

Page 72. Jam summus architectus . . .
Now God, the supreme architect, by the laws of His secret wisdom, created this earthly habitation of divinity, this most august temple that we behold. He adorned the supercelestial regions with intelligences, quickened the ethereal globes with eternal souls, and filled the outward and solid parts of this lower world with the many-natured animal host. But when the work was accomplished the artificer desired someone who would consider the nature of so great a work and love its beauty and admire its greatness. Therefore, when all things were completed (as Moses and Timaeus testify) He afterwards took thought of creating man. . . . Nor settled place nor proper form nor any peculiar gift did we give thee, O Adam, that what place, what form, and what gifts soever thou wouldst freely choose, these, by thine own will and purpose thou shouldst hold and possess. . . . We have made thee neither celestial nor terrestrial, neither mortal nor immortal, so that as the sculptor and moulder of thyself thou mayest shape thyself into what form thou most desirest. Thou mayest abase thyself unto things inferior, that is unto the brutes. Thou mayest, by thy soul's decision, be born again unto the things above, which are divine. O most great liberality of God the Father, O most great and marvellous felicity of man.

Page 73. Atque ita conatur . . .
Therefore he strives to be everywhere as God is. He strives also to be like God in being forever.

Page 74. Singuli namque homines . . .
For individual men, under one idea and in the same species, are as one man.

Page 75. Principio Deus . . .
In the beginning God creates of His own mind a substance [substantia] which we also call essence [essentia]. This, at the first moment of its creation, is formless and dark. But since truly it is born of God, it is turned back to God, its first cause, by an innate longing. Once turned unto God it is illumined by His light, and its desire is inflamed by the splendour of His beams. When its desire is kindled it cleaves wholly to God; and in so cleaving it receives its form. For God, who can do all things, depicts within the mind that cleaves to Him the natures of the things that shall be created. In it, therefore, are in a certain manner spiritually depicted all things that we perceive in these bodies. By these types are brought forth

the forms of the heavens, of the elements, of those vapours of whose nature are the starry globes, and of stones, metals, plants, and animals.

Page 78. . . . Ita Deus . . .

. . . as God, the centre of all things, who is simplest unity and purest activity, infused Himself into the universe, not only by being present to the whole but truly by implanting in all things by Him created a certain inmost part or power most simple and most excellent which is called the unity of their being (quae rerum unitas nominatur) and about which, as about a centre, all their remaining parts and powers depend.

Page 82. Quapropter nihil obstat . . .

Which things hinder not that love should be in all things, since as far as possible it penetrates through all.

Page 83. Cognoscere illum vere . . .

It is indeed possible now to know Him perfectly. For truly it is possible and easy to love what is known in any way. Those who know God please Him not unless knowing Him they love Him; and this not because they know but because whoso loveth is loved of God.

Page 84. quia sicut daemones . . .

because it is like the daemons who are midway between heavenly and earthly things.

CHAPTER IV

THE MEDICI CIRCLE (1)

POLIZIANO. THE *QUAESTIONES CAMALDULENSES* AND THE *ALTERCAZIONE*. LORENZO'S *SELVE D'AMORE* AND *LAUDE*. GIROLAMO BENIVIENI

THE poets of the Academy do not as a group show much real power or originality, and only two, Angelo Poliziano and Lorenzo de' Medici, have won any widespread fame. In them one may find a literary complement of the art of fifteenth-century Florence, although that art is perhaps more varied and profound than their work. Their range is, in fact, a severely limited one, though within it they often achieve exquisite results. Their poetry is not that of great passions or large conceptions. If one were seeking a hasty definition one might call it the poetry of delight; delight in natural beauty; in youth and gaiety; in country people and pursuits; in art and learning; in all the graces and pageants of a brilliant society; in the humour and at times in the crudities and vulgarities of life. The poets see their world through a tinted haze of literary reminiscence, but their feeling for the past is itself so vital that it does not spoil the freshness of their own perceptions, but becomes instead an essential element in them. The emotion that stirs them most deeply is regret that their joys cannot endure; and their loveliest lines are burdened with the sense of "the lapse of hours."

Though Lorenzo sometimes shows a warmer humanity, Poliziano was incomparably the greatest artist of the circle. Whether in a Latin "Sylva" or elegy, classical, yet as purely Florentine as a bas-relief of Donatello's, or in a "canzonetta," where the popular poetry of Tuscany has been refined to a quintessence by a scholar's touch, his verse has a melody, a finish, a precision, a delicate pictorial quality that make it perennially charming. He is so perfect that one is left with a thwarted wish that he were somehow greater.

His own predilections were mildly Aristotelian, but in subtler ways Ficino, of whom he always writes in terms of respectful discipleship, may well have been an inspiration to him. His purely scholarly and literary interests were too strong to allow him much time for philosophical studies.[1] As a poet he seems to have kept remarkably detached from the doctrines of the Academy; there are scarcely any direct references to them in his verse, and it is a debatable question whether or not they affected him.

His religious verse is fluent but conventional; his love poetry, with its echoes now of the "stil nuovisti," now of the popular songs of the countryside, is sometimes bantering, sometimes wistful, sometimes tender, as in the bird-like clarity and freshness of "La Brunettina mia"; but it rarely makes any attempt at a philosophical treatment of its subject. In the "Stanze" addressed by the ghost of a lover to his mistress there is a descant on a theme reminiscent of Cavalcanti and prophetic of Michelangelo, the idea that the beloved's beauty is an epitome of the beauty of the world.

> Costei ha privo il ciel d'ogni bellezza
> E tolto i beni di tutto il Paradiso
> Privato il Sol di lume e di chiarezza
> E posto l'ha nel suo splendido viso.

---

[1] "... sic ego nonnunque de philosophia quasi de Nilo canes bibi fugique" (A. Politianus, *Opera Omnia*, Basle, 1553, 1 vol., "Miscellaneorum," p. 310). But in the *Lamia: Praelectio in Priora Aristoteles Analytica*, p. 451, he defends himself against those who call him a mere "grammaticus." He was the pupil of Ficino and Argyropoulos and lectured in the Studio Fiorentino on Aristotle and other philosophers. His friendship with Ficino and Pico was no doubt one of the factors that helped to mould his peculiarly personal culture. Native genius he had in plenty, but the Neoplatonists' belief in the creativeness of the human mind, with its insistence that in knowledge if there are no limits there must be no stagnation, must have helped him to avoid the humanistic vice of worshipping the past too blindly. As Ficino said, Orpheus lost Euridice and Lot's wife was turned into a pillar of salt because they looked back instead of pressing forward. [*Opera*, Vol. I, p. 620.] In Poliziano's handling of his scholarship, so free, so vigorous, so touched by imagination and even by humour, one may see this aspect of Ficino's thought in action. He has made the past his own in no dead or mechanical sense; his learning and his personality are one thing, and express themselves as a unity.

> Al mondo ha tolto ogni sua gentilezza
> Ogni atto e bel costume e dolce riso.
> Amor le ha dato il guardo e la favella
> Per farla sopra tutte la più bella.[1]

Apart from this there is little until one comes to the celebrated *Stanze per la Giostra*,[2] and there, perhaps, in the picture of a world governed and linked up by love and permeated by secret sympathies and affections, one might see a translation into imaginative language of the thought of the *Heptaplus* or of Ficino's *Symposium*. It would be unsafe to press the point too far, for Poliziano had the traditions of the Golden Age and of the Earthly Paradise to draw upon, but continual association with the Neoplatonists may have coloured his conception and helped to create the delicately unreal and sentimental atmosphere of his poem. It is love "Quel che soggioga il ciel la terra e l'acque"[3] that dominates the *Stanze* and especially the whole exquisite description of the reign of Venus

> . . . ove ogni grazia si diletta
> Ove Belta di fiori al crin fa brolo.[4]

Here there are secret sympathies even between inanimate things, The wind plays lovingly through the grasses,

> . . . lascive aurette
> Fan dolcemente tremolar l'erbette.[5]

and the waters of the fountain feed the trees whose branches shade them from the heat, so that trees and fountain alike increase by mutual liberality.

---

[1] Angelo Poliziano, *Le Stanze, Orfeo, Le Rime*, ed. Carducci, 2nd ed., Bologna, Zanichelli, 1911. Cf. Cavalcanti, *Tu hai in te i fiori e la verdura*. Michelangelo, *Poi che le tue bellezze al mondo sieno*.

[2] The *Stanze* were written to commemorate Giuliano de' Medici's love for "la bella Simonetta" and to celebrate his success in a tournament. The poem was cut short by the murder of Giuliano in 1478. As it stands it tells only of the first meeting of the lovers, of Giuliano's instant infatuation, and of Cupid's triumphant return to the Kingdom of Venus, which is described in a long sequence of Poliziano's most delightful octaves.

[3] *Stanze*, v. 2.   [4] Ibid., v. 118.   [5] Ibid., v. 67.

> L'acqua da viva pomice zampilla
> Che con suo arco il bel monte sospende
> E per fiorito solco indi tranquilla
> Pingendo ogni sua orma al fonte scende
> Dalle cui labbra un grato umor distilla
> Che'l premio di lor ombre agli arbor rende:
> Ciascun si pasce a mensa non avara
> E par che l'un dell'altro cresca a gara.[1]

The trees themselves twine together in a loving embrace.

> ... l'arbor che già tanto ad Ercol piacque
> Col platan si trastulla intorno all'acque.[2]

While the beasts and birds and even the fishes in the stream are moved by the same force:

> Nè spengon le fredde acque il dolce fuoco.[3]

Even natural enmities are reconciled at the will of the god.

> Il cervo appresso alla massilia fera
> Co'pie levati la sua sposa abbraccia:
> Fra l'erba ove piu ride Primavera
> L'un coniglio coll'altro s'accovaccia
> Le semplicette lepri vanno a schiera
> Da'can sicure all'amorosa traccia
> Si l'odio antico e'l natural timore
> Ne'petti ammorza, quando vuole, Amore.[4]

Moreover, it is by the power of Love that the whole of this enchanted world is preserved and made eternal:

> Nè mai le chiome del giardino eterno
> Tenera brina ne fresca neve imbianca
> Ivi non osa entrar ghiacciato verno:
> Non vento l'erbe o gli arboscelli stanca:
> Ivi non volgon gli anni il lor quaderno;
> Ma lieta Primavera mai non manca;
> Che i suoi crin biondi e crespi all'aura spiega
> E mille fiori in ghirlandetta lega.[5]

---

[1] *Stanze*, v. 69. [2] Ibid., v. 79. [3] Ibid., v. 80.
[4] Ibid., v. 83. [5] Ibid., v. 87.

The same atmosphere pervades the passage in Lorenzo's *Selve d'Amore*, in which the poet, divided from his lady by misunderstanding, dreams of the early and untroubled days of his love and compares them with the Golden Age.

> La lepre e'l bracco in un cespuglio giace
> L'un non abbaia e l'altro ancor non geme:
> Tra il veltro e'l cavriol e'l cervo è pace
> Nè alcun ne piè veloce spera o teme:
> Scherzan tra lor e provocar lor piace
> Talor l'un l'altro: e se corrono insieme
> Non corron per fuggir il fero morso
> Ma sol per superar l'un l'altro in corso.[1]

A more curious example of an interpretation of nature that was directly derived from the Neoplatonists occurs in the *Canzoniere* of Girolamo Benivieni in a sonnet which, like more famous poems by Lorenzo and Poliziano, is addressed to a violet.

> Qual felice terren, qual vive fronde
> Ne formar l'alma e candida viola
> Che per le mani angeliche aprir sola
> Ne pote al cor quel che agli occhi hora si absconde—
> Forse che amor da le auree chiome bionde
> Della sua genitrice in ciel ne invola
> Così alcun fiore, onde per obscuro vola
> Per li humani pecti e imezo e così si infonde.
> Si gentil fior del ciel non di natura
> Opera certo fu: che el suo valore
> Lo effecto prova, io el sento, amor mel giura
> Così in virtù d'un semplicetto fiore
> L'alma più che altra libera e sicura
> Fa el dì che'n sua prigion la inchiuse amore.

The poem is conventional enough and would not claim one's attention if it were not for the commentary that Benivieni appends to it.

"Fra tutte le cose della natura nessuna certa quantunque minima quantunque vile e abiecta si trova in ella quale così come in ciascuna altra anchora che nobilissima, non resplende secondo

[1] Lorenzo de' Medici, *Poems*, ed. Ross and Hutton, London, 1912. Vol. I, *Selve d'Amore*, Pt. I, Stanza 17, p. 5.

el modo della sua capacità uno non so che admirabile e divino: per la quale può l'anima nostra quando è ben disposta e contemplando conoscere e conoscendo amare lo autore di quella cio è esso Dio.[1]

This touch of Wordsworthian sentiment was probably genuine in Benivieni in the days that followed his conversion, but it reads oddly in conjunction with the courtly little lyric it accompanies and suggests that the poet's Piagnone activities had a little dimmed his critical sense. Yet it shows that even the strictest and devoutest spirit of the group was prepared to justify his delight in natural beauty in the language of the Academy.

Traces of Ficino's influence are more numerous and more obvious in Lorenzo's verse than they are in Poliziano's, but one is confronted here as always with the capital problem of Lorenzo's sincerity. How far was his Neoplatonism a genuine conviction and how far a literary pose or a part of the politic identification of himself with the tastes and interests of his fellow citizens that made up so much of his success as a ruler?

The answer to those questions lies perhaps in the general character of his work. He gives one most commonly the impression of a gifted amateur, and of a man of quick but not profound imagination who entered readily into many moods, though he rarely felt any one of them with very great intensity. The dull vulgarity of the *Beoni* and the equivocations of the *Canti Carniaschialeschi* seemed to come as easily to him as the *Laude* and *Orazioni*. He is at his best in that graceful and half-humorous idyll *La Nencia di Barberino*, or in the celebrated *Trionfo di Bacco e d'Arianna*, which seems to be almost a symbolic utterance of his age, at once its paean and its elegy. In those lilting rhythms, warm with life and colour and movement yet penetrated by an undertone of melancholy, Lorenzo's evasive and enigmatic spirit appears for once to speak without disguise.

[1] Girolamo Benivieni, *Canzoniere dell'Amor Divino*, Florence, 1500, p. 25, Sonnet XIII. For the Canzoniere see the latter part of this chapter. The poem quoted above is one of the strangest instances of Benivieni's adaptation of his early verse to the religious ideals of his later life.

To a poet of his temperament it looks as if Ficino's Neoplatonism could have meant little; but before one dismisses his frequent references to it as insincere one must remember how intimately it was woven into his consciousness. He had learned it as a boy, side by side with the faith that his mother, Lucrezia Tornabuoni, had taught him, and some aroma of both the faith and the philosophy clung about him to the last. His Neoplatonism was perhaps an intellectual habit rather than a deep personal conviction, but it was, nonetheless, so closely identified with his mode of thought that he could never quite discard it, and could even, at different stages of his life, find in the distinctive language of the school adequate expression for his own emotions. Such a process can be traced fairly clearly in his poems. It is possible to distinguish three phases in his treatment of philosophical ideas, in the *Altercazione ovver Dialogo*, in the *Selve d'Amore*, and in some of the *Laude* and other religious poems; but they are phases of emotional intensity rather than of intellectual development. One is not concerned here with a poet who was also a thinker and whose work embodies a growing wealth of original thought. Lorenzo accepted the teaching of the Academy already fully matured and did not always succeed in making it his own. He is academic and passionate, lifeless and inspired by turns. In his early work, the *Altercazione*, he did little more than turn the second book of Landino's *Quaestiones Camaldulenses* into verse.[1] It can hardly

---

[1] The *Quaestiones Camaldulenses* (also called *Disputationes*) were written in 1470. The actual conversations are probably imaginary but must be typical, if idealized, versions of the ordinary proceedings of the Academy. The edition cited here is that of Mathias Schürerius, 1508. The principal speakers are Lorenzo himself, Leon Battista Alberti, and Ficino, but Landino and his brother Pietro, Giuliano de' Medici, Alamanno Rinuccini, and other frequenters of the Academy are also of the party. The *Altercazione* was probably written shortly after the dialogues.

For Landino see A. M. Bandini, *Specimen literaturae Florentinae*, saec. XV, 2 vols., Florence, 1751. A. Mancini, Arch. St. It., serie IV, Vol. XIX, 1887, p. 318. Landino (1424–97) encouraged Ficino to write his earliest work, the *Istitutiones Platonicae*, and was himself a great student of the Latin Platonists, but shows himself ready in the *Quaestiones* to borrow from his former disciple.

be said that he improved on his original, for the *Altercazione* is heavy reading and the *Quaestiones*, though there is no great novelty in their themes, form one of the most pleasing of humanistic treatises. The four dialogues deal respectively with the rival merits of the active and contemplative life, with the "Summum Bonum," and with the allegory of Virgil and, incidentally, of Dante. The first, which is touched upon in the opening of Lorenzo's poem, is an energetic presentation of the Academy's ideal of manhood . . . "ad recte agendum et ad verum investigandum natura producti simus."[1] In its conclusion that Martha and Mary are sisters dwelling under one roof, and that although Mary's virtue is the higher, both are pleasing to the Lord and neither can flourish without the other, there appears again in all its fervour the endeavour to understand the human spirit as a unity that must function in its completeness if it is not to be a mere travesty of itself.[2]

The lofty heights of contemplation can be attained only through activity "non datur igitur quies: nisi prius laboraveris."[3] The ecstatic state in which the soul is temporarily freed from the body is the utmost beatitude that man can know,[4] yet contemplation that does not issue in right action and notably in social action, is imperfect and, except with a few rare minds, may even be dangerous.[5]

The second book, *De Summo Bono*, was partly based on Ficino's *De Voluptate* (1457). In this, one of the earliest of his extant works, Ficino declares himself too young to arrive at any independent conclusion on the nature of true happiness, but sets out the opinions of the various schools of Philosophy, concluding with the Platonic, towards which he naturally inclines.[6] Landino evidently availed himself of the summary, but embodies Ficino's more mature

[1] *Q.C.*, Bk. I, p. A IV².
[2] Ibid., Bk. I, p. C II.
[3] Ibid., Bk. I, p. A IV⁴.
[4] Ibid., p. A IV⁴.
[5] Ibid., Bk. I, p. C¹. Sed mihi crede rarissimi erunt qui humanam societatem fugientes, soli apud se esse possint: id enim non nisi eius hominis est: qui iam hominis natura superata ad diviniora evolavit. Cf. p. B IV⁴.
[6] In Ficino, *Opera*, Vol. I, p. 986. See F. Gabotto, "L'epicurismo di M. F.," in *Rivista di fil. scientifica*, serie 2, Vol. X, pp. 428–42.

opinions in showing that Platonists and Christians are at one in saying that God is the sovereign good, and that He is to be known rather through the will than through the intellect.[1] Though he condemns "voluptas" or sensual pleasure, Landino looks upon true joy, which is attained through virtue and divine love, as the only thing in life that men seek for its own sake. In this he no doubt had Valla's work in mind and was perhaps trying to give the central thought of the *De Voluptate* a more purely ideal aim.[2]

Lorenzo's poem opens with a description of the valley to which the writer, flying from "l'aspro civil tormento," has withdrawn for peace. He hears a shepherd's pipe sounding in the distance and is soon greeted by the shepherd himself. Lorenzo thereupon begins to compare the simplicity and freedom of the shepherd's life with the perfidy of courts. The shepherd reproaches him for his inconsistency in not adopting the life he so much praises, and then points out its hardships and the troubles which it has in common with civic life.

> Ma credo appellar possa ad una voce
> Fortuna il mondo rigida e inimica
> Perché pende ciascuna nella sua croce.[3]

At this point Marsilio's lyre is heard. He soon appears and Lorenzo explains the question in dispute and asks for enlightenment. Marsilio replies

> . . . alcun non pensi
> Di trovar ben che sia perfetto o vero
> Mentre l'alma è legata in questi sensi.[4]

---

[1] *Q.C.*, Bk. II, p. D⁵. "Verum quoniam divinam essentiam non solum intelligendo attingimus: sed eam etiam expetimus, atque amamus, amandoque fruimur. . . ." See also pp. D II, E IV⁵.

[2] Ibid., p. E³ et seq. For Landino's defence of Epicurus see p. C III, and Saitta, "La Rivendicazione d'Epicuro nel Rinascimento" in *Fil. It. ed Umanesimo*, Venice, 1928, p. 81.

[3] The edition of Lorenzo's poems cited in the text is, unless otherwise indicated, the one edited by Janet Ross and Edward Hutton, London, 1912, 2 vols., Vol. II, *Altercazione*, Cap. I, p. 126.   [4] Cap. I, p. 127.

This has been ordained in order to keep us from cleaving to earthly things. "Il vero ben è un, ne più ne meno" and is reserved in heaven for those who have lived well. In the world there are three kinds of good.

> I primi la fortuna dà e toglie
> Gli altri quei ben che al corpo dà natura
> I terzi l'alma nostra in se raccoglie.[1]

The gifts of fortune and of the body are quickly dismissed. The first, "Dominazion ricchezza onore e grazia," are all vain. Dominion is a servitude, the desire for wealth is insatiable, and honour and grace, depending not on ourselves but on others, are matters of opinion merely. Bodily gifts—strength, health, and beauty—are easily lost; and beauty at least is of more joy to the onlooker than to the possessor. There remains then the gifts of the soul, which fall into two categories: the sensitive and the rational.

The gifts of the senses we share with the other animals, some of whom indeed possess them in higher perfection than we do. The pleasures of sense are "guerra eterna," accompanied by suspicion and followed by penitence and satiety. When we turn from these to the rational endowments of the soul we find that some are natural and some acquired, and of these the first receive all their value from the worth or vanity of the ends to which they are turned.

> Memoria audacia e dell'ingegno acume
> In questi non è il ben, chè son secondo
> Che gli fa l'uso e il buono o rio costume.

The greater these gifts are the more harmful they become when misused. By using these innate faculties well, however, the soul arrives at the acquired good of active and speculative virtue.[2]

The Stoics and Cynics held that happiness could be found in active virtue, but Marsilio points out that this is accompanied by pain and cannot, therefore, be an end in itself. Only in speculative virtue, the virtue of Mary, can the soul find the living water that can slake its infinite thirst for happiness.

[1] *Alt.*, Cap. II, p. 131. *Q.C.*, II, p. D II^i. [2] *Alt.*, p. 136. *Q.C.*, II, p. D II$_i$.

> Così la mente che contempla siede
> E quando al contemplato ben s'appressa
> Altro che contemplar giammai non chiede.[1]

Contemplation may occupy itself with terrestrial things, celestial things or super-celestial things. Democritus had placed the highest good in the contemplation of the laws of nature in the world.

> Ma il vero ben non è sotto la Luna
> Dunque non è nel contemplar di quelle
> Cose che si disfanno a una a una.[2]

Anaxagoras had maintained that the study of the heavens could reveal true happiness; but this study, though exalted, is yet inferior to the contemplation of super-celestial things which we may undertake either in the body or out of the body. Aristotle sets up the former as his conception of man's ideal state.

> Dice chi ben la sua sentenzia ha letta
> Che la felicità è l'operare
> Virtù perfetta in vita ancor perfetta.
> Ma se in due cose il vero ben dee stare
> L'una la volontà l'altra lo intendere
> Perfetta o l'una o l'altra non può fare.[3]

The soul, while it is in the body, cannot understand fully and still longs to advance further towards

> La pura verità formosa e bianca.

> All'alma avien come a certi animali
> Che manco veggon quel ch'è più lucente;
> Ancora gli occhi nostri al Sol son tali.
> E così l'occhio della nostra mente. . . .[4]

From this point the human mind cannot proceed unaided, but needs the help of heavenly wisdom. Perfection lies in separation of the soul from the body; and this is the joy reserved for the souls that have dedicated themselves to God. The contemplation of

---

[1] *Alt.*, p. 137. *Q.C.*, II, p. D II¹. [2] *Alt.*, p. 137. *Q.C.*, II, p. D IV.
[3] *Alt.*, p. 138. For views of various philosophers, see *Q.C.*, Bk. II, pp. C III et seq. [4] *Alt.*, Cap. III, p. 139.

super-celestial things may, however, fix itself upon one of two objects: the angelic nature or the Godhead itself. The angelic nature cannot satisfy the soul since it, too, is created, and it is our nature to search out the final causes of all things.[1]

The approach to God may be made either through the intellect or through the will (pel conosciuto ben godere Per mezzo del disio). Intellect and will are the two wings of the soul, but the will, which is one with desire or love, is the more perfect and the more richly rewarded, for true knowledge of God is impossible.

> Come error fa maggior e più espresso
> Chi ha Dio in odio che chi non lo intende;
> Cosi chi l'ama più più merto ha in esso.[2]

Love opens the gates of Paradise and cannot err, but speculation may induce pride, and so blind the seeker.

We seek to know the good in order to possess and enjoy it. Knowledge does not necessarily imply joy; but joy implies sight and understanding. Joy alone is desired for its own sake, and our minds become divine,

> . . . amando Dio, non sol vedendo.

Any intellectual vision to which man can rise is dulled and limited by the soul's own limitations.

> Aviene all'alma nostra, Dio intendendo
> Che a sua capacità tanta amplitudine
>   Contrae, e Dio in se vien restrignendo.

> Della divina infinità l'abisso
> Quasi per una nebbia contempliamo
> Benchè l'alma vi tenga l'occhio fisso;
> Ma d'un perfetto e vero amor l'amiamo,
> Quel che conosce Dio, Dio a se tira
> Amàndo, alla sua altezza c'innalziamo.

---

[1] *Alt.*, p. 141.
[2] Ibid., p. 143. *Q.C.*, II, p. D IV^5. Verum quoniam divinam essentiam non solum intelligendo attingimus sed eam etiam expetimus, atque amamus, amandoque fruimur: quae omnia in voluntate posita sunt, recte inter theologos dubitatum est esset ne in ipsa cognitione, an potius in voluntate tanta res ponenda.

The soul released by love from bodily fetters.

> . . . si converte in Dio
> E sopra Dio veduto si dilata.[1]

St. Paul tells how love raised him up to the third heaven; but above this there are realms of pure being to which we can only aspire after death. The poem ends in a long prayer for enlightenment addressed to the transcendent and yet present power who creates and cares for even those things that make no response, and whom alone we love in all the objects on which we set our affections.

> O venerando immenso eterno lume
> Il quale in te medesimo ti vede
> E luce cio che luce nel tuo nume. . . .
>
> Fonte di letizia e gaudio intero
> Io so che tu se'solo, ed in te giace
> Quel che appetisce il nostro desidero.
>
> Perchè se questo ovver quel ben ne piace
> non cerca il disio nostro o quello o questo
> Ma il bene in essi, dov'è la sua pace.[2]

In this cold and awkward poem Lorenzo expounds the doctrine whose quintessence he subsequently distilled into the first of his Laude.

It is one of the cases in which the influence of the Academy must be called definitely pernicious.

In the *Canzoniere*, though the poet has escaped from the academic stiffness of the *Altercazione*, the influence of the "stil nuovisti" is too strong to allow of any very original treatment of his themes.

There is some charming verse like the sonnet to the violets and *Lascia l'isola tua tanto diletta*, but the poems are on the whole too imitative to need extensive comment.

With the *Selve d'Amore*, however, one passes into a new atmosphere where Ficino's theories are fused with warm fantasy

[1] *Alt.*, Cap. IV, pp. 144-6.   [2] Ibid., Cap. IV, pp. 150-2.

and genuine emotion. The poem tells the story of Lorenzo's love for the Florentine lady, generally though not certainly identified with Lucrezia Donati. The exact amount of biographical fact it contains is debatable, nor for present purposes is it of the first importance. It is at least certain that it presents in fanciful guise the incidents of a real love affair.[1] The lovers meet and after a short time of happiness are separated. The lady is married to another and Lorenzo, after passing through an acute period of despair and jealousy, frees himself from these mortal passions; and from the personal and particular love rises to the love of abstract beauty which he sees "tutta accolta in un volto." The affair was not so serious as to prevent Lorenzo from wandering into long mythological digressions and delightful but often irrelevant descriptions of rural scenes. Yet the emotion that informs it, if never overwhelming, never strikes one as being wholly unreal.

The *Selve*, in spite of occasional tediousness, have a note of true poetry, a certain grace in their descriptions of nature, a lightness and fluidity in their rhythms, that mark them as far surer in inspiration than the *Altercazione*. Lorenzo was no longer under the obligation of formally expounding his philosophic tenets; but they would still rise in snatches to his lips when he was free to adorn and colour them as he pleased. In the *Selve* they seem to bud naturally out of the growing stem of the poem. The lady it celebrates is not only Lucrezia Donati, but a symbol of the beauty in which Lorenzo, the artist, delighted. The aesthetic side of Neoplatonism was one that could scarcely have failed to attract him; and there is probably some truth in the picture he paints at the beginning of the poem, of his youthful self searching for the perfect beauty among all forms through which beauty is diffused, as one might turn over the contents of a cabinet of gems in the search for one jewel rarer than them all. His catalogue of beautiful things,

---

[1] See N. Scarano, "Il Platonismo nelle poesie di L.," *N.A.*, August 1893, p. 606; September 1893, p. 49. I del Lungo. "Gli amori del magnifico Lorenzo," *N.A.*, May 1913. Lorenzo, *Poesie*, ed. Carducci, Florence, 1859, pp. 58-62. Prose commentary on *Rime*.

so reminiscent of Benozzo Gozzoli's frescos—gay, decorative, and slightly prosaic—reads oddly among his more fine-spun dreams.

> Non ornate di fronde apriche valli;
> Non chiaro rivo che l'erbetta bagni,
> Di color pinta bianchi rossi e gialli;
> Non città grandi o edifici magni;
> Ludi feri, stran giuochi o molli balli;
> Non legni in mar che Zeffiro accompagni
> Non vaghi uccei, nuovi animali o mostri;
> Non sculta pietra o gemme agli occhi nostri.
>
> In queste cose senza legge alcuna
> Givan gli occhi cercando lor pace
> Ascosa, e non sapevano in questa una
> Che conosciuta poi tanto a lor piace.
> Occultamente mia lieta fortuna
> Conduceva il disio, che nel cor giace.
> Condotto era il mio cor, e non sapeva
> A riveder chi gia veduto aveva.[1]

Through his wanderings he was, in fact, being led back to the idea of beauty innate in his own soul; and it was only when he first saw the lady of his love that he saw that idea incarnate. Earth and heaven and the goddess of love herself, who on that day leaned on the breast of Jupiter, rejoiced to see his discovery.

> Quando tessuto fu questa catena
> L'aria la terra e il cielo lieto concorse;
> L'aria non fu giammai tanto serena
> Nè il Sol giammai sì bella luce porse.
> Di fronde giovinette e di fior piena
> La terra lieta ov'un chiar rivo corse:
> Ciprigna in grembo al padre quel dì si mise
> Lieta mirò dal ciel quel loco e rise.[2]

Lorenzo paints with fine vigour and efficacy the early stages of his quest for this ideal beauty. Every trace of beauty in the world suggests the presence of the beloved and urges him into eager

[1] Lorenzo, *Poesie*, ed. Ross and Hutton, Vol. I, *Selve d'Amore*, Pt. I Stanzas 11–12, pp. 3–4.   [2] Ibid., Pt. I, Stanza, 17, p. 5.

pursuit like a hound in the chase. His words recall Ficino's simile of beauty as a delightful perfume that wins men to desire the unknown sweetness of the deity; and at the same time express the feelings of a youth "in love with love," who has not yet found a satisfying object for his affections.

> Nel primo tempo che Amor gli occhi aperse
> Questa beltate innanzi al disio pose:
> E poichè com'è bella me la offerse
> Ridendo, lasso, agli occhi la nascose.
> Con quanti pianti bellezze diverse
> Poi cercar, quanto tempo in quante cose!
> Talor vedendo pur l'afflitta ciglia
> Cosa la qual questa beltà simiglia.
>
> Allor siccome can bramoso in caccia
> Fra le frondi trovar l'occulta fiera
> Se vede terra impressa dalla traccia
> Conosce al segno ch'indi passata era;
> Perchè la simiglianza par che faccia
> Certo argomento alla bellezza vera
> Così cercando questa cosa e quella
> Amor mostrommi al fin mia donna bella.[1]

The poet's soul is satisfied in contemplation of the beloved even as

> . . . li beati spiriti intenti
> Stanno alla santa faccia sempre intorno.[2]

In fact, he almost goes so far as to identify the lady with the Absolute Beauty and to say that other things are beautiful only in so far as they participate in her.

> Anzi sempre si truova in ogni parte
> Chè ciò che agli occhi è bel da questa viene.
> Varie bellezze in varie cose sparte
> Dà al mondo il fonte vivo d'ogni bene!
> E quel che mostran l'altre cose in parte
> In lui tutto e perfetto si contiene:
> E se la simiglianza agli occhi piace
> Quanto è qui più perfetta ogni lor pace!

---

[1] Stanzas 24, 25, p. 6.   [2] Stanza 29, p. 8.

> Contrarie voci fanno un suon soave
> E diversi color bellezza nuova:
> Piace la voce acuta per la grave
> Nel nero il bianco la sua grazia trova.
> Mirabilmente l'alta bellezza ave
> Fatto che l'un nemico all'altro giova
> L'alta bellezza ch'ogni cor disia
> Ed io sol veggo nella donna mia.[1]

In the second part of the *Selve* Lorenzo is occupied with later and less happy vicissitudes of his passion. The lady is absent and Lorenzo, after crying at considerable length for death, falls a prey to "Disio, dispetto, invidia e triste cure" and to a desperate longing for the physical presence of the loved one.

> Me divida Fortuna allunga e smembra
> Dal suo bel viso e da tanta dolcezza:
> Nè bramo al mondo o prezzo se non quelle
> Membra e non posso udirne più novelle.[2]

Hope cheers him for a while with a promise of her return, which will make the Spring appear again on the earth; but the delicious reverie does not last and Lorenzo awakes to find that "resta con Amore Gelosia sola." The lovers are separated by inward as well as by outward barriers, so that they no longer find consolation even in Hope "Vita e conservazion di tutti i mali." It is at this point that Lorenzo makes his prayer for a renewal of the Golden Age, which is fused in his imagination with the rapturous and idyllic beginning of his love.

> In questi dolci luoghi in questi tempi
> Ponmi Amor con la belle donna mia
> Nell'età verde, ne'primi anni scempi
> Senza speranza e senza gelosia:
> Nè tempo mai l'età matura adempi
> Ma il nostro dolce amor eterno sia
> Non più bellezza in lei, non altro foco
> In noi; ma sol quel dolce tempo e loco.[3]

---

[1] Stanzas 27, 28, p. 7.   [2] Pt. II, Stanza 15, p. 13.   [3] Stanza 115, p. 36.

Yet if that time cannot come again he will be content with his lady's good will, since in her

> Concorre ogni virtute, ogni dolcezza
> E ciò che è bello è nella sua bellezza.[1]

Lapped in this purely contemplative mood he is blessed by a vision of the lady returning towards him and now she has almost ceased to be a mortal woman and become identified with the Idea of Beauty itself.

> O vaghi occhi amorosi
> Che in questo e'n quel bel viso
> Quando mirate fiso
> Vedete mille bellezze diverse;
> Mentre vi sono ascosi
> Questi due vaghi lumi
> Stolto alcun non presumi
> Aver veduto la bellezza intera.
> Qui è la belta vera
> Tutta accolta in un volto:
> Quinci l'esempio han tolto
> L'altre che in varie cose son disperse
> Chi questa belta mira
> Di eterno e dolce amor sempre sospira.[2]

Strangely enough, the finest expression of Lorenzo's Neoplatonism occurs not in any of his love poems but in the first of the series of Laude. These are of very varying merit, ranging from impudent reminiscences of "Canti Carnarcialeschi" to one poem of unquestionable beauty; and suggest on the whole that Monna Lucrezia had taught her son to "know his Bible" remarkably well and to speak fluently, if not always spontaneously, the language of orthodoxy. Here and there are hints of Ficino's theology; of man's dignity as arbiter of his own salvation,

> Chi senza te t'ha fatto
> Senza te stesso non ti vuol salvare,[3]

---

[1] Stanza 116, p. 36.　　[2] P. 39.　　[3] Vol. I, Lauda X, v. 4, p. 220.

of the Incarnation which took place not only that God should become man, but that man should become God,

> E'muor per darti vita
> E'diventa mortal per far te Dio,[1]

and the close identification of Beauty with the Deity.

> Con la tua bellezza tanta
> La bellezza innamorasti.
> O bellezza eterna e santa
> Di Maria bella infiammasti:
> Tu d'amor l'amor legasti
> Vergin santa dolce e pia.[2]

But the Lauda "O Dio, O Sommo Bene" stands alone among his poems, so completely alone as to be startling.[3] There is nothing to show what mood of despair and longing and frustration, what sudden imaginative lightening produced this outburst. If one is here again in personal contact with Lorenzo—and there is something in the poem that makes it hard to believe that one is not—it is with a Lorenzo very different from the poet of "Nencia" and the Carnival songs. That the two should have been one is simply one of the paradoxes of human nature. A state of mind like that revealed in the Lauda was certainly not habitual with Lorenzo; but there are phases of religious emotion that may come to the sinner as to the saint; and the desire for rest in the bewilderment of human passions, for permanence in the midst of change, for a perfection that even our worst faults cannot assail, are feelings that may flash upon the most heedless and perhaps gain in poignancy from the contrast between the flawed spirit and the beauty of holiness that it can neither attain nor quite renounce. It was the rascal Villon who wrote one of the tenderest of hymns to the Virgin, and the atheist Marlow who imagined that great last cry of Faust

> See where Christ's blood streams in the firmament.

Whatever moved Lorenzo in writing this poem it made him penetrate as never before to the very essence of his theme. The philosophy that supplied the flat dialectic of the *Altercazione* and

[1] Vol. I, Lauda X, v. 6, p. 221. [2] Lauda VI, v. 1, p. 213. [3] Lauda I, p. 204.

informed the fanciful love-traffic and sometimes trivial aestheticism of the *Selve* here becomes the natural language of the soul in a moment of high emotion. The poem, whether it be a "dramatic lyric" or a personal cry of despondency and exaltation, has the accent of truth. It opens with a couplet in broken rhythm full of desire and bewilderment; and the reiteration of the same rhymes at the end of each verse runs through it like a sigh of human weariness that passes at length into an affirmation of strong faith.

> O Dio, o Sommo Bene, or come fai?
> Chè te sol cerco, e non ritrovo mai.
>
> Lasso, s'io cerco questa cosa o quella
> Te cerco in esse, o dolce Signor mio.
> Ogni cosa per te è buona e bella.
> E muove come buona il mio disio.
> Tu sei pur tutto in ogni luogo, O Dio,
> E in alcun luogo non ti truovo mai.[1]

Beauty is at once the snare and the beacon light of the soul. It is the indefinable grace that makes the objects of sense appear in themselves lovable and precious; but if man tries to satisfy the infinite hunger of his spirit with those objects he will find only disillusionment. His need is for the light itself, not for the fragile vessels in which it shines as it lists. He can reach felicity only by that death to sensual things which is a new birth to eternal life.

> La vista in mille varie cose volte
> Te guarda e non ti vede e sei lucente
> L'orechio ancor diverse voci ascolta
> E'l tuo suon è per tutto e non ti sente.
> La dolcezza comune ad ogni gente
> Cerca ogni senso e non la truova mai.

---

[1] Cf. *Orazione*, II, p. 197.
Santo Dio, il qual sol se'conosciuto
Da'tuoi familiari, e santo se'
Che nel Verbo ogni cosa hai constituto
Santo Dio, del quale sol immagin è
Ogni natura; santo per essenzia
Perchè mai la natura formò te . . .

> Deh, perchè cerchi anima trista ancora
> Beata vita in tanti affanni e pene?
> Cerca quel cerchi pur; ma non dimora
> Nel luogo ove tu cerchi, questo bene:
> Beata vita, onde la morte viene
> Cerchi; e vita ove vita non fu mai.
>
> Delli occhi vani ogni luce sia spenta
> Perch'io vegga la vera luce amica:
> Assorda i miei orecchi acciò ch'io senta
> La disiata voce che mi dica:
> Venite a me, chi ha peso e fatica
> Ch'io vi ristori, egli è ben tempo omai.

The lines gain in force and music as the poet turns from the thought of his own weakness to that of the serenity and unalterable loveliness of invisible beauty, rising to a sonorous climax and sinking back at last in an assurance of peace.

> Allor l'occhio vedrà luce invisibile
> L'orecchio udirà suon ch'è senza voce
> Luce e suon che alla mente è sol sensibile
> Nè il troppo offende, o a tal senso nuoce.
> Stando i piè fermi correrà veloce
> L'alma a quel ben che seco è sempre mai.
>
> Allor vedrò, o Signor dolce e bello
> Che questo bene o quel non mi contenta:
> Ma levando dal bene e questo e quello
> Quel ben che resta il dolce Dio diventa:
> Questa vera dolcezza e sola senta
> Chi cerca il ben: questo non manca mai.

The upward impulse of love that had served elsewhere as matter for an erudite discourse here becomes the inward fire and breath of the poem. By a strange fate Lorenzo, who had consummately expressed the careless and pleasure-loving aspects of his age, became also an interpreter of its most intimate disquietude and its deepest aspirations. The weariness he voiced did not proceed from boredom or ascetic renunciation; it was the restlessness of eager and richly endowed minds, conscious of immensities hitherto unexplored in the visible world, in the past history of mankind, and in the intricacies of the individual soul, but unable to find in any of them a full satisfaction for their own tremendous longings. Side by side with much indifference and unbelief and moral corruption there ran through the Renaissance the passionate quest for a faith or a philosophy capable of unifying all the manifold varieties of existence and experience and of showing God, man, and nature as participating in a single life. Such a philosophy Florentine Neoplatonism attempted to supply. Its sincerest followers so loved the beauty of the world and the greatness of the human spirit that they hungered to believe them both divine, and yet were aware of something vaster than either, continually apprehended behind the mutable variety of things, but continually evading their most ardent pursuit.

> Tu sei pur tutto in ogni luogo, o Dio
> E in alcun luogo non ti truovo mai.

Moments of defeat and even of despair are incident to such an endeavour. It is possible to believe in human perfectibility, but no honest man can believe that the world and he himself are perfect as they are. The mere possession of an ideal is a negation of such a claim; and to betray that ideal, whether it be regarded as a divinely proffered gift or as implicit in the soul itself, brings inevitable pain. The urgency of Lorenzo's lines suggests not intellectual dissatisfaction only, but repentance.

The Neoplatonists were, however, fundamentally optimistic and such a mood could never have with them the tragic intensity that it assumes in a Jacopone or a Thomas à Kempis. They lay little emphasis on the agonies of penitence, much on the quiet perfecting of the inner life and on the ultimate assurance of victory.

Man is an active spiritual principle, striving continually, in obedience to the law of his own being, to identify himself with the glory whose image he perceives in his own soul and in the world around him. The objects of sense must be left behind, not because they are evil in themselves—for they too participate in the divine—but because they are limited and man's infinite spirit cannot rest in any but an infinite life, which is at once its utmost goal and its most immediate treasure.

> Stando i piè fermi correrà veloce
> L'alma a quel ben che seco è sempre mai.

In Girolamo Benivieni the interpretation of Neoplatonism is exclusively religious, but the fact makes of his *Canzoniere del Amor Divino* one of the strangest documents of the age. Benivieni in his youth wrote a considerable number of love-lyrics in the Petrarchan-Neoplatonic tradition, but after his conversion to the opinions of Savonarola he bitterly repented of these early effusions and did his utmost to suppress all copies of them. When he found this to be impossible he adopted the curious expedient of collecting the poems and publishing them with a commentary that explained them all as expressions of Christian sentiment.[1]

For instance, in the first sonnet of all the lady is described as a personification of "essa increata bontà," and the means by which this is apprehended by the soul are represented by the five senses. We "feel" the Good by the outward sense, "hear" by the inward sense, "understand" by "la parte rationale," "taste" "quanto allo affecto," and "see" "quanto allo acto dello intellecto."

> La donna mia non è cosa mortale
> Che si possa vedere sensibilmente
> Ne imaginar, che nostra inferma mente
> Nostro concepto human tanto non sale.

---

[1] I have not seen the original MSS. Sessoriano 413, but from Caterina Re's account of them in her study *Girolamo Benivieni*, Città di Castello, 1906, pp. 81 et seq., and from all that is known of Benivieni's life and characters it does not appear that the poems, even in their unregenerate state, can have been particularly "lewd lays." It was probably easy enough to transpose them into a purely religious key; a few, like the sonnet *Dove nudo si vede ogni pensiero*, do not read like adaptations at all. The *Canzone dell'Amor Divino* may perhaps be taken as a sample of Benivieni s "pagan" manner.

> Le sue parole, el suo bel volto han tale
> Virtù: che chi l'un vede e l'altre sente
> Subito il cor quasi oro in fiamma ardente
> Purga: e da gire al ciel gli son date ale.
> Questo mi dice amor, che in terra fede
> Giurando all'alma fa de beni di quella
> Che come el sol le stelle ogni altra excede
> L'anima semplicetta che gli crede
> Un non so che divin mentre favella
> Di lei sente, ode, intende gusta e vede.[1]

Such fruition of the soul's desire is not, however, often to be known during the period of mortal life. The sense that the earth is a place of exile is strong in Benivieni, stronger on the whole than his consciousness of its being "ombra di Dio." True, the material world is the last pale and imperfect image of the glories that the divine mind beholds in itself and gives by participation to its creatures; but since our nature became corrupted by sin it has lost the power of passing easily through sensible things to the divine and finds a hindrance in the very things that were given it for guides

> Et così va che in ciascun ben terreno
> Una esca è tale che quanto più al cor
> Tanto più el nutre di letal veneno.[2]

It is a common experience for the soul to be abandoned to its unaided strength partly to test its virtue and partly to reveal to it its own weakness and the unsatisfactoriness of the earthly shadows it pursues. The quest for the absolute Beauty that exceeds all forms and all definitions is interwoven throughout the *Canzoniere* with the feeling that the inward discipline is no mere contemplative exercise but a battle with the powers of darkness that will not end till death.

On one hand there is the familiar picture of the soul, exiled from its native place, but stirred with a desire to return there by

---

[1] *Canzoniere dell'Amor Divino*, Florence, 1500, Pt. I, Son. I, and Commentary, p. 9. [2] Ibid., Pt. II, Son. IIII, p. 45a.

the sight of the vestiges of the divine that it beholds in the sensible world, in itself (l'ombra scolpita nella mente)[1] and in the celestial world and the powers of heaven.

> Quando per che veder l'alma smarrita
> In tanto exilio il suo sposo dilecto
> Non può, contempla in questo e in quello obiecto
> L'ombra talhor di sua beltà infinita.
> Sotto se de suoi doni per lei vestita
> Vede la terra, i se el proprio intellecto
> Sopra a se il ciel, e qualunque altro aspecto
> Dentro a quel che al suo ben la tira e'nvita.
> Et ben cieco è colui signor che in tanta
> Luce non vede: e sordo è chi non sente
> Tue voci: e muto e chi di te non canta.
> Ma stolto è più chi ciascun ben presente
> Lampeggiar vede al tuo increato sole
> Et nol cerca, disia, teme: ama e vuole.[2]

Here, as Benivieni explains in his commentary, are described the six stages by which man may arise to union with God. First, he contemplates the divine in the creation; then he passes to some general abstract notion of God's power and goodness; and then he beholds Him in "el proprio intelletto."

"Dico adunque come poi l'anima, lasciate le cose estrinsece tutte, in ella sua mente si raccoglie, vede allora non solo per se, ciò è mediante le sue operazioni e virtù, la imagine di Dio, che è el terzo grado di cognitione."

When this stage is reached the soul begins to understand her own nobility as co-heir with Christ and temple of the Holy Ghost, and may ascend to the first mode of contemplation, meditation on the essential nature of God, unity, perfection, eternity, and other divine attributes. Finally, it can contemplate the union of God and man in Christ and "Sciolta in tutto e resoluta si andrebbe."[3]

[1] *Canzoniere*, Pt. I, Son. XVI, p. 32.
[2] Ibid., Pt. I, Son, II, p. 10a.
[3] Ibid., Commentary on Son, II.

THE MEDICI CIRCLE

But this freedom is the result not of "otio" but of "fera pugna."

Among Benivieni's best sonnets is one in which he cries out against the "rebel powers" not of the flesh only but of his own recalcitrant spirit.

> Spirti miei ingrati, e tu perfida mente
> Che l'interno mio mal conosce e vedi:
> Occhi miei ingordi: e tu cor, che a quei credi
> Cieco: e ben morte a lei che lo consente
> Rustica lingua, e tu poca prudente
> Alma, che aiuto ad questa ingrata chiedi:
> Van disio, sordi orrechi, infermi piedi
> Per cui son tracto al mio martyr sovente
> Onde vi da tanta baldanza e core?
> Che vi fa contro ad me d'error si pieni
> Contro ad me, che pur son vostro signore?
> Ingrata turba che a morir mi meni
> Et non ti accorgi ben che'l tuo dolore
> Cerchi: e che meco insieme a morir vieni.[1]

There is a note of moral earnestness in his work that derives immediately from his religious principles. The choice between the world and the spirit is no academic one with him; it is a vital decision on which hangs the soul's eternal destiny. The cleavage between soul and body is austerely marked, with no suggestion of the half apology for the latter that appears in Ficino and gains ground in his successors in the sixteenth century.

For Benivieni the soul that has once descended into matter is inevitably subject to error and by no means sure of finding its freedom.

> Questa nostra non vita
> Ma morte inganna ognun che a lei si piega
> Chi el mondo un tracto lega
> Raro e talhor non mai quindi si scioglie.

Now and then it may recognize in the world a reflected gleam of the primal light; but mortal weakness is such that the very

---

[1] *Canzoniere*, Pt. II, Son. XII, p. 56a.

beauty sent to guide it may mislead the soul into clinging to the shadow instead of passing onward to the reality.

> ... Ma perchè ovunque esurge
> Fra noi quaggiù quel sol, con esso nasce
> Un non so che, che pasce
> L'alma d'un fragil ben che lui simiglia
> Nostra mente smarrita
> Ben disia el vero sole: ma l'ombra piglia.

Benivieni confesses that he himself is

> ... un di quelli
> Che per troppo disio del primo viso
> Mi misi a guardar fiso
> Quella beltà che l'universo adombra
> Et così solo quella ombra
> Che in pria si offerse all'hor per mio ben presi
> Misero, nè già intesi
> Che al suo primo splendor salir conviensi.[1]

Or, as he puts it in his commentary:

"Si impari, dico, el vero e legittimo corso della vita Christiana: el quale corpo e la quale vita quanto essere debba da ogni voluptà del senso aliena assai per se ce lo insegna la croce di Cristo: en ella quale quasi libro certissimo e da chi ben lo intende per tal modo descripta la regola e lo exemplo imitabile d'ogni virtù; che impossibile è fuori di quello in alcuno altro più perfettamente e con maggiore brevità acquistare alcuna quantunche minima perfezione."[2]

Yet his asceticism did not, as has already appeared, destroy his delight in natural beauty. Nor did his sense of man's weakness shatter his belief in the dignity of the being in whom the material and spiritual worlds are linked together.

"E infra queste due nature quasi media è posta la natura humana: la quale perchè sempre nel mezzo partecipa della proprietà de'suoi estremi, ha con l'una e con l'altra creatura spirituale e corporea convenientia e proportione: Imperoche essendo l'huomo composto di materia e di forma ciò è di anima e di corpo, quanto alla anima è conforme alla prima creatura, ciò è alla creatura angelica: quanto

---

[1] *Canzoniere*, Pt. II, Canzone II, pp. 57a et seq.
[2] Ibid., Commentary on Canzone II, p. 65a.

al corpo alla ultima ciò è alla creatura totalmente corporea."[1] The mere fact that man, by his double nature, is called upon to take up the bitter struggle for moral perfection confers upon him an excellence that the angels themselves do not share. Benivieni is at his happiest in his descriptions of the end of the soul's pilgrimage, on which he seems to have brooded often and intensely. At times he uses the common language of mysticism and speaks of the ultimate ecstasy under the negative images of silence or darkness or under that of unimaginable light.

. . . la fiamma occulta
Che nell' abysso della tua infinita
Caligine arde a nostri occhi sepulta.[2]

Yet he evidently did not regard the eternal world as formless or indeterminate. If the bliss of disembodied spirits consists sometimes in the ineffable rapture of the beatific vision it does not mean that the individual soul is annihilated. Rather it lives with a fullness and freedom unknown during its sojourn in the flesh among the inexhaustible riches of the intelligible world where all that has true being exists not in its semblance, as on earth, but in itself. There the soul sees the Ideas which are in God as flowers are in a garden, and there it mingles with other blessed spirits in a life of unflawed love and understanding which is described in lines that suggest Plotinus' phrase "All is each and each is all and the glory is infinite."

Dove nudo si vede ogni pensiero
Penetrando l'un cor l'altro, en ciaschuno
Un amor una mente un desidero
Un amor che d'amor creato in uno
Amor vive: uno amor che fruendo ama
Amando frue, d'amor sempre digiuno.[3]

---

[1] *Canzoniere*, Pt. I, Commentary on Son. VI, p. 17a. Cf. "Come per la proportione e convenientia che lui ha con tutto lo universo e con le sue parte è chiamato minore mondo; così per la medesima transumptione si può convenientemente chiamare esso universo maggiore uomo" (Commentary, p. 27a).

[2] Ibid., Pt. I, Introduction, p. 5.   [3] Ibid., p. 6.

Involved as the lines are they are warmed by something more than conventional sentiment. The poem is not dated, but it may not be too fanciful to suppose that it was inspired by the memory of Pico. Even this apotheosis of human affection is, however, less perfect than the love with which the soul dies to itself and lives in the "sposo dilecto" for whose sake it had formerly rejected all the joys of earth.

> Qui alloggia il cor che per lui more
> Non pur reforma e vivo all'alma el rende
> Ma li veste ale, onde sospeso ascende
> Con la sua scorta in braccio al mio signore
> Qui lieto arde, indi e' belli occhi inspira
> Onde amor prima in lui discese, e forma
> L'alma per quei di sua novella stampa.
> Quivi, perche all'amato si conforme
> L'amante: e ciasuun suo simil desira,
> Nostro human pecto amor formato avampa.[1]

If the *Canzoniere* is a statement of Neoplatonism in the language of a fervent "Piagnone" the *Canzone dell' Amor Divino*, with Pico's commentary, became almost as famous as Ficino's *Symposium* as a treatise on Love. The work was begun in 1486, but was abandoned because it appeared to the two friends as too pagan, and they doubted its fitness for Christian readers. It was evidently known in manuscript, however, and when the first edition of Pico's works was published at Venice in 1495, Benivieni was importuned into allowing the treatise to be printed, and added a preface explaining the circumstances in which it had been begun and left unfinished, and acknowledging its debt to Ficino.[2]

---

[1] *Canzoniere*, Pt. II, Son. XVI, p. 28.

[2] The *Canzone dell' Amor Divino*, with Pico's commentary, is in *Pici Opera*, Basle, 1573, Vol. I, pp. 734 et seq. The passages quoted in English are from the translation by T. Stanley [Gardner's ed.]. See *A Platonick Discourse upon Love written in Italian by John Picus Mirandula in Explication of a Sonnet by Hieronymo Benivieni*, in poems by T. Stanley, London, 1651. Reprinted with introduction by Edmund Gardner in *The Humanist's Library*, Merrymount Press, Boston, U.S.A., 1914.

The Canzone, like the more famous ones of Guinizelli and Cavalcanti, was written as a poetic summary of a complex theory. Its theme is the origin, nature, and functions of Divine or Intellectual Love, and it is so involved and obscure that Pico's elucidations were certainly necessary.

> Quando dal vero ciel converso scende
> Nell'angelica mente il divin sole
> Che la sua prima prole
> Sotto le vive frondi illustra e'riforma
> Lei che'l suo primo ben ricerca e vuole
> Per innato disio che quell'accende
> In lui riflessa prende
> Virtù che'l ricco sen dipinge e forma.[1]

Here, according to Pico, the "divin sole" represents the first emanation from God, in other words the Ideas which, when poured into the Angelic mind, make it revert to God and desire the perfection of those Ideas. The more she possesses this perfection the more fervently she loves it, and this desire is Celestial Love in its pure form. The "vero ciel" is God who includes all created things as the Heavens include all sensible ones; the "vive frondi" refer to the Orchard of Jupiter, where the Ideas were first planted, and are called "living" because they have in themselves the principle of Understanding or Wisdom, which is the noblest spiritual life. The ideas "adorn and inform" the mind which receives them, but they are not merely external but "the Substance of the Minde" and so are not accidents to the soul but "her first intrinsical act," which is what Benivieni means when he calls her desires "innate." Love transforms the lover into the beloved, as Ficino had already demonstrated.[2]

The Soul, when it enters the body, forgets the intellectual Beauty of which it was formerly conscious; but awakened to love

---

[1] The Canzone, *Pici Opera*, Vol. I, p. 746, Stanza III
[2] Pico, Commentary, o.c., p. 735, Ch. XII.

by the beauty of sensible forms it is gradually led back to the fountain of beauty, God.[1]

Man is human by his rational soul, and akin to the angels by his intellectual nature. When he gives himself over to intellectual love he dies as man and lives again as an angel in a fuller and sublimer life, continually loving and desiring the divine beauty whose image he first dimly perceived in the recesses of his own soul. "Sensible light is the act and efficacy of corporal, spiritual light of Intelligible Beauty. Ideas in their descent into the inform Angelick Minde were as colours and figures in the night. As he who by moonlight seeth some fair object, desires to view and enjoy it more fully in the day; so the Minde, weakly beholding in herself the Ideal Beauty dim and opacuous [which our author calls "the skreen of a dark shade"] by reason of the night of her imperfection, turns (like the moon) to the eternal Sun to perfect her Beauty by him; to whom addressing herself she becomes Intelligible light; clearing the beauty of Celestial Venus and rendering it visible to the eye of the first Minde.

"In sensible Beauty we consider first the object in itself, the same at midnight as at noon; secondly the light in a manner the Soul thereof: the author supposes that as the first part of sensible Beauty (corporal forms) proceeds from the first part of Intellectual Beauty (Ideal forms) so sensible light flows from the intelligible descending upon Ideas."[2]

Corporal beauty consists first in proportion of parts, then in fitness of colour and form, and then in a certain Grace or indescribable radiance that shines through all that is fair. Those who say that Beauty is dependent only on fitness of form and colour are easily confuted; since many persons faultless in these respects

---

[1] Canzone, Stanza IV. Love is pictured as continually pursuing the traces of the divine beauty in the world.
>Questi perche nell'amorose braccia
>Della bella ciprigna in prima nacque
>Sempre seguir gli piaque
>L'ardente sol di sua bellezza viva.

[2] Gardner's ed., p. 71.

THE MEDICI CIRCLE

lack the final grace that moves love in others. Therefore this grace must come from the soul which, when it is fair and lucid, begins to transform the body into its own likeness. Moses' face shone when he came down from the mount of vision, and Porphyry has recorded the extraordinary light that showed in the face of Plotinus when he was uplifted by divine contemplation. Plotinus himself claimed that outward beauty was always allied to inward perfection.

> Quando formata in pria dal divin volto
> Per discendere quaggiù l'alma si parte . . .

it brings with it an idea of beauty which it does its best to express in its body. It is moved to love when it sees the same idea expressed in another person; and from this love of corporal beauty it ascends by six stages.

The first and lowest is delight in the outward beauty of an individual. Then the soul makes an inward image of its beloved which it renders more beautiful by the light of its own virtue. By the aid of the "intelletto agente" it then abstracts and contemplates an idea of corporal beauty in itself, apart from particular forms, and this is the highest stage it can reach while it remains in contact with matter.

If, however, the soul reflects on its own operation, which reveals the existence of a universal beauty not wholly contained in any single object, it begins to see that this universality is to be found not in outward things but in its own "intrinsical Power." Therefore, if it has light in itself by which to see ideal beauty in the dim glass of material forms, how much more clearly will it behold it if it looks into the bright mirror of its own substance? There it finds the image of ideal beauty communicated to it by the Intellect. From the Idea intrinsic to herself the soul ascends to the Celestial Venus, "Who in fullness of her Beauty, not being comprehensible by any particular Intellect, she, as much as in her lies, endeavours to be united to the first minde, the chiefest of Creatures and general Habitation of Ideal Beauty."[1] Here she comes to rest and finds her abiding place for ever.

There follows in the Commentary a note on the theory of the affinity of souls with the heavens. Some souls proceed from Saturn, others from Jupiter, others from the other spheres, and have a likeness to the soul of the particular planet from which they have descended. It was a common belief among the Neoplatonists that the soul descending from its star in its "Vehiculum Caeleste" formed a body for itself and was united to it by the sort of "astral body" that it brought with it from its sphere. Each soul brings with it from its star a special formative virtue by which it infuses into its body the likeness of itself. Yet matter is so variously disposed to the impressions given it by the soul that two persons of like temperament may be totally unlike to outward view, the matter from which the one had to form his body having been more tractable than that allotted to the other. Love tends to spring up between persons born under the same star as they have the same innate idea of beauty and desire to complete and perfect it by uniting it with the same idea in another person. The lover believes the beloved object to be more beautiful than it really is, since he sees

[1] Gardner, o.c., p. 74. Pico, o.c. Canzone, Stanza VIII, p. 746.

> Quinc'Amor l'alm'in quest'el cor diletta
> In lui, com'in suo parto anchor vaneggia,
> Che mentre el ver vagheggia
> Come raggio di Sol sott'acqua el vede.
> Pur non so che divin ch'en lui lampeggia
> Benche adumbrat'el cor pietoso allecta,
> Da questa ad più perfecta
> Beltà ch'n cima a quel superba siede.
> Ivi no l'ombra pur ch'en terra fede
> Del vero ben ne dia scorge, ma certo
> Lume e del vero sol più ver effige
> Quinci mentre el pio Cor l'alma vestige
> Seque, entro alla sua mente el ved inserto.
> Indi a più chiaro apperto
> L'un appresso ad quel sol sospeso vola
> Dalla cui viva, et sola
> Luce informat'amando si fa bello
> La mente, l'alma el mondo e dio ch'en quello.

it in the mental image that he has formed of it, separate from matter and glorified by the kindred idea of beauty implicit in his own soul.

It will be seen that in all this no mention is made of profane love, which Pico regarded as unworthy of consideration by a teacher of the Platonic mysteries.[1]

---

[1] Although the Platonic Academy numbered among its frequenters many poets besides those discussed above, its influence (except upon the writers of "poemi visioni" treated in the next chapter) was mainly negligible.

Peregrino Aglio, although described by Ficino as "conphilosophus suus," gives little evidence of his philosophical powers in the compositions that have been preserved. His poems are mostly praises of friends and patrons, personal outcries and complaints of the needy humanist and the young man of parts whom the world has used hardly. Most of his writings are contained in Magl., VII, 1025, 131; Laur. LIV, 10, c. 97^r; and Laur. LXV, 52, 16^t. The small essay, *P.A. confilosofo di Marsilio Ficino*, by F. Flamini, Pisa, 1893, may be consulted for his life.

Naldo Naldi seems to have been almost the unofficial laureate of the Medici. Most of the persons and events of Lorenzo's Florence were celebrated by him in a multitude of tedious Latin elegies and epigrams. He also wrote Latin love poems of Petrarchan inspiration. Ficino, who evidently admired him, addressed several letters to him, but beyond returning compliments, contained in them, Naldi did not respond to his friend's influence.

His poems are scattered through many MSS., but the principal collections are Magl., VII, 1057, and Laur. XXXV, 34.

Alessandro Braccesi, the friend of Pico and Savonarola, shows on the whole more literary merit than Naldi. In his *Liber Amorum* (Cod. Laur. 40 and 41; Cod. Plut. XCI) he relates the vicissitudes of what was probably a genuine passion. He is indebted to Petrarch but shows no specific sign of the influence of the Neoplatonists either in the *Liber Amorum* or, according to Bice Agnoletti, who has written a careful monograph on him (*Alessandro Braccesi*, Florence, 1901) in the *Carmina*, contained in Cod. Vat. Lat. 10681. The *Canzoniere* of Giovanni di Francesco Nesi (Cod. Ricc. 2962) is definitely Neoplatonic but has no markedly original features. Its prevailing tone is moralistic and religious, showing some affinity with Benivieni. Neither the poems of Antonio Pelotti (Cod. Ricc. 834, c. 187^r) nor those of Luca and Bernardo Pulci contain anything of note.

TRANSLATIONS

Page 91. *Costei ha privo il ciel* . . .
　　She hath despoiled heaven of loveliness
　　And stolen all the wealth of Paradise;
　　Beggared the sun of light and radiantness
　　And gathered them into her glorious eyes.
　　All earth's most gracious gifts she doth possess,
　　Sweet laughter, fair and lofty courtesies;
　　And love hath given her his own look and tone
　　To make her fairest of all fairs alone.

Page 92. *Quel che soggioga* . . .
　　He who subdues the earth and sky and sea.

Page 92. . . . *ove ogni grazia si diletta* . . .
　　. . . where every Grace rejoices
　　Where Beauty crowns her locks with woven flowers.

Page 92. . . . *lascive aurette* . . .
　　. . . light amorous breezes make
　　The little tender grasses gently shake.

Page 93. *L'acqua da viva pomice zampilla* . . .
　　The water bubbles forth from living stone
　　That on its arch upholds the lovely hill,
　　And gently flowing through a flowery zone
　　Paints all its downward-moving course, until
　　It reach the fount whence cooling dew is thrown,
　　Repaying to the trees their shadows chill.
　　Each takes its fill of an unstinted feast,
　　And seems, by mutual rivalry, increased.

Page 93. . . . *l'arbor che già tanto ad Ercol* . . .
　　. . . the tree that so delighted Hercules
　　Sports with the plane along the watery leas.

Page 93. *Nè spengon le fredde acque* . . .
　　Nor can chill waters quench the precious flame.

Page 93. *Il cervo appresso alla massilia fera* . . .
　　The stag beside the wild beast lingering
　　With feet uplifted doth his mate embrace;
　　Among the grass, full in the smile of Spring,
　　One coney by the other finds his place;
　　The gentle hares, in number hastening

To amorous sport, fear not that hounds will chase.
Thus Love where'er he wills in every breast
Old hate and natural fear can lull to rest.

Page 93. Nè mai le chiome . . .
There comes nor hoar frost light nor chilling snow
To dim the eternal garden's locks to white.
Therein the frozen Winter dare not go,
That grass, those trees, no blasts unfriendly blight.
There the revolving years no changes show
Since joyous Spring takes never hence her flight,
But loosens her bright hair upon the winds
And myriad blossoms into garlands binds.

Page 94. La lepre e'l bracco . . .
The hare and brach in one self covert lie,
One bays not yet nor doth the other moan.
'Twixt deer and hound and roe is amity;
Nor hope nor fear in swiftness have they known,
But sport together and delight to vie
With one another, for they run alone
To vanquish one another in the race
And not to flee the fierceness of the chase.

Page 94. Qual felice terren . . .
What favoured soil, what living leafage nursed
This well-beloved and snowy violet
That at the touch of angels opened first,
Moving the heart while to the eyes hid yet?
Perchance Love shook it from the golden hair
Of his progenitrice in Paradise
That so to human breasts it might repair
When earthward borne through far obscurities.
So fair a flower did heaven, not nature, mould,
For of its worth doth the effect approve;
I feel it, Love confirms it certainly.
Such virtue doth this humble floweret hold
That since the heart was held in bonds by Love
It feels above all hearts secure and free.

Page 94. Fra tutte le cose . . .

Of a truth among all the offspring of nature there is nothing howsoever small or howsoever lowly and base in which, even as in each thing most noble, there shines not, according to the measure of its capacity, I know not what of admirable and divine, by which our soul, if it be rightly disposed, may in contemplating know, and in knowing love, the author of its being, that is God.

Page 97. . . . *ad recte agendum* . . .
    We are brought forth by nature in order that we may act virtuously and search out truth.

Page 97. *non datur igitur quies* . . .
    therefore repose is not granted unless thou hast first laboured.

Page 98. *Ma credo appellar possa* . . .
    I think that all men with united tongue
    May fortune call unfriendly and severe
    Since each by her upon his cross is hung.

Page 98. . . . *alcun non pensi* . . .
    . . . let none look
    To find the true and perfect good, while yet
    The soul is fettered in its fleshly nook.

Page 99. *I primi la fortuna* . . .
    The first does fortune give and take again
    The next by nature to the frame are given
    The third the soul does in itself contain.

Page 99. *Memoria audacia* . . .
    Courage and memory and strength of wit
    Are not that good, since each is but as use
    And good or evil conduct fashions it.

Page 100. *Così la mente* . . .
    In contemplation thus the mind is still,
    And as it nears the good it gazes on
    To contemplate for aye would be its will.

Page 100. *Ma il vero ben* . . .
    But since true good is not beneath the moon
    'Tis not in contemplation of such things
    As one by one dissolve and vanish soon.

Page 100. *Dice chi ben* . . .
    They say who have his lesson rightly read
    That our felicity is but to do
    Works of pure virtue in life justly led,
    But if the sovereign good consist in two
    Perfections, of the reason and the will,
    Or one or other vainly we pursue.

Page 100. *La pura verità* . . .
>The pure truth stainless and beautiful. . . .
>Our souls are ever as those beasts that see
>Least clearly whatsoever shines most bright.
>Such eyes to look upon the sun have we;
>And such, too, is our intellectual sight.

Page 101. *Come error fa* . . .
>As he who hateth God commits more great
>And certain fault than who discerns Him not
>So who most loves Him wins the loftiest state.

Page 101. *Aviene all'alma* . . .
>Thus fares the soul when God it strives to know;
>In its own bounds it cribs His amplitude
>And God into itself contracteth so. . . .
>
>Even as through a cloud we contemplate
>The chasm of His divine infinity,
>Though hard the mind's eye strive to penetrate.
>But let us love Him well and perfectly;
>Who knows God, God into himself doth draw,
>Loving, we soar to His high majesty.

Page 102: . . . *si converte in Dio* . . .
>. . . returns to God
>And in beholding God itself dilates.

Page 102. *O venerando immenso* . . .
>O venerable vast eternal light
>Who dost Thyself within Thyself behold
>Illumining whate'er in Thee shines bright.
>
>Fount of felicity and joy entire
>We know Thou art alone and hast in Thee
>Whatever moves the springs of our desire,
>For though this good or that alluring be
>Nor this nor that doth our desire pursue
>But the true good, our peace, which there we see.

Page 104. *Non ornate di fronde* . . .
>Not opening valleys all in leafage dight
>Not the clear stream that bathes the tender grass
>Purfled with hues of yellow, red, and white;
>Not cities wide nor buildings' stately mass;
>Soft dance, outlandish games or strenuous fight

Nor ships that o'er the sea with west winds pass;
Nor monsters nor fair birds nor beasts of price
Nor graven stone nor gem so greets our eyes.

Through all of these without or guide or aim
Wandered mine eyes, seeking their peace unknown,
And knew not that among them hid to fame
Was she who soon should be my joy alone.
Through secret ways my happy fortune came
Leading desire that in the heart had grown.
My heart was guided all unwittingly
To see again what it long since did see.

Page 104. *Quando tessuto fu* . . .

When first this chain was woven earth and air
And heaven did in harmony combine,
For never was the atmosphere so fair
Nor did the sun with lovelier lustre shine
Filling glad earth with flowers and leaflets where
There flowed through all a river crystalline.
Cypris that day leaned on her father's breast
Laughing and with her joy that region blest.

Page 105. *Nel primo tempo* . . .

In that first time when Love mine eyes unsealed
This beauty to my hopes he did display,
And soon as her perfections he revealed
Laughing he snatched her from my sight away.
Then with what tears I searched the various field
Of other beauties, for how many a day!
Till some reminder of that loveliness,
Would haply come these wretched eyes to bless.

Then as a hound that in the chase is fain
To find the hidden quarry 'mid the leaves,
And when it sees the ground some print retain
The other's passing by that sign perceives;
So, since each likeness seems to pledge again
That the true beauty is, and ne'er deceives,
Now this and now that other thing I sought
Till Love my beauteous lady to me brought.

Page 105. . . . *li beati spiriti intenti* . . .

. . . as the blessed souls for ever
Enraptured wait about the face divine.

Page 105. *Anzi sempre si truova* . . .
>Thus all that speaks of beauty to the eye
>Comes from her ever, in that form or this.
>The various beauties that dispersèd lie
>Flow from the living fount of every bliss;
>And that which other things in part supply
>Perfect in Him and undivided is;
>And so, if each resemblance charm the sight
>How far more perfect here the eyes' delight!
>Contrasting voices make delicious sound
>And diverse hues a loveliness unknown;
>White shows its beauty on a sable ground
>The treble pleases, matched with deeper tone,
>For sovereign Beauty wondrously hath bound
>One foe to be the other's benison;
>That sovereign Beauty which all spirits crave
>And in my lady fair alone I have.

Page 106. *Disio, dispetto, invidia e triste cure* . . .
>Anger, desire, envy, and bitter cares.

Page 106. *Me divida Fortuna* . . .
>By Fortune am I parted now and torn
>From her fair face and from such dear delights;
>Nought else on earth I prize and nought implore
>But that one form of which I hear no more.

Page 106. *resta con Amor* . . .
>with Love abideth only jealousy.

Page 106. *Vita e conservazion* . . .
>The life and preservation of all ills.

Page 106. *In questi dolci luoghi* . . .
>To those dear haunts in that departed time
>Oh Love, restore me with my lady fair,
>In those unsullied years, that tender prime,
>Of neither jealousy nor hope aware.
>Let not our days to ripe fulfilment climb
>But let our love become eternal there.
>No other fire in us, nor other grace
>In her; but only that sweet time and place.

Page 107. *Concorre ogni virtute* . . .
>In her all virtue and all sweetness meet
>And in her beauty, Beauty shines complete.

Page 107. *O vaghi occhi amorosi* . . .
    Oh, eager amorous eyes
    Who now on this, now that, fair countenance
    Looking with searching glance
    A thousand individual beauties see.
    E'er yet before you rise
    These shining orbs and fair
    Let none, presumptuous, dare
    Claim to have seen beauty's entirety.
    Here the true beauty is,
    All harboured in one face,
    And every scattered grace
    In other forms its pattern takes from this.
    And who doth this behold
    Sighs ever with such love as grows not cold.

Page 107. *Chi senza te t'ha fatto* . . .
    Who without aid of thine
    Made thee, without thee wills not thee to save.

Page 108. *E'muor per darti vita* . . .
    He dies to give thee life
    And mortal He becomes to make thee God.

Page 108. *Con la tua bellezza tanta* . . .
    Beauty's self for thee did burn
    Such thy beauty free from stain;
    Beauty, sacred and eterne
    Thou for Mary's grace wast fain;
    Thou to love didst Love constrain
    Virgin gracious, mild and holy.

Page 109. *O Dio, o Sommo Bene* . . .
    Ah God! ah Sovreign good! how dost Thou ever,
    That I, who seek Thee only, find Thee never?

    Alas, if this or that I look to win
    Thee do I seek in it, most gracious Lord.
    Desire is wakened for the good therein
    And all that's good and fair Thou dost afford.
    Thou wholly art in every place, true Word,
    Yet in no place can I discern Thee ever.

Page 109. *La vista in mille* . . .
    The sight, to thousand various objects veering,
    Fixed on Thee sees Thee not, though Thou art bright.
    The ear innumerable voices hearing
    Perceives not thine whose sound is infinite.

The sweetness common to each living wight
Each sense pursueth still and findeth never.
Alas, unhappy soul, why dost thou chase
Felicity among such toils and woes?
Seek if thou wilt; but not in any place
Where now thou seekest doth that good repose.
Thy true felicity thyself dispose
To seek in death; and life where life was never.
From these fond eyes be every light retired
That I the true befriending light may see.
Be deaf, mine ears, that so the voice desired
I now may hear, saying in verity
"Weary and heavy laden come to me
Full time it is I should refresh thee ever."

Page 110. *Allor l'occhio vedrà luce invisibile* . . .
Then shall the eye see light invisible
The ear perceive sounds uttered voicelessly,
Both by the mind alone discernible
Causing no surfeit and no injury.
The feet shall stay, but swift the soul shall fly
Unto that good which dwelleth with it ever.

Then shall I see, oh Lord benign and fair,
That nor this good nor that can stay my need,
But that the gracious God abideth where
The good from this or that disguise is freed.
This true and single bliss he feels indeed
Who seeks the good; this only faileth never.

Page 111. *Tu sei pur tutto in ogni luogo* . . .
Thou wholly art in every place, true Word,
Yet in no place can I discern Thee ever.

Page 112. *Stando i piè fermi* . . .
The feet shall stay, but swift the soul shall fly
Unto that good which dwelleth with it ever.

Page 112. *La donna mia non è cosa mortale* . . .
My lady is not mortal, nor to be
Beheld by sense nor by imagining,
For the conceptions of humanity
In these frail minds reach not so high a thing.
Her words, her lovely face such virtue hold,
That who sees one and who the other hears
Makes pure his heart as flame-refinéd gold
And gets him wings to mount the heavenly spheres.

> Love thus instructs me who doth make on earth
> Pledge of her grace and to the spirit tells
> That as the sun the stars she all outshines.
> The simple heart that trusteth in her worth
> Some nameless grace of heaven while it dwells
> On her, feels, sees, tastes, hearkens and divines.

Page 113. *Et così va che in ciascun ben* . . .

> So is it that in every earthly bliss
> There lurks a snare which, gathered to the heart,
> That heart with deadly venom nourishes.

Page 114. *Quando per che veder l'alma smarrita* . . .

> When the lorn spirit in such sore exile
> Is powerless her beloved Spouse to see
> Now here, now there, she contemplates awhile
> The shadow of His fair infinity.
> She sees the earth which He for her hath dressed
> Beneath her; and herself with mind endued.
> Above her heaven and its powers who best
> Draw and invite her to beatitude.
>
> Blind is he truly, Lord, who in such light
> Sees not, and deaf who heareth not Thy call.
> And dumb is he who lauds not Thee aright
> But foolish he who sees these blessings all
> Forth-flashing from Thy uncreated fire
> And doth not seek it, love, fear and desire.

Page 114. *Dico adunque* . . .

I declare then how the soul, forsaking all external things, recollects herself within her own mind and there beholds the image of God, by herself alone, that is by her own operations and virtues; and this is the third stage of knowledge.

Page 114. *Sciolta in tutto* . . .

Would depart hence wholly free and unfettered.

Page 115. *Spirti miei ingrati* . . .

> Ingrateful powers and thou, perfidious mind,
> That all my inward ill dost see and know;
> Gross eyes, and heart eye-credulous and blind,
> And thou that bringest all that trust thee low,
> Unruly tongue, and spirit indiscreet,
> Who to this graceless one dost look for aid,

> Hopeless desire, deaf ears, uncertain feet,
> That to my ruin have me oft waylaid;
> What doth such heart and vigour you afford
> That thus with errors you beset me round,
> Beset me, who am yet your sovreign Lord?
> Ye lead me to my death and have not found
> That so ye seek your doom, unthankful horde,
> Nor that with me yourselves are death-ward bound.

Page 115. Questa nostra non vita . . .

> This our not life but death
> Deceives whoever to its law doth bend.
> Who makes the world his friend
> Rarely or never freedom wins again.

Page 116. . . . Ma perchè ovunque esurge . . .

> . . . but since where'er that sun
> Rises upon us here, with it doth rise
> Some power that supplies
> The soul with phantoms in its image made,
> Our spirit, led astray,
> Desires the true sun, but doth clasp the shade.

Page 116. . . . un di quelli che per troppo desio . . .

> . . . one of those who overmuch
> Longing to look on the Eternal's face
> Did set myself to trace
> That beauty which creation dimly shows,
> And thus, unhappy, chose
> That shade which first appeared to be my bliss,
> And knew not that it is
> Needful to mount unto the primal splendour.

Page 116. Si impari, dico . . .

Let us learn, I say, the true and lawful course of the Christian life. How far removed from every sensual delight that body and that life must be the cross of Christ doth most surely teach us; in it, as in a most faithful treatise, the rule and exemplary pattern of every virtue is so justly set forth by one well versed in the matter that it is impossible, by any means apart from this, to acquire any perfection howsoever limited, more perfectly or with greater speed.

Page 116. E infra queste due nature . . .

And between these two natures, human nature is placed being, as it were, an intermediary; which, because it is ever in the midst, participates in the qualities of its two extremes and has with both spiritual and corporeal creatures affinity and congruence. For since man is compounded of matter and form, that is of body and soul, he is akin, through his soul, to the first creature, that is to the angel, and through his body to the last, that is to the creature wholly corporeal.

Page 117. . . . *la fiamma occulta* . . .
   . . . the secret fire
   Which is the abysm of Thine infinite
   Darkness burns on, hid from our eyes' desire.

Page 117. *Dove nudo si vede ogni pensiero* . . .
   Where every thought without disguise is known
   As hearts do each the other penetrate,
   In each one love, one mind, one will alone
   One love that lives in love by love create.
   One love that loves rejoicing in its own;
   Loving, enjoys, of love insatiate.

Page 118. *Qui alloggia il cor* . . .
   Hither He brings the heart that for Him dies,
   Not changed alone and to the soul restored,
   But girt with wings, that soaring, it may rise
   With her to the embraces of my Lord.
   Joyful it burns, and doth itself inspire
   From those fair eyes whence Love did first descend.
   And by their power the soul new form assumes.
   There, since the lover seeks himself to blend
   With the beloved, and like doth like desire,
   Our human heart transforming love consumes.

Page 119. *Quando dal vero ciel* . . .
   When from true heaven the sacred sun
   Into the Angelick minde did run
   And with enlivened leaves adorn,
   Bestowing form on his first-born;
   Enflaméd by innate desires,
   She to her chiefest good aspires;
   By which reversion her rich Breast
   With various figures is imprest.
         Platonick Discourse, p. 53.

Page 121. *Quando formato in pria* . . .
   From the Sun's most divine abode
   The Soul descends into man's heart.
         Platonick Discourse, p. 56.

CHAPTER V

THE MEDICI CIRCLE (2)

THE *POEMA VISIONE*

THERE is considerable evidence of a cult of Dante among the members of Lorenzo's circle, and especially among those most affected by Neoplatonic doctrines. Florentine humanism, generally speaking, held Dante in honour as one of its greatest forerunners, though its more pedantic scholars like Niccolo Niccoli might dismiss him as a "poeta da calzolai" and bold spirits like Maffeo Vegio might try to improve the *Commedia* by translating it into Latin verse. Boccaccio's hero-worship, however, was the beginning of a more enduring tradition, appealing as it did to the sound instinct for preserving native culture that marks the Florentine Renaissance, and to the natural delight of an artistic race in a supreme artist.

The latter part of the fifteenth century saw a great revival of interest in Dante, fostered no doubt by the civil wisdom of the Medici, and having its most enthusiastic champions among the followers of the Academy. They felt, rightly enough, the affinity between much of Dante's thought and their own; he was not only a mighty poet and man of letters but a prophet desiring the revelation that they themselves had seen. In Lorenzo and Poliziano, indeed, the interest he aroused was mainly literary, and appears in many poetic echoes and in the youthful eagerness of Lorenzo's essay on the early Tuscan poets; but Ficino stated the philosophic view when he wrote in the preface to his translation of the *Monarchia* "Dante Alighieri . . . benchè non parlasse in lingua greca con quello sacro padre di filosofi Platone, nientedimeno in ispirito parlò con lui, che di molte sentenze platoniche adornò i librisu oi. Tre regni troviamo scritti dal nostro rettissimo duce Platone: uno de'beati, l'altro de'miseri e il terzo de'peregrini. . . . Questo ordine platonico prima seguì Virgilio; questo seguì Dante dipoi col vaso di Virgilio beendo alle platoniche fonti. . . . Del regno de peregrini viventi trattò nel libro da lui chiamato 'Monarchia.' "

Cristoforo Landino, who dealt at length with the Platonic allegory of Virgil and Dante in the third and fourth books of the *Quaestiones Camaldulenses*, was also the author of an exhaustive commentary on the *Commedia*, which appeared first in 1481 with a prefatory elegy by Girolamo Benivieni. It was probably for this edition that Botticelli began his exquisite series of drawings, still the most satisfying pictorial interpretation of the poem. Other works of his show traces of Dantesque inspiration, and Michelangelo has left in two sonnets the expression of his love for his "famigliarissimo Dante."[1]

In such an atmosphere it is hardly surprising that some writers should have been tempted not merely to praise but to imitate. Not all of these imitations were Neoplatonic, but it is to the endeavour to combine the manner of Dante with an exposition of Neoplatonic doctrines that *La Città di Vita* of Matteo Palmieri, the *Poema Visione* of Giovanni Nesi, the *Paradisus* of Ugolino Verino and, to some extent, the poems of Lorenzo Bonincontri, owe their being. In the case of Nesi and Verino one may add the visionary and apocalyptic utterances of Savonarola. In spite of the laudatory criticisms passed upon these poems by their authors' friends it would seem that they struck even contemporaries as anachronisms. It does not appear that they were ever widely read.

---

[1] Lorenzo's essay on the early vernacular poets may be seen in the Crusca edition of his poems, Vol. I, Florence, 1825, and in Carducci's ed., Florence, 1859. Landino's Commentary on the *Divina Commedia* was first published at Florence in 1481 by Niccolò di Lorenzo della Magna and passed through various other editions, notably those of 1491 and 1578, Venice (v. Bibliography). The most easily accessible complete reproduction of Botticelli's drawings is A. Venturi's *Botticelli e Dante*, Florence, Lemonnier, 1922. The quotation from Ficino is taken from his preface to the translation of the *Monarchia*, ed. Turin, 1853, pp. 3 et seq. Vegio's translation of the opening of the D.C. into Latin is in the same MS. as Verino's *Paradisus*, i.e. Laur. XXXIX, 40, p. 135. The sonnets by Michelangelo are Nos. CIX, 37, and CIX, 49, in *Poesie*, ed. K. Frey, Berlin, 1897.

None of them, if one excepts the *De Rebus Caelestis* of Bonincontri, which had a certain scientific interest, were printed in their own day. Even manuscripts are few, and it has remained for later generations to disinter them.

In the case of Matteo Palmieri the cause of this contemporary neglect might lie in the taint of heresy that attached to his work; but the real reason lay deeper, and affected them all. The mentality that had created and enjoyed the huge visionary literature of the Middle Ages had passed or was passing. Heaven and Hell to the new generation were taken for granted but were rarely pressing realities. The bantering treatment of the supernatural in Pulci and Ariosto shows how far mediaeval forms had been emptied of significance. The *Commedia* could still find appreciative readers, because it was also a great work of art and a great storehouse of human insight and varied interest, but the value of the average didactic "poema visione," whether as a means of instruction or as an authentic picture of the life beyond the grave, was rapidly disappearing. Perhaps no form of literature calls for a rarer combination of qualities in the author if it is not to be merely tedious and unconvincing. If the poet has not wings to soar with he is digging himself a bottomless pit of oblivion.

It cannot be said that the Florentine poets here under discussion escaped this danger. Their works are not so much poems as literary curiosities. They belong, in fact, to that order of books whose one chance of survival lies in their finding a witty parodist or a critic at once humorous and malevolent. Even this dubious kind of immortality seems to require more pronounced characteristics in the victim than any that these poems can boast. They are not exactly ludicrous in their badness. They have none of the kind of pungent absurdity that brought prolonged fame to Mr. Robert Montgomery's poems. Theirs is the unforgivable literary sin; they are dull, and even Luigi Pulci in his skirmishes with the Academy makes scarcely an attempt to treat them individually.

Matteo Palmieri's long philosophic poem, *La Città di Vita*, belongs to the early phase of Florentine Neoplatonism rather than to its full development.[1] It was written between 1455 and 1464, and was, therefore, completed when Ficino's translation of Plato and perhaps the *Theologia Platonica* were only begun. It may have been indebted to the lost *Istitutiones Platonicae* and the miscellaneous translations and short essays of Ficino's early years; but Palmieri owed his initiation into the Neoplatonic doctrines principally to Marsuppini and Traversari, with whom he was at one time on terms of great intimacy. The numerous astrological elements in his poem probably had their origin in a series of conversations which he held with Traversari and Paolo Toscanelli the mathematician at some time about 1430.[2] To Traversari may also be partly due the more conservative and ecclesiastical tone of Palmieri's thought; if one contrasts him with the boldest of the humanists he appears curiously mediaeval. Yet the *Città di Vita* owes almost all its fame to a heresy, and conceals here and there among its tedious and antiquated involutions hints of the new connotation that the Florentines were beginning to read into familiar words. The prose treatise, *Della Vita Civile*, shows how far Palmieri identified himself with contemporary thought when it came to laying down principles for the practical conduct of life.

La *Città di Vita* takes the form of a vision in which the poet, guided at first by the Sybil of Cuma, and later by a good spirit called Calogenio, passes through the unseen world and hears the mysteries of faith and philosophy expounded by the way. It is written in very obvious imitation of the *Divine Comedy*, but the likeness, it need hardly be said, is purely external. Palmieri's poem is abstract and colourless; a theologico-philosophical disquisition in verse that can be called a poem only for convenience.

[1] See preface by M. Rooke to the edition of the first book and first fifteen cantos of the second book published in *Smith College Studies in Modern Languages*, Nos. 1-2, Northampton (Mass.), 1927. The poem exists in two MSS.
(1) Laur. XL, 53, 1464-5. The original MS. was given by Palmieri to the Guild of Notaries. It contains a commentary by Leone Dati and has been considerably damaged by fire and water.
(2) Magl., II, 11, 41. A copy dated 1466. The second MS. has been used. The third number in all references is that of the terzina.   [2] *Della Torre*, p. 226.

The landscape of his spiritual world is nebulous and uncertain, and neither the author nor his guides nor the other dwellers in the universal City are much more clearly individualized than figures seen through a fog.

Yet if the *Città di Vita* is scarcely an adventure to read it has had an adventurous history. Palmieri himself realized that it contained matter of offence and was careful to give the manuscript, sealed, to the Guild of Notaries, with instructions that it was not to be opened until after his death.[1] As he had feared, his work was banned by the Church. The manuscript passed through many vicissitudes but attracted little notice until the nineteenth century, though it is briefly mentioned by several writers before that period and quoted by Bandini in his catalogue of the Laurenziana. Only one manuscript copy was taken and it was not until within the last few years that anything more than a few detached fragments has been printed. The general purport of the poem was evidently fairly well known to Palmieri's contemporaries, but the concealment of the text makes it unlikely that the other "visions" were directly imitated from it.

The principal heresy of which Palmieri was accused was not wholly unconnected with his Neoplatonism. In his account of the creation of souls he adopts the theory put forward by Origen concerning the fate of the neutral angels.[2] Instead of placing them as Dante did, among the damned, he asserts that they were sent to earth in human form and given once more the choice between good and evil; and that those who chose rightly would, after death, be restored to their old places in the heavenly hierarchy. Origen, as appears notably in the famous case of Pico's nine hundred theses, was the one of the early Christian authors to whom the Florentine Neoplatonists most frequently had recourse. He was cherished by humanist theologians like Erasmus for a spirit more gracious, liberal, and humane than that of many other philosophers

---

[1] For M. P.'s heresy see esp. M. Rooke, o.c., and G. Boffito, *L'eresia di M. P. cittadino fiorentino*. G.S., Vol. XXXVII, p. 1.
[2] In *La Città di Vita*, Bk. I, Cap. V.

of the primitive church. Among his debts to the Alexandrian school one may perhaps include a more hopeful and merciful attitude towards the whole problem of sin and retribution than the one generally accepted by the Church. He was, in fact, in modern terms, a Universalist, a believer in "the final restitution of all things." If he did not go to the length of explaining away evil as simple negation, the mere deadness and formlessness of matter, he had strong sympathy with the belief that the soul contained an inmost divine principle incapable of sin and bound, therefore, after whatever age-long process of purification might be necessary, to be reunited to its source. This was an idea that all the Florentine Neoplatonists, and especially Ficino, caressed in their moments of enthusiasm and denied in their moments of orthodoxy; and that led them to mitigate current opinion regarding the permanence of evil and the possibility of final estrangement between the Divine Spirit and the inferior spiritual beings of its creation.

Palmieri was far from denying the existence of Hell—he devotes most of the second book to the subject—but he had no desire to see it thickly populated. He may have argued subconsciously, though he never definitely voices the opinion, that if all spirits were created in pure love by a Being incapable even of willing evil, it is unlikely that any but the most obstinately recalcitrant will be cast away for eternity.

> Questo beato nel suo sancto sito
> fu sempre ed era ed è si liberale
> in altri egli ha suo proprio bene partito.
> Sopra ogni altro potere è questo tale
> Che come e vuole in tutto puo giovare
> sanza potere di voler far male.[1]

Angels and men were created only so that they might, by the right use of reason and free will, desire to know God and enjoy Him for ever.

> Intelligenza bisognò facesse
> Con lume di ragione e immortale
> Ad chi l'eterno ben tutto si desse.[2]

---

[1] *Città di Vita*, I, 5, 17.   [2] O.c., I, 5, 19.

The first and most luminous of the angels loved himself more than God, and so fell, along with others of his kin who had chosen evil instead of good. The rest of the angels remained in bliss, with the exception of those who

> . . . ad Dio non fur nemici
> Ne seguaci della divina voglia
> Ma stetter dubbi ad chi si far amici.[1]

These waverers did not deserve either Heaven or Hell until they had made their choice. They were therefore sent to dwell in the Elysian Fields or Paradise, the region in which the souls of men are created; and in due course took their way to earth, passing downwards through the spheres. Like human souls, they formed for themselves material bodies, and in these lived their allotted time and made the vital choice between good and evil. Those who chose aright would return to their old places in heaven, but as men with resurrected bodies instead of as pure spirits.

> Ad questo tutte per voler sapere
> Se vera luce od tenebre l'apprende
> Le chiama Idio e manda ad grandi schiere.
> Cosi l'amore in lor libertà pende
> Celata nella lor purità prima
> Ciascuna insieme col suo corpo rende
> Et mostra quante nel peccato infima.[2]

There existed another possible charge of heresy against Palmieri, much more definitely Neoplatonic in character.[3] Luigi Pulci, who

---

[1] *Città di Vita*, I, 5, 24. [2] O.c., I, 5, 49.
[3] The first heresy was repeated in the picture of the *Assumption*, formerly the altar piece of the Palmieri chapel in the Church of San Piero Maggiore and now No. 1126 in the National Gallery. The picture was at one time attributed to Botticelli, but is now generally supposed to be the work of Botticini. It shared the condemnation pronounced on the poem. The Palmieri chapel was placed under an interdict and its altar-piece veiled until the final demolition of San Piero in 1745. The picture represents heaven, opened to receive the glorified figure of the Virgin, with the Holy Trinity enthroned in the midst of the nine orders of angels. The faithful angels are depicted as winged beings robed in the traditional colours of their orders or bearing traditional symbols; but scattered through their ranks are other figures of purely human aspect, bishops, cardinals, kings, friars, warriors, and a number of women saints. Some of these figures appear in every grade of the angelic hierarchy except

satirized all those "poeti e filosofi e morali" who claim to have immediate revelations from the other world, singles out Palmieri for special blame as a believer in the transmigration of souls.[1] The charge was probably unfounded, at least in the sense in which Pulci understood it; but there is something refreshing in the disgust of his blunt and humorous bourgeois mind at those members of the Academy whose propensity for recording visions was not always balanced by a corresponding faculty for seeing them.

> E se Paulo già vide "arcana Dei"
> Fu per grazia concesso a qualche fine
> Accio che quel potessi i Farisei
> Confondere colle sue sante dottrine
> Ma gli spiriti infernal malvagi e rei
> Privati son delle virtù divine
> Ma perchè pur molti secreti sanno
> Per virtù naturale gran cose fanno.
>
> Vanno per l'aer come uccel vagando
> Altre spezie di spiriti folletti,
> Che non furon fedeli ne rei quando
> Fu stabilito il numer degli eletti.
> Non so se'l mio Palmier qui venne errando
> Che par di corpo in corpo ancor gli metti
> Onde e'punge la mente con mille agora
> Esser prima Euforbio e poi Pitagora.
>
> E forse qui s'inganna il Tianeo
> Che si ricorda, dice, esser pirato
> E come e'prese un altro in mar piu reo
> E come gentilezza gli ebbe usato.[2]

---

the highest, since there was a tradition that all the seraphim remained faithful. See D. Angeli, "Per un quadro eretico," *Arch. St. dell'Arti*, 1896. J. Cartwright, "A Heretical Picture," *Magazine of Art*, London, 1883.

[1] In *Morgante Maggiore*, Canto XXIV, vv. 108 et seq., ed. Volpi, Florence, 1863, 3 vols., Vol. III, p. 148.

[2] The mention of the *Life of Appollonius of Tyana* may refer to the translation by Alamanno Rinuccini in MS. Laur. Plut. LXVII, No. VIII. Mentioned by Bandini, *Specimen*, Vol. II, p. 3, as having had some diffusion, and published by Aldus in 1502. Rinuccini was a friend and admirer of Palmieri's and pronounced his funeral oration. See G. Richa, *Notizie istoriche delle Chiese fiorentine*, Vol. I, p. 153, Florence, 1754.

One of the passages that Pulci had in mind was, no doubt, the fifteenth canto of the first book, where Palmieri describes the descent of the soul into matter by way of the spheres. From each sphere it takes something of its special characteristics, varying the quantity according to its own choice. Finally, upon reaching the earth, it forms for itself a material body. In a later passage of the poem Sybilla explains how the soul, on entering the body, drinks of Lethe and so forgets the truths it saw in the eternal world; and how, after it has wandered for a while in ignorance, its memory may be stirred to recollection and cause it to begin the upward struggle to its former home.

> Sybilla "intendi" disse "ove noi siamo
> Tornati al fiume ove si fa sicura
> L'anima entrando pel cammino strano.
> Sopra esto fiume la trovasti pura
> Di lume hornata tal, se lo tenesse
> Conoscerebbe el vero eterno dura.
> Ma come possa par che non vedesse
> Quel vero in ciel che certo ella vi vide
> Prima che in Lethe oblivion bevesse
> La qual beuta la memoria uccide
> Del ver già seppe, a metterla nel forse
> Fache opinando el suo parer divide.
> Questa ignoranza quel baglior le porse
> Prese nel fiume el qual passando scese
> Ne, quel passato, del calar s'accorse
> In selva obscura pare stran paese.
> Salvo se errando per sinistra via
> Nel cammin primo ver lo'nferno scese.
> Poi per tornare onde ella venne pria
> Riprese lesta per salir al monte
> Conduce al ben che suo fin desia.[1]

Now this passage, though it undoubtedly asserts a pre-existence of the soul need not, and pretty certainly did not, imply for Palmieri a belief in the transmigration of souls as that is commonly understood. All that he definitely says is that the individual soul exists in the eternal world before its descent into the body, and that once

[1] *Città di Vita*, III, 24, 5.

it has entered the realm of matter, which seems to it "stran paese," its whole existence becomes a struggle between the false opinions and lures of the senses that drag it downwards, and the innate desire for divine truth and perfection that causes it to strive towards the blessedness of its former life. Neither in the case of the neutral angels nor of the rank and file of human souls is there any indication that the struggle continues through a sequence of incarnations. On the contrary, Palmieri plainly shows that the fate of each soul is conditioned by its own exercise of free will during its time in the body, and sealed at the end of the individual life. Of course a belief in the soul's pre-existence as a separate conscious entity might savour of heresy to orthodox minds who regarded each soul at the moment of its coming into the world as a new creation "ex nihilo."

Apart from his heresies Palmieri was soaked in Neoplatonic doctrines. The opening cantos of his poem are devoted to speculations "della prima essentia la quale è idio," though it cannot be said that his metaphysics are particularly original. He begins by describing the Deity, eternal and perfect in unity and simplicity, giving life to all things and containing them all, though Himself contained of none.

> Eterno potere uno sempre e solo
> Solo e da cui e dal suo verbo spira
> Amore ardente nel excelso polo.
> Questo al eterno tutto in che si gira
> Vita donde ogni cosa in esso vive
> E sempre vixe quel s'intende o mira.
> Questa essentia che non si circumscrive
> El mondo guida e tutto in se contiene
> Nulla lasciando fuor delle sue rive.[1]

Men cannot understand why God was moved to create the world; they must simply accept the fact and believe that it came about through the pure goodness of the Creator and that all things are made in accordance with the archetypes that He beholds in His own mind.

[1] *Città di Vita*, I, 2, 3.

> Et come e volle si è creder pio
> Fascese il tempo la misura e'l mondo
> Nel suo incommutabile disio
> Generato nell'abysso profondo
> Dove s'asconde la potenza eterna
> Exemplar primo d'ogni mondan pondo.
> Nel quale tutto quello che si squaderna
> Come in ello e così convien si torni
> Dovunque sia o dove che si cerna.[1]

The divine nature is reflected in the angels and by them infused into the lower orders of being.

> Chi poi riceve l'adornato amore
> Lo'nfonde ancora in altre creature
> Nuntie celesti al vostro buon valore.
> Da queste sono in voi scintille pure
> Date perchè natura al sommo bene
> Vi meni sciolte da le adverse cure.[2]

We are endowed with free will, without which there could be no merit; and all spirits, angels, or men, are citizens of a single city.

> Tutti gli spiriti in questi versi decti
> El popol fanno alla città di dio
> Creati buoni e non in tutto electi.[3]

Some writers, indeed, claim that on account of the fall of the angels there must be two cities, but Palmieri refutes the idea. Nothing, he says, can be outside the First Being. Therefore, all creation (the evil as well as the good he would seem to imply) is, as it were, the body of one spirit, moved by a single indwelling life.

> E volendo al suo centro pervenire
> Poi ch'uno esser non puote e questo ancora
> Fa si convien un corpo solo unire.
> Questa è la gran città dove dimora

---

[1] *Città di Vita*, I, 2, 14.   [2] O.c., I, 2, 24.
[3] O.c., I, 2, 30. Cf. III, 32, 1.

> El primo desider che l'alma mena
> Altro non è che di felice vita
> Sempre di bene per eterno piena.

> Tutto quel vive intende sente o spira
> E quel si danna o per lo mondo honora.
> Vita infinita tutta questa gira
> Contienla tutta e salda unisce e legha
> Sinche ogni parte in ogni parte tira.[1]

Yet though all things are in Him, He is Himself outside space and time, perfect and whole without any deficiency, movement, or change.

> La vita sempre vixe nella mente
> Che l'universo circulando move
> Vero lume era splendido e lucente
> El ben tutto che da l'eterno piove
> Era in essentia carità divina
> Vivente per amore un sommo giove.[2]

From Him proceed all life and all forms, but He is Himself above every form and definition. He manifests Himself to His creatures in many ways; but their apprehension of Him is in strict relation to their capacity, that is to the purity and sanctity of their souls.

> Dota è la più solenne della mente
> Data per grazia solo all'alma sancta
> Vede essa più che quel chel senso sente.[3]

Sometimes God makes Himself known as whiteness purer than snow, or as light, or cloud, or the voice of thunders; sometimes through joy or love or a rapture that transcends speech and can only be suggested by a paradox:

> Hor ombra di splendor più che lucente.

Palmieri, in common with the rest of the Neoplatonists, insists on the immediacy of the relation between God and the soul. Though the Deity is for him almost as impersonal as "The One" of Plotinus or the ineffable God of Dionysius, it is yet present to the individual conscience, whose admonitory voice is, therefore, in a real sense divine. It would be foolish to read into Palmieri such a conception of immanence as appears in Ficino, but there is perhaps more potential heresy in the following lines, with their

[1] *Città di Vita*, I, 2, 38.   [2] O.c., I, 3, 1.   [3] O.c., III, 26, 4.

emphasis on the authority of individual experience, than in the errors of which he was convicted.

> Ad chi pensando, ad chi vien improviso
> Peregrin viene e vien com'ortolano
> Ad questo in terra ad quello in paradiso.
> Vedesi in monte o in diserto o piano
> Ad chi nel tempio di sua coscienza
> Dove e'fa pacto col giudicio umano.[1]

Our souls were, indeed, first created for a timeless life of contemplation, and it was only after the Fall that man was subjected to temporal weaknesses and limitations (Queste qualità quando dove e come). His true state should be that of the angels:

> Sempre son questi ad dio tucti vicini
> Hornando l'opra alla bellezza eterna
> Gli elesse e volle a sua primi confini
> Sanza mistura d'altra cosa esterna
> Pura bellezza del divino ornato. . . .[2]

The desire for happiness, that is for the unhindered fruition of the vision of God, is innate in man, and he can discern and choose the way to it through his powers of reason and free will. Yet in a world of shifting semblances he may easily be deluded into following shadows of real good, instead of good itself. The damned are those who have abandoned themselves so completely to false good and false opinion that they have permanently estranged themselves from God.

To the wise man, however, the objects of sense act not as fetters but as spurs; they urge him on to seek a reality behind themselves. The "seconda essenzia," the world, was created by God in time, and must be in some sense like Him, or at least like some type existing in Him.

> Tutto il visibil si contien nel mondo
> Ne fu prima da Dio creato fusse
> El creator fu sempre alto e profondo
> Per questo dice alcun che chi condusse
> Opus magnum non avendo altro exemplo
> Se simigliando in acto lo produsse.[3]

---

[1] *Città di Vita*, I, 3, 18.   [2] O.c., II, 18, 4.   [3] O.c., I, 4, 10.

There is latent here the idea of the macrocosm, created, like man the microcosm, in the image of God; but the idea is not elaborated. Palmieri, taking a hint from the *Timaeus*, describes the world as a vast animal, informed by a "World Soul" that binds all its members into one body.

> Et che ella vive già Platon non niegha
> Perchè vivendo ogni animal, ragione
> Gli par sia vita in quel che gli conlegha.[1]

The material world is for ever changing, but all created things renew themselves by generation, so that the temporal, though imperfect, continues from age to age as the "moving image" of the eternal.

The real pilgrimage of the poet and Sybilla only begins after the canto of the Fallen Angels; and its outward incidents may be passed over quickly. The two make a journey through Hell and see the punishments meted out to the many different categories of sinners.[2] From thence, guided by Calogenio, they begin the ascent of the mount of Purgatory. Calogenio, like Beatrice, represents grace coming to the aid of human reason [Sybilla]

> Però qualunque voglia spirituale
> Libera vien al punto che divide
> La buona via, e quella va nel male.
> . . . Della vita è l'eterno padre duce
> Per l'altra va ciascun come ad se piace
> Chiudendo gli occhi al lume che più luce.[3]

Palmieri does not here allot to Reason such a high place as it holds in Ficino's philosophy, though in a later passage he comes near to doing so. The soul, unillumined by grace, has no more

---

[1] *Città di Vita*, I, 2, 41.

[2] It is interesting to note how M. P., for all his Neoplatonic leanings, condemns Zoroaster and Apuleius for their traffic with the Magic Arts. [Bk. II, caps. 31–32.] In this Palmieri is more orthodox than the Academy in general. Pico and others inclined on the whole to condemn astrology, but favour "natural magic." Ficino never made his position entirely clear, but was far more indulgent towards the prophecies of the astrologers than Pico, and often cast horoscopes himself.

[3] O.c., III, 1, 3.

than the bare faculty of choice between good and evil. It cannot forge for itself a genuine, if limited, perfection. Still the capacity for choice is of fundamental importance and the gift of grace is dependent on its exercise. Only a voluntary turning back to God can save the soul that has let itself go to evil; but once it is set upon the way of salvation the divine light begins to pour into it from above. This is symbolized by a light that streams down from above the purgatorial mount and illumines all the upward way. Yet by reason of the dual tendencies of the soul the business of purification is necessarily toilsome and many hindrances must be met and overcome.

>Et quanto del piacer più s'abbandona
>Tanto l'è più spedito esto cammino
>Et meno andando con alcun tentione
>Spesso el disagio tanto l'è vicino
>Ch'andar sanz'esso per niun modo puote
>Non tucta astratta nell'amor divino.
>Da questo advien che andando i piè percuote
>Duolle el cammin e par le gran fatica
>Lasciar le voglie all'apetito vuote
>Et ben che'l ben sia quel che la nutrica.
>El senso mal contento si ribella
>Et la combacte come sua nimica.
>Quando ella vince si rifa più bella
>Peregrinando in su per questo monte
>Colle virtù la fan salir più snella.[1]

At the end of the long ascent the soul is at length set free and passes into forgetfulness of its earthly desires as complete as its forgetfulness of heavenly truth during its immersion in matter.

>Verso la terra più non volge voglia
>Ma quella oblisce, come nel calare
>Quel vero obli convien in ciel si coglia.[2]

The soul, which was made for heaven, cannot find peace till it returns to its true home; but it is not left without guidance during its earthly wanderings. The eternal ideas are present at every

[1] *Città di Vita*, III, 3, 27. [2] O.c., III, 24, 25.

stage of its journey; obscurely discerned through the things of sense, clearly manifest in the purgatorial regions, perfect and wholly to be enjoyed in heaven. On earth man is granted only a partial revelation, so that his faith and virtue may be tested.

> Le buone cose fur da dio create
> Per guidar l'alme in cielo e farle electe
> Fuor desta entrata son tutte aloggiate
> Et sono essenzie tancto benedecte
> Sanza altra qualità per modo astracte
> Qui sendo tucte sono in ciel perfecte.[1]

Perfect happiness consists in complete freedom from all passions, which may be found in faithful contemplation of heavenly things. It is a passive state rather than the active process of fusion between the mind and its object that is characteristic of Ficino's teaching.

> L'anime più fedeli e più devote
> Aver non posson premio più felice
> Ch'esser per sempre d'ogni passion vote.
> Quando all'anima aver questa non lice
> Vien sol da lei, che verso el ciel non mira
> Et sol per questo fassi peccatrice.[2]

To arrive at this state of felicity man must order his life by the right use of reason which is understood as the divine principle in the human soul, and whose office it is to discipline the lower faculties just as the divine reason orders and subdues the chaos of the universe. Man's reason is, in fact, an image of the universal reason and is governed by the same laws. As in his *Vita Civile*, Palmieri here emphasizes the soul's capacity for maintaining itself in virtue and happiness by the practice of that moral philosophy which is "tutta nostra" and in which even the "natural man" may be blessed.

> Quella ragion intendo che s'eterna
> Coll'esser primo nel crear produsse
> Quel che far volle che s'intende o cerna.
> Questa ragione e quella che condusse
> Nell'uom la parte fa che l'uom avanza

---

[1] *Città di Vita*, III, 2, 16.   [2] O.c., III, 29, 38.

THE MEDICI CIRCLE

> Ogni animal che in terra facta fusse:
> Et sopra agli altri dàgli tal prestanza
> L' unisce ad dio e fallo che el ciel merta . . .
> Di vie maggior honore ancor l'acerta
> Facendol possessor di questo bene.
> In corpo humano divina parte inserta
> Dalla quale è una ragion che viene
> All'uom da quella che si posa in dio
> Si ch'una legge l'uno e l'altro tiene
> Con ordin tal lo'mperadore, e prio
> In ciel e terra esta ragion commanda
> L'uomo ubedisce s'esser non vuol rio.
> Convien da questo una ragion si spanda
> Per cielo e terra, e pigli l'universo
> Per che sol questa per lo tutto manda.
> Da questo, quel dover che e puro e terso
> In quel primo exemplare, in Dio si pose
> Quello, e nell'uomo, e tucto el mondo asperso.[1]

Reason becomes almost identical with Palmieri's conception of Uranian love, which is the power that subdues the carnal affections and turns the soul towards the contemplation of truth.

The ascent may indeed begin through love of the beauty or truth manifest in the world, but when the soul has learned from them all that they have to teach it puts them away, recognizing that all knowledge gained through things that have no real existence or permanence must be itself imperfect and cloudy.

> Facta scienza delle cose umane
> Quelle spregiando come vil rifiuta.[2]

Withdrawing from these things it finds within itself a principle of true knowledge, independent of earthly conditions and discernible only by an act of pure reason.

> Già muor vivendo e cerca in altro lato
> Vivere sciolta, l'alma di se lieta
> Che'l corpo, a, quasi senza se lasciato. . . .
> Gode di se, ch ogni altra voglia acheta.[3]

---

[1] *Città di Vita*, III, 21, 6. Cf. *Vita Civile*, ed. Giunti, 1529, p. 19 verso.
[2] O.c., III, 25, 12.
[3] O.c., III, 25, 26.

In this state of true self-possession the soul is no longer troubled by the importunate demands of the body, or even by the inclination to sin.

> Nulla miseria humana più le move
> Ad cose far non sieno in cielo electe.[1]

It passes beyond itself and begins to participate freely in the divine by a mingling of knowledge and love.

> Solo alla mente questo lume è dato
> La qual di ciel colla nostra alma scese
> Per che tornasse in ciel con questo ornato.
> Sol dal divino questo l'alma prese
> Et come la mente ancora è la vita
> Divina, po che sol far questo intese.[2]

The mind, that has purified itself by the aid of its own inner light, becomes capable of true prayer, that is of a complete conversion of itself to God. In this state it may be for a time released from the body, and raised, like St. Paul, to the third heaven.[3]

It is not, however, until after death, when the bondage of the flesh has been completely shaken off that the soul enters into the fullness of its joy. Then it passes to heaven and beholds the Idea of Justice, the perfect righteousness that consists in knowing and loving God, and existing in absolute conformity with His will. It is the eternal principle of goodness to which the several virtues that man must practise on earth are simply approximations.

> Eterna facta immobile e sicura
> Questuna sola ogni virtù riceve
> Quanto esser puote in ciel purgata e pura. . . .
>
> La mente in ciel questa giustizia vede
> In quelle creature che son degne.[4]

From the company of the eternal Ideas and of "angeli sempre stabili in letizia" the blessed spirit is uplifted to the vision of the "Sommo Bene" itself. This excels even the glory of the Ideas

---

[1] *Città di Vita*, III, 25, 30.   [2] O.c. III, 25, 3.   [3] O.c., III, 25, 48.
[4] O.c., III, 31, 15.

and the poet confesses himself powerless to describe it and passes into the accustomed language of mysticism.

> Et quando più nel sommo ben contemplo
> Tanto più mancan le forze e lo ingegno
> Ad dir quel vidi nel celeste templo.
> Lustrava luce in universo al regno
> Rifusa in tucto, si che tucti spiriti
> D'essa lucean ognun com era degno.[1]

The *Poema Visione* of Giovanni Nesi may be found in two of the Codici Riccardiani in an obscurity in which it might be more charitable to leave it.[2] Nesi was one of the members of Ficino's circle who came under the influence of Savonarola; and he wrote, besides the long poem under consideration, a "Canzoniere" of no particular originality and some "Sermoni Morali." The poem is constructed on the model of the other Dantesque visions. It opens with an account of how the author, on awaking from sleep, was caught up into a divine rapture.

> Guardai in alto et vidi molto allunge
> O architecto del divino esempio
> La luce ove occhio mortal non giunge.
> Vidi un si glorioso e vago tempio
> Che quanto più'l miravo più crescea
> La voglia di vederlo a scempio a scempio
> Un ampla sphera qual non si scorgea
> Di che natura fussi o quarta o quinta
> Che'l raggio di mia vista trasparea
> Bene era in dieci cieli quella distincta
> Pel centro passa un axe et nelli estremi
> Duo poli avean collegata e vincta.[3]

---

[1] *Città di Vita*, III, 34, 3.

[2] The MSS. are (*a*) Cod. Ricc. 2722. Original MS. Handwriting not easily legible and full of erasures and corrections; 174 numbered pages. (*b*) Cod. Ricc. 2750 [O, IV, 32]. A copy in a beautiful hand, cited here. Both MSS. are undated and contain no reference to any external event that would place them exactly, but the denunciations of the sins of the world in Canto X, with their accompanying threats of judgment to come, possibly indicate that the poem was written while its author was under the influence of Savonarola, most probably, therefore, between 1489 and 1498.

[3] *Poema Visione*, Cap. I, p. 1 verso.

From this exaltation the poet looks down to earth and considers the vanity of mortal things and the permanence of heaven. He sees the four elements, peopled with their several orders of beings, and Chaos in which all forms exist potentially.

> . . . ogni seme congesto
> Le forme che il factore et prima et poi
> Creò e di creare li sono incluse
> Et tra le fuori el sol co'raggi suoi.[1]

All these forms are reflections, more or less perfect, of types that exist eternally in the Divine Intellect, and the creation is only, as it were, the shadow of God

> Quel motor infinito, eterno e pio
> In ogni ben creato se dipigne
> Ch'altro non è ciò che è ch'ombra di Dio.[2]

The most perfect sensible image of God is the starry sphere which resembles Him in its simplicity, purity, changelessness, and all-embracing greatness.

> Giove mi par che in quel sua imago infundi
> Vive in se puro ne ha materia externa
> Et di luce e calor in altri abundi
> In se non luce; in se non arde; alterna.
> Vice non ha: anzi sempre in un modo
> Sua forma vive semplice et eterna
> Questa è di nostra vita un fermo chiodo
> E tanto ha di vigore et si activo
> Che più nature lega in un bel nodo
> Luce nè mixta et in sè di luce è privo
> Tutto comprende et da nulla è compreso
> Per cui diventa in mortal corpo vivo.
>
> * * *
>
> Questo è l'ardente muro e questo il velo
> Che le cose quaggiù cinge et raffrena
> Si che in sè convertille ha giusto zelo.
>
> * *
>
> Questa è l'ultima spera e più vicina
> Che molto porge senso anima et vita

---

[1] *Poema Visione*, III. D 10 v.   [2] O.c., VII, pp. 21-22.

THE MEDICI CIRCLE

> A quei che come Anteo la terra affina
> Quì è l'artefice e quì son le dita
> Et qui il pennel che pinge ciò che'scripto
> Nel primo ciel ch'a tal opra l'invita.[1]

His vision convinces the poet that the Platonic theory of the creation is the most in harmony with the Christian revelation

> Hor se la tua Lyra havessi Orpheo
> Canterei come et gli elementi et il mondo
> Ditermino et infinito il signor feo.
> In numero creò misura et pondo
> Tempio sì bel che tre persone sembra
> Nume divino mirabile et profondo.[2]

In the next canto he speaks of the angelic hierarchies and of their functions, with a strange mingling of the system of Dionysius with the demon lore of the Neoplatonists, and the demi-gods of paganism.

> Vidi in ciascun suo cerchio un stuolo alato
> Di varie menti. Quì eran semidei,
> Angeli qui, heroi dall altro lato
> Demoni vidi anchoro ond'io temei
> Di loro aspecti en si diverse genti
> Parte buoni mi parieno e parte rei.
> Chi lume porge et chi spegne sovente
> Al genio humano, et chi di quello ascende
> Nel sen purgato d'heroico mente.[3]

There are three worlds, angelic, celestial, and terrestrial. Spiritual beings are divided into nine legions that rule over the nine spheres under the governing power of the Almighty.

> L'intelligibil ciel sono e'miei throni
> Et le sphere che vedi son la cetra
> Che l'angelica man volgendo suoni
> Questo mondo sensibil benchè tetra
> Caligin sia et il mio sacro scabello
> Ove la pianta mia per l'huom s'impetra

---

[1] *Poema Visione*, VII, p. 24 v. [2] O.c., VIII, p. 25. [3] O.c., VIII, p. 26.

> L'un sembra l'altro: et sembran tutti quello
> Che nella mente tua già scrivo et segno
> Cui darai il mio color con tuo pennello.[1]

All creatures were made through the pure goodness of God, who desired to let all things participate, as far as was possible, in His own blessedness. The Son was begotten from eternity of God's love for Himself.

> L'idea universal si trahe di pecto
> Un raggio ehe percuote et torna in suso
> Che l'universo in si bel nodo strecto
> In questa ha il cielo ogni gioia rinchiuso
> Che dentro a se possiede; in questo ha Giove
> In questo han gli altri Dei suo lume infuso.[2]

This idea is repeated in the description of the seven heavens through which the poet passed in the subsequent course of the vision.

> Bene eran septe cieli; ma trasparea
> Ciascuna in forma ch'a la vista cede
> Onde lor qualità meno scorgea
> Ma percotendo in el più denso riede
> In giù il raggio el tornando in suo fonte
> Di quel vide lassù quaggiù fa fede.[3]

It is not necessary to describe the constellations and their several legends or Nesi's adventures in the paradise of the sages or the paradise of the heroes, which occupy the central cantos of the poem. The only point worthy of note is the passage on the operation of the heavens, and the influence that they exercise on human affairs.

> Nulla ociosa è quivi et nulla dorme
> Ogni cosa opra et di mysterio vaca
> Nulla fu in cielo a Dio tanto conforme.
>
> * * *
>
> Quinci viene il tuo ben, quinci la noia
> Quinci il fato celeste a noi discende
> Quinci tua vita e quinci opo è che muoia.
> In tanti corpi il ciel non un comprende

---

[1] *Poema Visione*, IX, p. 28.   [2] O.c., XII, p. 38.   [3] O.c., XIII, p. 47 v.

> Ch'altra figura altro parto produce
> Et tutto il mondo in tutto il ciel risplende
> Ivi son raggi, ivi lumi, ivi luce
> Chi più chi meno; et secondo l'aspecto
> Diversa stella diversa opra induce.[1]

Nesi, however, was too thorough a disciple of Ficino to admit that the influence of the stars made man helpless or irresponsible. The will, fixed upon the highest good and perfected by grace, can make him master over all the complex entanglements of circumstance, inclination, and illusion, which are his human portion but are not of his own making. Our dispositions and fortunes come to us from the stars, but we can free ourselves by setting our hearts on God and so receiving power to escape from the snares of sense.

> Ne senza te ad te già venir puossi
> Tu'l fin, tu'l mezzo se'di tua bontate.

> Potente è il ciel a mover gli umani acti
> Et imprime la sua stampa in vostri pecti
> Onde par che talhor l'ingegni abbacti.
> Non che servino a quel vostri intellecti
> Che l'imperio mortal loco hanno in mano
> Ne sono in alcun modo a lui suggecti
> Che quando l'occhio interno ha il veder sano
> Commanda al senso et vince quella forza
> Che spinge el cielo benche ne sari invano.[2]

In the heaven of lovers the writer sees the spirits of those who loved on earth miraculously united, each living in the life of the other.

> Cosi l'amante nell'amato vive
> Che si trasforma in quello, e diventa una
> Come in sua fronte amor chiaro descrive. . . .

> Felice morte che due vite accoppia
> Felice vite che in sì bel suggecto
> In altri accende amore, e in se lo alloppia.[3]

---

[1] *Poema Visione*, XI, p. 34 v.   [2] O.c., XXI, p. 71 v.–72.   [3] O.c., XXII, p. 72.

There, too, is the temple of Venus Urania, set in the garden of the Ideas, which was the birthplace of love. Nesi hails the Goddess as the power through whom all things are brought into being and preserved,

> Salve dunque, sacrata e vera dea
> Per cui è ciò che è et per cui vive
> Ogni vita vivente in tua idea,[1]

and passes on to describe the garden in which all forms known on earth exist in their primal beauty and perfection.

> Ciò che mai il cielo dal sacro seno scorse
> Di quel vivo splendor nel terren grembo
> Hor l'una hor l'altra idea destò et morse.
> Chiodate ivi parieno in aureo nembo
> Gemme infinite: et quelle immortai forme
> Porton ciascun, ascose nel suo lembo.
> Queste piantono in terra a pena l'orme,
> Et di mortale amanto veston quelle.
> Che nude sono in cielo al ciel conforme.
> Non credo sien lassù già tante stelle
> Quante son queste idee: al fine in uno
> Ristrecte sopra il ciel, del ciel più belle.
> Ciò che nutre quaggiù o sole o luna
> Da le forme celeste han lor semente
> Et que dal fonte ove ogni ben s'aduna.
> Ciò che è si truova in quello; ivi ogni mente
> Ogni alma ivi, ogni vita et ogni vero
> Essere albergo, et fuor di lui niente.
> Et se mai sia'l tuo volo alto et leggero
> Vedrai ben che tu se'o fusti sempre
> Una ombra sanza lui, un sogno, un zero,
> Et più et men come il suo pennel tempre
> Per ritrarti il pittor da quello exempio
> Che'l ciel col suo rotar già mai distempre.

* * *

> Nel ampia vesta sua [del cielo] l'imago è sculpta
> Dello exemplar divino: onde ella adorna
> La nuda pria nutrice arida et inculta.[2]

---

[1] *Poema Visione*, XXIII, pp. 75, 77 v. [2] O.c., XXVI, p. 860.

The first heaven receives the direct impress of the divine Ideas and here dwell the Hours and the Seasons. Yet the lower world is no less a mirror of God's glory, so formed that its beauty wins the soul back to the unseen beauty of the spiritual world.

> Questo è lo specchio et la tuba ch'invita
> A contemplare in sè la tua bellezza
> A fruir sopra sè te eterna vita
> Questa tua ombra a veder l'alma avezza.[1]

In like manner all human art and wisdom are but echoes and inspirations from the eternal harmony of the Muses' heaven.

> Quivi una voce d'echo quasi sente
> Il genu humano in terra: ma qui in cielo
> Il canto d'este muse apre ogni mente.[2]

There is little more originality of thought but considerably greater literary merit in the *Paradisus* of Ugolino di V. Verino than in the work of either Nesi or Palmieri. Verino also is borne upward through the heavens in a dream.

> Namque videbatur stellis ardentibus aether
> Conburj et totus fumare est visus olympus
> Sydereo at postquam steteram sublimis in axe
> Unde aer liquidus neptuniaque arva videri
> Unde urbes posterat et tristia tartarum ditis.[3]

Below him he sees the earth, and after lamenting over its discords and corruptions, he is shown the halls of the gods in a vision strangely mingled of classical reminiscences and the Apocalyptic description of the new Jerusalem. The Deity himself is described under the familiar type of the sun,

> Non aliter quam si ferventis apollinis orbem
> Cum purus sine nube dies estate serena . . .
> Non potuere pati mortalia lumina tantum
> Splendorem cecidi quoties spectare volebam,[4]

---

[1] *Poema Visione*, XXIV, p. 78 v.   [2] O.c., XXIV, p. 78 v.
[3] Ugolino di V. Verino, *Paradisus de rebus supernis e de beatorum splendore e maxime de his qui optime rem administra rem*, Ugolini Veri, 1489, Laur. XXXIX, 40, p. 83.   [4] O.c., p. 85.

and there follow several passages on the creation of angels and men parallel to those already quoted from Palmieri and Nesi.

The angels were created by God to participate in His light, and those who remained faithful fulfil eternally their several functions.

> At divina cohors caelique exercitus omnes
> Partim hymnos partimque levesque agitare choreas
> Flectereque ingirum psallantes ordine miro
> Hi laudes domini cantabant voce sonora.[1]

Others, again, are the guardians of man and bid him

> ... vanos vitae mortalis honores
> Spernere, virtuteque sequi per mille labores.[2]

Each man has also his evil angel who tempts him with honours, wealth, and sensual pleasures; but he is free to choose between these counsels and to guide his two horses like a good charioteer. To the good man death, which releases him from the body, is the supreme good fortune. Verino's picture of the life of paradise is, however, Elysian rather than philosophical and bears a remarkable likeness to the "Regno di Venere" in Poliziano's *Stanze*, by which it was, no doubt, suggested.

> Quattuor in partes non hic distinguitur annus
> Eternum ver est; sed nullis nubibus aether
> Nigrescit, nullus caelestes irrigat imber. ...
> Carpebant lepores florentia prata fugaces
> Et timidi passeri posita formidine dames.[3]

Apart from these passages there are scattered through the *Paradisus* those reflections on the nature of the Deity which had become the commonplaces of Neoplatonism. It is scarcely necessary to give a summary of them again, and they are epitomized adequately enough in Verino's epigram entitled *Quid sit deus et quod sit formatur*, which occurs in the second book of the collected epigrams contained in the same Laurenzian manuscript as the *Paradisus*.

[1] *Paradisus*, p. 88.   [2] O.c., p. 89.   [3] O.c., pp. 92–93.

THE MEDICI CIRCLE 161

> Scire cupis superum quae sit substantia regis
> Ens sine principio, ens sine fine deus
> Omnipotens, simplex immobilis omnia volvens
> Et faciem illius nemo videre potest
> Ipse auctore caret qui conditor omnia verbo
> Et nichil est quod non fecerit ipse deus.[1]

In contrast with the theological and philosophical aims of Palmieri, Nesi, and Verino, the purpose of Lorenzo di Giovanni Bonincontri's verse was mainly scientific.

Bonincontri, a Florentine by birth, was a professional astrologer and mathematician, whose intimacy with Ficino and Pontano may well have turned his mind towards writing astrological poems with a Neoplatonic background. Besides his poems he wrote a number of astrological and mathematical treatises, and the *Astronomicon*, an edition of Manilius with elaborate commentaries, which was published at Rome in 1484. It contains numerous references to Plato and the Neoplatonists, and is interesting in its endeavour to confute Manilius' Stoic fatalism with the energetic Neoplatonic doctrines of free will. Several manuscript copies of Bonincontri's poems exist, but only the *De Rebus Caelestis* has been printed in its entirety.[2]

The *Rerum Naturalum* contains little that is remarkable. In dealing with the creation the poet closely follows the Biblical narrative; and his cosmography is the traditional system of the ten concentric heavens, of which the utmost is the clearest image of God.

> Illic sublimes animas consistere certum est
> Quas non atra dies, nec nox obscura malorum

---

[1] O.c., p. 16.
[2] Laur. XXXIV, 52, c, is the most important MS. B. Soldati, in *La Poesia Astrologica nel* 400, p. 155 [Florence, 1904], mentions several other MSS., chief among them Vat. Lat. 2844, which contains a commentary. The poem was written and dedicated to Lorenzo not earlier than 1469. See Soldati, o.c., p. 158.
The editions of *De Rebus Caelestis* are:—
    (1) Venice, De Sabio, 1526.
    (2) Basle, Robert Winter, *c.* 1540.
    (3) Basle, in *Opera Lucae Gorici*, 1575.

> Compulit infernas sceleratas labier oras:
> Hunc Pater omnipotens divina mente creatum
> Concelebrat fulgore suo.[1]

The *De Rebus Caelestis* opens with an exposition of the mysteries of the faith, the doctrines of the Trinity, the Incarnation, and the Atonement. The creation took place "ex nihilo." God is perfect purity and simplicity, but all things are full of Him.

> Simplex esse Deus non ulli cognitus unque
> Purior excessu mentis qui fine coheret
> Principia: et cunctis connectit singula rebus
> Quem primum constat rebus, formisque creatis
> Invenisse viam, de quo nunc dicimus: hic est
> Qui caelum et terras et cuncta animalia fecit.
> ... nec conferre locum poteris: spaciumque naturae:
> Quod non ille sua describat imagine Plenum
> Qui quoque caelum et terras aquosque profundum
> Ambit: et immenso spaciatur margine mundi
> Non tamen ille locum signat: sed nos quia summa
> Purior est caeli sedes et purior orbis
> Dicimus ardentis peragrare volumina caeli.[2]

Bonincontri insists again, as he had done in the *Astronomicon*, on the free will of man, who must not blame the stars for his defections. Souls are created pure, and only became tainted with sin on entering the body, though they acquire special temperaments on their downward passage through the spheres. The evil influences of the stars are punitive, but not malign, and every man is attended by his good and evil angel who try to influence his conduct, but cannot touch the sovereign independence of his will. The only point on which Bonincontri shows himself at all unorthodox is in a lightly implied belief in metempsychosis, which may have earned him a place in Pulci's gallery of philosophers.

> ... post corpora prima
> Hic modus est illis infundi in corpora semper
> De que novo genitis vita adveniente creari
> Donec longa dies senio confecerit orbem.[3]

---

[1] Laur. XXXIV, 52, c, 1 b.   [2] *De Rebus Caelestis*, Venice, 152, p. 1.
[3] Laur. XXXIV, 52, c. 24 b et seq.

His chief interest, however, lies in the actual configuration and mechanism of the heavens rather than in the philosophical import of his scheme.

The Neoplatonists lucubrated, and their fellow citizens on the whole listened to them with respect; but there was one poet, living in close contact with the group, who refused to take them seriously. Luigi Pulci, the story-teller, jester, friend, servant, and boon companion of the Medici, represents that solid plebeian Florence of the bottega and the piazza and the tavern which probably remains in all ages essentially the same. It was a Florence to which Lorenzo and his circle were far from irresponsive, even if they were self-conscious enough to view their response a trifle satirically. The *Morgante Maggiore* must have made delectable reading for the author of the *Beoni* and the *Nencia*; and it is not difficult to understand the bond of sympathy that held Luigi and his patron together.

There were, however, aspects of Lorenzo's complex nature that Pulci did not so well appreciate. The man who enjoyed a hunting party, a broad jest, or a disreputable adventure, was equally ready, at other times, to write allegorical sonnets or talk metaphysics with Ficino. If our friends are more or less perfect incarnations of our ideas, Pulci and Ficino might well appear as visible symbols of two opposing elements in Lorenzo's personality or, in Neoplatonic language, two attendant daemons who drew him into opposing paths. Between Pulci and Ficino's disciples some hostility existed, though how far that hostility was serious is still open to debate. The chief evidence of it is to be found in the letters of Pulci and Matteo Franco, and in the virulent series of sonnets that passed between them; but it is probable that a good deal of verbal warfare took place of which no record has been kept. Pulci twitted the Academy; and the Academy disapproved of Pulci and cast reflections on his moral character and his religious orthodoxy which finally caused him, in the second edition of the *Morgante*, to attempt a fairly systematic reply.

Lorenzo continued to favour both parties, and no doubt found their quarrels amusing.

Pulci's qualities—his noisy humour, his rambling inventiveness, his command of racy Tuscan speech, his rich sense of comic character and low life—are not those most commonly allied with a taste for abstract speculation. They do not, certainly, exclude a capacity for serious thought, as may be seen in the work of Folengo or Rabelais; but one need not expect to find in Pulci a satirist of this quality. It is doubtful if he can be called a satirist at all, if true satire imply a moral or reforming aim in the writer. There is no trace of any such aim in the sonnets against Ficino; and if it exists in the *Morgante* it is extremely difficult to define.

On the contrary, Pulci's attacks on the Neoplatonists seem to have proceeded from personal irritation rather than from any sense of outraged truth or any desire to express a cherished opinion. This is emphatically true of the sonnets, though it might need some qualification with regard to the *Morgante*. One can see how to Pulci's mind, with its firm grasp of mundane, roystering life, and its restless humour, the discourses of the Neoplatonists must have invited ridicule. All this familiar talk of the unseen, of contemplation, and ecstasy, and bodiless beauty and ideal love must have seemed to him high-sounding humbug. There is a touch of guttersnipery in his sonnets, as of the street urchin prancing and grimacing and making long noses before these portentous gentlemen who, to his thinking,

> Say a very foolish thing
> In such a solemn way.

Some of the sonnets are directed personally to Ficino, the "venerabil gufo soriano," others have a more general application. The former are little more than somewhat vulgar accusations of incompetence and plagiary that might be matched and overmatched in a dozen humanistic quarrels. Two short quotations will suffice to show their quality and to justify the annoyance they caused Pulci's victims.

> Marsilio questa tua filosofia
> Non se ne sente in bocca mai a persona
> Che tu la metti donde il dopo nona
> E riesce poi in chiasso o in pazzeria.
> Che di'tu ? Che traduci ?
> —Platone—Sia col mal che Dio ti dia!
> O tu bestemmi la filosofia!
> Nani nani ; bugia
> Tu ne recesti un dì tanta a Careggi
> Che tu non n'hai se tu non ne releggi.

Or again

> Bestia fuggita qua dalle maremme
> Non ti vergogni, vil traditor vecchio
> Usurpar l'altrui gloria e l'altrui gemme
> E la virtù d'un sol che al mondo è specchio
> Or sturati l'orrecchio
> Che tu se pur lo dio delle cicale.

It certainly required a fair equipment of boldness and impudence to address the "alter Plato" of Florence in this strain; and even Pulci may have balked a little at his own audacity. In the edition of the sonnets printed during Ficino's lifetime these poems are headed "Ad un geometra" and slightly bowdlerized to correspond with the title. The text as quoted here is that reprinted by Volpi from Cod. Trivulziano 965.[1] No doubt the original versions were known to those immediately concerned, but even if they had not been, there was always another poem of more general application that contained ample matter of offence.

> Costor che fan si gran disputazione
> Dell'anima ond'ell entri o onde l'esca
> O come il nocciol si stia nella pesca
> Hanno studiato in su n'un gran mellone.
> Aristotile allegano e Platone
> E voglion ch'ella in pace requiesca
> Fra suoni e canti, e fannoti una tresca
> Che t'empie el capo di confusione.

---

[1] Volpi, "Luigi Pulci," G.S., Vol. XXII, p. 30; at pp. 47, 48.

> L'anima è sol come si vede espresso
> In un pan bianco caldo un pinocchiato
> O una carbonata in un pan fesso
> E chi crede altro ha il fodero in bucato
> E que'che per l'un cento hanno promesso
> Ci pagheran di nocciole in mercato.
> Mi dì un che v'è stato
> Nell'altra vita e più non può tornarvi
> Ch'appena con la scala si può andarvi.
>   Costor credon trovarvi
> E beccafichi e gli ortolan pelati
> E buon vin dolci e letti sprimacciati
>   E vanno dietro a frati.
> Noi ce n'andrem Pandolfo in Val di Buja
> Senza sentir più cantar Alleluja.[1]

Impertinences of this kind could not be passed over in silence and Franco attacked the "pessimo Tersite" in sonnets so violent that Luigi said they gave him the fever. It has been suggested that the whole tenzone was an elaborate joke, but it seems too full of genuine bitterness and spite to have been entirely a make-believe, even allowing for the immense licence accorded to jesters at that time. Quite apart from the question of the sonnets, Lorenzo's more serious friends may well have felt both jealousy and disapproval at the favour shown to the scapegrace Luigi, and Franco may have been the spokesman of an outraged Academy when he wrote:

"Gigi è importuno, Gigi è fastidioso, Gigi ha pessima lingua, Gigi pazzo, Gigi arrogante, Gigi seminator di scandali, Gigi ha mille difetti secondo voi, e nondimeno senza Gigi non si può respirare in casa vostra. Gigi è animella delle vostre palle. Havete tolto a mostrare la magnificentia et humanità vostra in tenere a grazia questo dispecto della generatione humana."[2]

Perhaps the most convincing argument for the genuineness of the antagonism is that Pulci should have troubled to write a defence so long and elaborate as the episode of Astarotte. His own attitude

---

[1] In *Sonnets of L. Pulci and M. Franco*, Lucca, 1759, No. CXLV, Volpi, o.c., p. 34. [2] *Lettere di L. P.*, ed. S. Bongi, Lucca, 1886, No. 53.

towards ultimate problems is debatable. It is fairly certain that he was by no means a religious minded man or one much given to serious thinking; it is not so certain that he was wholly indifferent in such matters. Probably he liked in most moods to consider himself an "esprit fort," or at least a practical man with too much common sense to be hoodwinked by either priests or philosophers. He led a sufficiently irregular life and allowed his famous tongue to play very freely with reverend names; but he was determined to ensure his own safety in both worlds. He treated established religion with enough observance to escape serious scandal, and the possibility of consequences more remote but possibly more unpleasant. Now and then he seems even to have been moved by genuine feeling.

In 1473 he was "converted" through the influence of Nannina de' Medici, having previously, according to Franco, remained for twenty years unconfessed. The same authority affirms that the good effects of the conversion were short-lived.

The literary fruit of this episode was the *Confessione*, which has the appearance of sincerity.[1] It may well be that Pulci's fits of repentance and his pious invocations of the Virgin and the Saints at the opening of the cantos of the *Morgante*, were genuine while they lasted. Side by side with his somewhat careless and superstitious acceptance of popular theology, which he often treated with amazing irreverence, he seems to have had some fitful but real awareness of a supreme governing power in the world.

When he came to answer the critics who had accused him of irreligion, it was on this conviction that he based his defence. Yet it is doubtful if his beliefs would ever, in themselves, have been urgent enough to demand expression, if he had not been goaded into speech by the irritation he felt at Ficino and the other Neoplatonists who took on themselves the mystery of things and professed to map out the unseen. Beyond the rather conventional invocations at the beginnings of the cantos there is little in the

[1] The *Confessione* was published by Volpi, o.c., p. 55, from Magl., II, IV, 678 (c. 51 v). For this aspect of Pulci see also Burckhardt, o.c., pp. 476, 516; Geiger, o.c., Bk. I, Ch. 10, pp. 55–60.

first edition of the *Morgante* at all analogous to the twenty-fourth canto.[1]

Pulci, indeed, formulated his ideas rather from a desire to badger his opponents than from any inner need of his own; but provocation, while it sharpened his wit, seems to have deepened whatever seriousness he had. The episode of Astarotte is built of passages of unexpectedly dignified verse, through which there plays and flickers something of the witty and startling profanity of the *Vision of Judgment*.

The mouthpiece of his opinions is the fiend Astarotte, who is sent by the enchanter Malagigi to bring Rinaldo and Ricciardetto from Egypt to Roncevaux. The choice of speaker ought perhaps to make one cautious of attaching overmuch value to these remarks, but one remembers that the devils, thanks to their antecedents, were generally supposed to have a good deal of inside information on matters necessarily baffling to human ingenuity. Astarotte, too, is so dignified and courteous a figure that he seems intended for a serious personage.

In one speech he evidently harks back to the old difficulty of the neutral angels, explaining to his audience the difference between the fall of man, who sinned ignorantly, and that of the angelic intelligence "La qual peccò come natura dotta." Man may be saved by penitence and grace, but the fallen or indifferent angel "non più può ritornar perfetta e intera."

Origen, the favourite theologian of the Neoplatonists, comes in for further censure for his hope that Judas himself might be saved.

---

[1] The opening of the speech of Antea, daughter of the Soldan, in Canto XVI, v. 6, is the only important parallel:—
> Quel primo Dio che fece cielo e terra
> E la natura e stelle e sole e luna
> Ed a sua posta l'abisso apre e serra,
> E fa, quando e'vuol l'aria chiara e bruna
> E ch'è pietoso e giusto e mai non erra
> Benchè ciascun pur gridi alla fortuna.

The first edition of the *Morgante* in 23 cantos appeared at Florence in 1482. The second edition, with additional cantos, was published in the following year. References are given to Volpi's edition, Florence, 1863, 3 vols.

E non sarebbe anche Giuda dannato
Chè se pentì, ma la speranza manca,
Sanza la qual nessun mai fia salvato
E'l detto d'Origen non lo rinfranca
Nè sia chi l'altra opinion conchiuda
In diebus illis salvabitur Giuda.[1]

Pulci cuts a strange figure as a champion of orthodoxy, but he plays his part with evident relish. He next turns to rebuking the presumption of those who take it on themselves to explain the ordering of the universe and to determine the causes of God's acts and the disposition of the heavenly hierarchies. No names are mentioned, but a good many readers could recognize themselves, under the general categories of "poeti e filosofi e morali," as a part of that misguided humanity "che vuol saper, sanza saper niente."

E poeti e filosofi e morali
Queste cose ch'io dico anche non sanno
Ma la presunzion vuol de'mortali
Saper le gerarchie com'elle stanno;
Io ero Seraphin de'principali
E non sapea quel che di qua detto hanno
Dionisio e Gregorio ch'ognun erra
A voler giudicar il ciel di terra.[2]

But how could they do otherwise than err, asks Pulci, with one of his quick, mischievous turns of fancy, when they are led astray by "spiriti folletti," those elusive spirits of air whose life consists in deceiving their victims with all manner of falsehood? Here he was treading on delicate ground, for he himself had undoubtedly dabbled in various forms of magic and occultism; but that may possibly have served to convince him that the spirits were not always trustworthy.[3] He describes their activities with malign

---

[1] *Morgante*, ed. c, Vol. III, Canto XXV, vv. 153 et seq.
[2] Ibid., vv. 156-9.
[3] For evidence of Pulci's interest in occult arts see *Morgante*, Canto XXI, Episode of Creonta; Canto XXII, v. 102; Canto XXIV, vv. 112, 113; *Letters*,

relish, hinting that they are the true inspirers of the philosophers and extremely busy at their task.

> ... non vengon costretti
> Nell'aqua o nello specchio, e in aria stanno
> Mostrando sempre falsitate e inganno.
>
> Vannosi l'un con l'altro poi vantando
> D'aver fatto parer quel che non sia
> Chi si diletta ir gli uomini gabbando
> Chi si diletta di filosofia
> Chi venire i tesori rivelando
> Chi del futuro dir qualche bugia
> Si ch'io t'ho letto un gentil mio quaderno
> Chè gentilezza è bene anche in inferno.[1]

So far Pulci's negations; but when it comes to making positive statements, which may presumably be taken to represent his personal views, he speaks with the voice of the Neoplatonists themselves. He expounds, in fact, something remarkably like Ficino's conception of natural religion, and emphasizes again the theistic tendency implicit in his system. God is all-creating and all-pervading, exalted even above the Son in wisdom, the source of all movement, power, knowledge, and light. The world is ordered by Him with perfect righteousness, but foreknowledge, or understanding of final mysteries, is not conceded even to the angels who most nearly approach Him.

ed. Bongi, pp. 49, 53, 56, where a sort of familiar spirit is mentioned; Volpi, o.c., pp. 30–3.

Bonincontri, in the *De Rebus Caelestis*, ed. c, p. 10 v., ascribes to the neutral angels a character not unlike that given by Pulci to his "spiriti folletti."

> Sed quisquis sceleri largas non movit habenas
> Et tacitus voluit suspenso incedere passu
> Donec longa dei patientia substulit arma:
> Errantes fluitare polo nec sistere in alto
> Aspicies: imas terrae nec ferre tenebras
> Nubiferos gravioris aquae demictere nimbos
> Ad terram: et rigido caelum convolere fumo
> Saepius ad magicos soliti discendere cantus.

[1] *Morgante*, XXV, vv. 60–1.

> Dicea Malagigi: Tu m'hai pur detto
> Un punto che mi tien tutto confuso
> Che il Figliuol tutto non sappi in effetto.
> Io non intendo il tuo parlar quì chiuso.
> Disse Astarotte: Tu non hai ben letto
> La bibbia, e parmi con essa poco uso;
> Chè interrogato del gran dì il Figliuolo
> Disse che il Padre lo sapeva solo.
>
> Or nota Malagigi se tu vuoi
> Ch'io dico pur la mia definizione
> E domanda i teologhi tuoi poi:
> Voi dite in una essenzia tre persone
> O vero una sustanzia, e così noi,
> Un atto puro sanza ammistione:
> Però che questo di necessitate
> Convien che sia quel che tutti adorate.
>
> Un motor, donde ogni motor deriva
> Un ordin donde ogni ordin sia construtto
> Una causa a tutte primitiva,
> Un poter donde ogni poter vien tutto
> Un foco donde ogni splendor s'avviva
> Un principio onde ogni principio è indutto
> Un sapere donde ogni sapere è dato
> Un bene donde ogni bene è causato.[1]

Further on Astarotte tells his hearers that the world extends far beyond the pillars of Hercules; and Rinaldo asks if the people of these unknown countries are all also the children of Adam, and if they will be saved. Astarotte replies:

> Sappi ch'ognun per la croce è salvato
> Forse che'l vero, dopo lungo errore
> Adorerete tutti di concordia
> E troverete ognun misericordia.
>
> Basta che sol la vostra Fede è certa
> E la Vergine è in ciel glorificata
> Ma nota che la porta è sempre aperta
> E insino a quel gran dì non fia serrata,

---

[1] *Morgante*, vv. 141–5.

E chi farà col cor giusto l'offerta
Sarà questa olocausta accetata
Chè molto piace al cielo la obbedienza
E timore osservanza e riverenza.

Mentre lor ceremonie e divozione
Con timore osservarono i Romani
Benchè Marte adorassino e Giunone
E Giuppiter e gli altri idoli vani
Piaceva al ciel questa religione
Che discerne le bestie dagli umani
Tanto che sempre alcun tempo innalzorno
E così pel contrario rovinorno.

Dico così che quella gente crede
Adorando pianeti adorar bene:
E la giustizia sai così concede
Al buon remunerazio, al tristo pene;
Si che non debbe disperar merzede
Chi rettamente la sua legge tiene:
La mente è quella che vi salva e danna
Se la troppa ignoranza non v'inganna.[1]

Religion then is not so much the acceptance of a definite historical revelation as a disposition of the mind. It is a faculty inherent in human nature, the acknowledgment and adoration of a higher power by which man exalts himself above the brutes. This natural religion is imperfect till illumined by grace, but it is not wholly unworthy, and when devoutly practised it is acceptable to heaven. Sincere worship and moral uprightness outweigh any mere intellectual error. The pagan gods were "idoli vani" and yet not mere stocks and stones or devils leading men astray; they were rather adumbrations of the truths that the human heart dimly apprehends of itself, though it can only find their fulfilment in the Christian revelation.

That this point of view had its dangers Pulci fully realized, and he guards himself against possible attacks by insisting that it

[1] *Morgante*, vv. 233-6.

is one thing to do one's best by natural intuition when no clearer
light is vouchsafed, and another to reject true knowledge when
that is available. The obstinate unbeliever who has heard the truths
of Christianity and will not accept them is in far great danger
than the pagan who has served God well according to his capacity.

> Nota ch'egli è certo ignoranza ottusa
> O crassa o pigra accidiosa e trista
> Che la porta al veder tenendo chiusa
> Ricevette invan l'anima e la vista;
> Però questa nel ciel non truova scusa
> "Noluit intelligere" il Salmista
> Dice d'alma tanto ignorante e folle
> Che per bene operar, saper non volle.[1]

"La mente è quella che vi salva e danna." Man by his innate
perceptions of truth and right can mould his own destiny, and it
is neither through fate nor any injustice on the Creator's part
that we are what we are and believe what we believe.

> Dimmi, rispose Malagigi, ancora
> Chè tu mi pare qualche angel discreto
> Se quel primo motor, ch'ognuno adora
> Conosceva il mal vostro in suo segreto
> E vedeva presente il punto e l'ora
> E par che sia qui ingiusto il suo decreto
> E la sua carità qui non sarebbe
> Perchè creati e dannati v'arebbe.

> Crucciosi come un diavol Astarotte
> Poi disse: E'non amò più Micaelle
> Che Lucifer quel giusto Sabaotte
> E non creò Cain peggior che Abelle;
> Se l'un superbo fu più che Nembrotte
> L'altro è tutto disforme a Gabrielle
> E non si pente, a non esclama Osanna
> Libero arbitrio l'uno e l'altro danna.[2]

Then, immediately after uttering these solemn asseverations,

---

[1] *Morgante*, vv. 237, 238.   [2] *Morgante*, vv. 148–50.

Pulci is at his pranks, defending himself comically over a shameless piece of plagiary.

> Altro certo offerir non ti possa ora:
> L'alma chi la diè credo sua sia,
> Il resto tutto sai convien che mora:
> O sommo amore, o nuova cortesia!
> (Vedi che forse ognun si crede ancora
> Che questo verso del Petrarca sia
> Ed è gia tanto e'lo disse Rinaldo
> Ma chi non ruba è chiamato rubaldo.)[1]

From this note of wounded innocence the poem slips back into its accustomed bantering mood; and again one wonders how deeply Pulci really felt this profession of faith. Was it simply a defiance flung out by his restless and mocking spirit, a proof that he, with no hieratic status, as it were, was capable of knowing as much and writing as nobly in laudable matters as any of those who made these things their special concern? Did he "only do it to annoy"? Everything that is known of him might incline one to think he did; but the fact remains that some of Astarotte's speeches have a dignity and solidity that suggest something genuine behind them, a spring of seriousness, deeply hidden and habitually neglected, that has been drawn upon for once in self-defence.

[1] *Morgante*, v. 283.

TRANSLATIONS

Page 135. *Dante Alighieri* . . . *benchè non parlasse* . . .

Dante Alighieri . . . although he discoursed not in the Greek tongue with Plato, that sacred father of the Philosophers, did none the less in spirit hold converse with him, since he adorned his books with many Platonic sayings. Three kingdoms do we find described by our most trusty guide, Plato; one being of the blessed, one of the damned, and one of the pilgrim spirits. Virgil first followed this Platonic order; which Dante did also follow, drinking of the Platonic springs from Virgil's cup. . . . In the book which he called *Monarchia* he treats of the pilgrims in this present life.

Page 166. *Gigi è importuno* . . .

Gigi is importunate, Gigi is tiresome, Gigi has a vile tongue, Gigi's crazy, Gigi's arrogant, Gigi is a scandal-monger, Gigi has a thousand faults according to you, but none the less one cannot draw breath in your house without Gigi. Gigi is the marrow of your bones. You have taken it upon you to display your greatness and liberality by favouring this offscouring of the human race.

(NOTE.—For verse translations to this chapter see Appendix, p. 279).

CHAPTER VI

THE "TRATTATO D'AMORE"

MUCH has already been written on the "trattato d'amore" of the sixteenth century, and it would be obviously impossible, even if it were desirable, to follow in the present chapter the methods of Lorenzo Savino, or T. F. Crane or Menendez y Pelayo.[1] It may be said at the outset that these treatises, with the single exception of the *Dialoghi d'Amore* of Leone Ebreo, show very little originality of thought. Their fundamental ideas were taken from the works of Ficino and Pico, and the modifications that they underwent at the hands of different authors were, for the most part, of presentation and atmosphere rather than of substance. It is from this point of view that they are treated here.

The first question that suggests itself is "Why did the Neoplatonic 'trattato d'amore' become so immensely popular in the early part of the sixteenth century?" Treatises on the nature and art of love were, of course, no new thing in Italy; they existed before the Renaissance and continued to be written after the Renaissance proper was past. In some form they may probably be found in all literatures and all ages since they are after all concerned with one of mankind's perennial interests. Classical literature presents two outstanding points of view, the philosophical treatment of love that has ever since been known as Platonic,

[1] Lorenzo Savino, *Di alcuni trattati e trattatisti d'amore italiani. Studi di letteratura diretti da E. Percopo*, Naples, 1909–14, Vols. 9–10. T. F. Crane, *Italian Social Customs of the Sixteenth Century*, Newhaven Yale U.P., 1920, esp. Chs. III and IV. Marcellino Menendez y Pelayo, *Historia de las ideas esteticas en Espagna*, tom. I–II, Madrid, 1890–1. These three standard works contain not only careful analyses of the more important treatises but a wealth of information—historical, biographical, and bibliographical—regarding them and their authors. Useful general studies are contained in Flamini, *Il Cinquecento*, pp. 372–82. M. Rosi, *Saggio sui trattati d'amore del '500 Recanati* 1889, and *Scienza d'amore, idealismo e vita pratica*, Milan, 1904. P. Lorenzetti, *La bellezza e l'amore*, Annali di Pisa, 1920.

and the frankly sensual view of the *Ars Amandi*. The Middle Ages recognized a sacred and a profane love; the sacred love of the soul for God, of which love towards one's fellow creatures was a kind of secondary product, and the profane love of the senses, sweet in enjoyment but leading the soul to Hell. The most general treatment of love in mediaeval literature was moral and allegorical, but feudal society, especially Provençal society, evolved a distinctive ideal based upon its own organization.[1] The lady to whom the Provençal poet addressed his poems was regarded as a feudal superior who received from her lover the same honour and service as were given by a true knight to his liege-lord. In return she was expected to be gracious to him and to encourage him in all courtesy and valour. The proper relations of the lover to his lady gave rise to innumerable "questions" that were frequently and minutely debated in Provençal society and literature.[2]

The introduction of Provençal poetry into Italy produced at first a number of close imitations of the troubadours' manner; but the essentially civic society of the peninsula, where feudalism had never really taken root, could not fully assimilate the chivalric conception of love. Instead, the Italian poets, especially after Guido Guinizelli, transformed the chivalric ideal into a philosophical one. The beloved, from being simply the liege-lady of the troubadours, becomes a being of more than earthly perfection who raises the lover towards the bliss of paradise.

He contemplates and adores and is purified by his love, which wakens virtue in his heart as the influence of a star infuses virtue into a precious stone. In the writers of the "stil nuovo" the lady and the passion she inspires tend to become more and more etherialized till in such a poem as Guido Cavalcanti's *Donna mi*

[1] This does not, of course, mean that love was not often treated directly and imaginatively in both classical and mediaeval literature; it is merely a statement in the most general terms of the main theories that were current regarding it.

[2] For an erudite summary of this question see Crane, o.c., Chs. I and II. It would be an amusing but not perhaps very profitable piece of research to compare a list of Provençal or sixteenth-century Italian "questions" with some of the discussions that rage in our present-day newspapers.

prega they are simply abstractions for the intellect to subtilize and refine upon. The best work of the school expresses a mood of ecstatic worship in which the lady appears as a heavenly visitant or as one in whom the beauty of the world is concentrated.

Cavalcanti's own sonnets, *Chi è che viene ch'ogni huom la mira* and *Tu hai in te i fiori e la verdura*, are glowing examples of this type of verse. In the *Vita Nuova* the ideal of the "stil novisti" is transcended in a peculiarly original vision. Dante's love is contemplative and philosophical; it is also human, and it is recorded in the most imaginative of spiritual autobiographies where abstract ideas are personified and dramatized and where external events are charged with the strange significance of a dream. Beatrice herself is no abstraction; she has definite individuality, though it is suggested by touches so delicate that they can escape a superficial reading, and the love and grief that Dante felt for her have an unmistakably personal quality. But she remains essentially "la gloriosa donna della mia mente," the being around whom the most ideal aspirations of his mind could centre.

Dante's love was as rare a phenomenon as his genius, and even his greatest successor was not able to make the vision his own. Petrarch's poems reveal a mind troubled by a very mortal passion trying to subdue itself to the Dantesque ideal and finding itself in repeated conflict with it. Their originality and their profound difference from the work of the "stil novisti" lies precisely in the realization of this conflict and in the exquisite precision with which the poet fixes his own fluctuating moods. That he himself was not deceived as to his own feelings is proved not by the *Rime* alone but by the *Secretum*, where he protests that he loves only the spiritual beauty of Laura which leads him heavenward, and St. Augustine replies that he ought first to love God and then to love Laura for His sake. At bottom his ideal is akin to the one formulated by his beloved Cicero in the *Tusculanae*, where love is defined as a passion and is, therefore, to be shunned; but "love in virtue," or friendship based on the beauty and moral worth of the friends, is permitted. This theory of Petrarch's, with slight individual modifications, carries the Platonic tradition down to the time of Ficino. Its influence is apparent in such a book as the *Polisofo* of Filippo Nuvolone, or in the four epistles of Coluccio Salutati to Pellegrino Zambeccari.[1] Even after Ficino's works were published Petrarch continued to be the handbook of writers on love, more especially of lyric writers, and much of the so-called "Platonism" of the sixteenth century is in reality Petrarchism.

Other attitudes towards love of course existed. There was the frankly voluptuous and pagan view, thinly veiled by Dantesque imitations in Boccaccio, open and unashamed in Valla and Pontano; and the "civic" view in which love was exalted as the basis of family life and civil order and which found exponents in Salutati and Giovanni Dominici, Maffeo Vegio, Alberti, and many others.

Although philosophical disquisitions on love were common long before the days of the Platonic Academy the fact remains that the "trattato d'amore" arrived at a peculiar stage of development during the late fifteenth and early sixteenth centuries that separates it from earlier and later treatises on the same topic. To understand that development one must visualize the conditions that fostered it. Italian society was at this period essentially a society of courts, but of courts where intellectual gifts were valued quite as highly as nobility of birth. There was a large leisured and cultured class which found two of its principal recreations in light literature and conversation and which must have possessed, if the records that remain of it are true, a high general level of wit and intelligence and an unusual capacity for taking up any subject and discussing it skilfully if not profoundly.

The sexes met on equal terms and women took a prominent and sometimes a distinguished part in courtly life. Questions of love and gallantry and of the respective merits and social functions of men and women were favourite topics for arguments which,

[1] Coluccio Salutati, *Epistolae*, ed. Novati, Vol. III, pp. 1–52. G. Zonta, *Filippo Nuvolone e un suo dialogo d'amore*, Modena, 1905. The introduction is useful for theories of love before Ficino, esp. Ch. VI, p. 82.

if they were sometimes fairly serious, passed often into an ingenious game.

Such a state of society provided in perfection the elements necessary to bring the "trattato" to its fulfilment as a literary form. It emerged almost inevitably from that peculiar interplay of social and literary life. The place it occupied must have been not unlike that of the novel and the popular press to-day. It combined a certain more or less superficial discussion of abstract questions with pictures of contemporary life and often with considerable liveliness in the portrayal of character and the handling of dialogue.

It exploited the fashionable philosophy much as our modern newspapers exploit psycho-analysis or the theory of relativity. The Neoplatonic theory of love was attractive, especially to an age in which beauty in all its manifestations was so eagerly pursued, and it provided an excellent opportunity for the display of rhetoric and literary skill. The philosophical elements, in fact, soon became stereotyped, and the drawing of manners and character and discussions on extraneous questions became more and more prominent. Many of the treatises had a definite complimentary aim, and served to glorify a particular social circle by introducing the members of it as speakers in the discussions. They were written to please, and often show considerable vivacity and grace of style, besides flattering their readers' intelligence by presenting abstruse matter to them in a palatable form. As the sixteenth century advanced the growth of countless formal academies and the more exclusively erudite character of the audiences to which the later treatises were consequently addressed did much to rob the "trattato" of its livelier qualities. With the moralizing influences of the Counter-Reformation there crept in also a horrible didacticism that expressed itself in innumerable treatises, *Del Perfetto Matrimonio*, *Della Perfetta Verdovanza*, and the like.[1] In polite society the topic of

---

[1] See G. Rossi, "La collezione Giordani della Bib. Communale di Bologna," *G.S.*, XXVII, 372-90. The Neoplatonic strain, however, persists in the dialogues of Tasso, Manso, Vito di Gozze, etc.

love tended to lose such intellectual interest or coherence as it possessed in Bembo or Castiglione, and to trail away into an infinity of small questions and "conceits" of which the *Paradossi* of Ortensio Lando are the classic example.[1]

The treatises of Ficino and Pico have already been discussed and it is not necessary at the moment to recapitulate their contents.

They were written, as has been seen, primarily in an attempt to explain a philosophico-religious problem, but they had also a practical end in view, a reform of the deep-rooted moral corruption that was common in contemporary Italy. It does not appear that they had any marked effect on morals, but it may be that, against their authors' will, they lent some countenance to the worst vices of the age. Platonic love in its original form was not love between the sexes but a philosophical ideal built upon the Greek conception of heroic friendship. This love of man for man, having as its object the encouragement of military and civic virtue, was an institution of Greek life and was in many states regulated by strict laws which did not, however, prevent its degenerating very far from its ideal aim. Socrates, according to his ancient commentators, tried to restore to the emotion its proper moral value, and Plato further elaborated and philosophized his principles.[2] The love depicted by the Neoplatonists is still, on its human side, essentially a heroic friendship, and the relations of Ficino and Cavalcanti or of Pico and Benivieni are instances of the feeling at its best. Unfortunately, in the society that surrounded them, the most shameful depravity came sometimes to be qualified as "amor socratico."

While Neoplatonism remained in what one may call its philosophical state it left the classical view unchanged, but as soon as it began to pass into popular literature it was modified by the mediaeval Christian tradition, especially as that was manifested

---

[1] Crane, o.c., Ch. V, for this vermiculate Platonism. The *Paradossi* were published at Lyons in 1543.
[2] J. A. Symonds, "The Dantesque and Platonic Ideals of Love" in *In the Key of Blue and Other Prose Essays*, John Lane, London, 1893, pp. 55–86.

in Petrarch, and by the actual conditions of a society where women were conspicuous.¹

Ficino's ideal persists in his disciple, Francesco Cattani da Diacceto. "Soleva, says Varchi, ancora Messer Marsilio, mentre che egli trovandosi hoggimai oltra coll'età leggeva a suoi discepoli, dire io me ne vo, ma se bene mi parto, io vi lascio lo scambio, intendendo di Messer Francesco, il quale si chiamava per sopranome il Pagonazzo."² Diacceto does in fact repeat his master's teaching without adding to it anything material. There is the same division of being into God, angelic intelligence, soul, and matter, and the same latent idea of universal animation, expressing itself in the picture of the world or macrocosm as a great animal whose activities are repeated in man the microcosm.³ Love is defined as ". . . desiderium perfruendae et effigendae pulchritudinis in pulchro

---

[1] See p.e. *Asolani*, ed. Aldus, Venice, 1505, p. f. IIII, for praise of women and description of the complementary rôles of the sexes. *Il Cortigiano*, ed. Cian, pp. 266 et seq. Speron Sperone, *Dialogo d'Amore*, in *Opere*, Venice, 1740, 5 vols., Vol. I, p. 36. "Ama adunque la donna gioia e diletto dell'universo, non per diletto che le succeda ma acciò che dilettando e giovando ella allo amante la virtù sua e la sua cortesia non ancor nota sia celebrata e lodata, questo è il bene questo è il premio, questo è il fin della donna amata e del suo amore verso l'amante."

[2] "I tre libri d'amore di M. Francesco Cattani da Diacceto Filosofo et Gentil Huomo Fiorentino con un Panegirico all'Amore et con la vita del detto autore fatta da M. Benedetto Varchi" (*Ven. G. Giolito de'Ferrari*, 1561, p. 183). The *Panegirico dell'Amore* was published separately at Rome, 1526, in 4° and dedicated to Giovanni Corsi and Palla Rucellai. Diacceto's complete Latin works were only published in 1564. Fr. *Catanei Diaccetii, Patricii Florentini Philosophi summi Opera Omnia*, Basileae, MDLXIIII. All these publications were posthumous, as Diacceto died in 1522. He carried on Ficino's tradition of oral teaching in the gatherings of the Orti Oricellari and is frequently mentioned, together with his master, in the works of their contemporaries and successors.

[3] *Opera*, Basle, 1564. *De Amore libri tres*, Bk. III, Ch. 5, p. 114; Bk. I, Ch. 2, p. 94. Here Diacceto, after pointing out that the elements move of their own nature while plants have vegetative life, animals power of movement, senses, and power of distinguishing between things dangerous or profitable, and man, besides possessing these powers, has also the contemplative faculty, adds a passage on the animation of the heavens, "quinimmo ubi tam exquisite moventur, necesse est, ab anima divinissima moveri."

quemadmodum dicitur in Symposio";[1] and the distinction between Venus Urania and Venus Dione is restated, together with the immeasurable superiority of ideal beauty over its material manifestations.[2] Beauty is of different kinds, but it is always the flower of goodness, the object of our visual faculty, material or intellectual. Wherever it exists it does so as an "accident" since it is not intrinsic to those things through which it is revealed.[3] Both the angel or "mundus intelligibilis" and the soul desire not only to enjoy beauty but to express it "Ex quo mundus intelligibilis undequaque pulcher fit," and the soul expresses itself through matter as far as matter is capable of receiving its impress.[4] Perfection for every creature consists in possessing God in so far as it is able not by intellect alone nor by the will alone, but by the whole mind.[5] The human mind, being itself divine, is present where it works and works where it is drawn by affection or by its innate need of activity, so that when it gives itself to divine things it lives as a god, independent of time and change and perfect in understanding, and may be called a coadjutor of the World Soul.[6]

The *Panegirico dell'Amore* repeats the main ideas of the longer work in a more rhapsodical style. Diacceto is perhaps easier to read than Ficino, but presents no novelty either in his thought or in his mode of presenting it. Leon Battista Alberti's two little treatises, *Hecatomfila* and *Deifira*, make no attempt at a philosophical discussion of love, but may owe some of the warmth of their apology for the passion to the inspiration of Ficino's work.[7]

[1] O.c., Bk. III, Ch. 1, p. 119.
[2] Quemadmodum igitur artificiosa habent dupliciter ut sint, tum in artifice, antequam prorumpit in opus: tum seipsis, ubi artifex in opus processit (verbi gratia Minervae Phidiae habet, ut in Phidiae mente primo, tum deinde in marmore fit; verumtamen quando primum est in Phidia longè melius quam in marmore habet), o.c., Bk. I, Ch. 4, p. 98. See also Bk. II, Ch. 6, p. 115; Ch. 7, p. 117.
[3] O.c., Bk. III, Ch. 2, p. 121.
[4] O.c., Bk. I, Ch. 7, p. 106; Bk. III, Ch. 4, p. 128.
[5] O.c., Bk. I, Ch. 7, p. 106.   [6] O.c., Bk. II, Ch. 7, p. 117.
[7] The *Hecatomfila* and the *Deifira* may be found in *L.B.A. Opuscoli morali*, ed. Cosimo Bartoli Ven. Franceschi, 1568, pp. 398 et seq. In *Daelli Biblioteca*

The great prototype of the courtly Neoplatonic treatise is the *Asolani* of Pietro Bembo.[1] It is a carefully balanced and dignified piece of writing, deliberate in style and aristocratic in atmosphere, though leavened with a certain gaiety that makes it less frigid than most of Bembo's work. It was written while he was still a young man with a fresh enthusiasm for Ficino's doctrines though with no speculative desire to expand them. He makes some parade of expounding new ideas; but his treatment of them is essentially an aesthetic one. They form part of a harmonious picture in his mind, blending with the groves and fountains of Asolo, and the conversations and "canzoni" of the "lieta brigata," in a golden light of retrospection. In the opening scene three damsels of the court sing songs on different aspects of love which set the tone for the three discourses into which the book falls. The first, which deals with the pains of love, provides a starting-point for Perottino, the

Rara, Milan, 1863, Vol. VI, and in *Opere Volgari*, ed. Bonucci, Florence, Vol. V. The poems of Lorenzo probably played a large part in the diffusion of Neoplatonism. They show much of the mingling of philosophical, personal, and aesthetic elements that characterizes the "trattato."

[1] Cardinal Pietro Bembo (1470–1547), son of the Venetian Bernardo Bembo, the friend of Ficino. As a child B. accompanied his father to Florence and was present at a meeting of the Platonic Academy. He achieved immense popularity and prestige not only by the *Asolani* but also by his poems and linguistic studies. The *Asolani* were first sketched in 1496, the conversations on which they were based having taken place probably in the same year or the year before. They were re-cast probably about 1498 and first published by Aldus in 1505. (For dates of composition, etc., see Savino, o.c., pp. 240 et seq.) Other editions are Aldus, 1515, 8°; De Sabbio, Venice, 1530, 4°; Scoito, Venice, 1553, 8°; Venice, *Opera*, 1729.
I have used the first edition.
For Bembo see besides Savino, Vol. IX, pp. 237 et seq. Gaspary, *Storia della let. it.* (trans. Rossi), Turin, 1891, Vol. II, P. II, pp. 60–7, Bibliography, pp. 284–5. Crane, o.c., Ch. III.

The scene of the *Asolani* is set at the court of Caterina Cornaro, the ex-Queen of Cyprus, at Asolo. The conversations take place on three succeeding days during the wedding festivities of one of the Queen's ladies. The three principal speakers, Perottino, Gismondo, and Lavinello, and their ladies, Lisa, Sabinetta, and Berenice, are members of the court under fictitious names. Praises of the Asolan circle run through the whole work and the background of the castle and its gardens is effectively touched in.

despised lover, whose discourse tells an often-repeated tale of sighs and tears, despair and wretchedness. It is punctuated with small questions, especially on punning etymologies such as the relations of "amare" and "amaro," "donna" and "danno," "giovani" and "giovano," and by a fitly lugubrious canzone.

These lamentations are answered on the second day by Gismondo, who makes himself the advocate of that "amore umano," which is content to rest in the senses of sight and hearing, and of love as a natural force and a civilizing influence. To abuse it is to abuse nature who has infused it into every form of being. To love another person is simply to love another part of ourselves and to desire our own completeness.[1] Love may, indeed, be rational or irrational and so the cause either of honest and temperate desire, joy, and fear, or of disordered passion; but it is the generator and preserver of all creatures, and the foundation of all civil usages; family and civic life, laws, friendship, and all the arts and amenities by which man has excelled the brutes.[2]

The delights given to the eye and ear are continually new and never painful. The praise of sight introduces a description of the ideal of womanly beauty, incarnate in the speaker's lady Sabinetta. One is tempted to think that the type had long since been established by Petrarch. This creature of golden hair and starry eyes, of cheeks "con la colorita freschezza delle matutine rose," of soft and opulent grace, is Laura and no other.[3]

With the third book comes the crown of Bembo's virtuosity. His art becomes more careful and deliberate; he seems to be exalting and isolating his theme, giving it the romantic setting of the lonely

---

[1] *Asolani*, pp. f. IIII et seq. Gismondo illustrates his remarks with the legend of the double human beings, and makes them the occasion for a review of the complementary functions of the sexes. [2] O.c., pp. f. IIII^4, g. IIII^3 et seq.

[3] O.c., p. h. The type persists in Renaissance treatises; the descriptions become more minute, but the ideal is the same. One may trace it in the *Bellezza delle Donne* of Firenzuola, in the *Ritratti* of Trissino, in the *Libro della Bella Donna* of Luigini, in the *Leonora* and *Dialogo Amororo* of Betussi, in the *Discorsi* of Annibale Romei, and in creations of the poets such as Ariosto's Alcina and Sannazzaro's Amaranta.

mountain side where the hermit instructs Lavinello in the mysteries of divine love; and modulating his style to a statelier cadence.

The hermit exhorts the young man to rise from the love of particular and earthly beauties to the contemplation of the supreme beauty to which all visible things recall our thoughts. The love of earthly objects is only justifiable as a step in that upward progress. The middle way of mortal love, though not to be wholly condemned, is unsafe, since it is always easier for men to fall than to rise. Men who despise mortal things as if they were themselves divine, and aspire to divine things with mortal eagerness, and men "che hanno alla sempiternità pensamento," are already gods, though they still linger in the flesh.[1] Such liberty is, however, generally the prerogative of age, which may truly be called the health of our life, while youth, with its passionate unrest, is rather a time of fevered delusions. While we pursue those things that have no true being, we cannot know contentment, for who "nel mezzo delle sue più compiute gioie non sospiri alcun altra cosa"?[2]

"Ma perciò che egli in questa prigione delle membra rinchiuso più anni sta che egli lume non vede alcuno mentre che noi fanciulli dimoriamo et poscia dalla turba delle giovanili voglie ingombrato ne terrestri amori perdendosi può del divino dimenticarsi, esso in questa guisa lo richiama il sole ogni giorno, le stelle ogni notte la luna vicendevolmente dimostrandoci. Il quale dimostramento che altro è senon una eterna voce che ci grida 'O stolti che vaneggiate! Voi ciechi dintorno a quelle vostre false bellezze occupati a guisa di Narciso vi pascete di vano desio: et non vi accorgete che elle sono ombre della vera che voi abbandonate. Gli vostri animi sono eterni: perchè di fuggevole vaghezza gl'innebriate? Mirate noi, come belle creature che siamo; et pensate quanto dee esser bello colui di cui noi siamo ministri.'"[3]

In the world we are all dreamers, but those whose dreams are of the external beauty will awake to see the reality, like those lovers of the Queen of the Fortunate Islands who, on coming to her court, were sent into an enchanted sleep from which they

[1] O.c., p. p 11¹.   [2] O.c., p. m ii.   [3] O.c., p. m.

awakened with the subject of their dreams written on their foreheads. Those who had dreamed of sensual pleasures were sent to dwell with the beasts; those who dreamed of power and civic activity were sent out into the world again to bear rule in families and states; but those who dreamed of the Queen herself remained for ever in her court, rejoicing in her beauty and her wisdom.[1]

There is nothing new in Bembo's discourse, but there is a touch of poetry that few of his imitators retain. He makes no attempt to develop an independent philosophy from Ficino's theory; apart, perhaps, from the second book, he does not try to relate it to practical problems. He regards it as a thing beautiful in itself and satisfactory to contemplate, a lovely abstraction shining in its own distant and rarefied air.

A marked contrast to the *Asolani* appears in Mario Equicola's staggering work the *Libro di natura d'Amore*.[2] Among the treatises of the age it stands, fortunately, alone. It aims, in fact, at being an encyclopaedia of the whole subject of Love, in its most trivial as well as in its loftiest aspects, and its contents range from flabby metaphysics to chapters that might serve as light reading for Freudians. The framework is a simple repetition of the scheme that the Florentines had made familiar, but it is stuffed out and distorted with miscellaneous information of every conceivable kind. In the first book Equicola collects and summarizes the opinions of all the most important writers on love from the Middle Ages down to his own contemporaries, citing, among others, L. B.

---

[1] O.c., p. m iii.
[2] Mario Equicola (1470–c. 1525), secretary to Isabella d'Este and noted both as a bibliophile and as a writer and courtier. The *Libro di natura d'Amore* was begun in 1494 in Latin and afterwards translated, but was not published until 1525 at Venice. (Savino, o.c., Vol. X, pp. 6–10.) I have used the second edition, "Libro di natura d'Amore di Mario Equicola Di nuovo con somma diligenza Ristampato e corretto da M. Ludovico Dolce," in *Vinegia appresso G. Gioliti de Ferrari et fratelli* 1554. Another edition was printed by the same press in 1563. On Equicola see besides Savino, o.c., Flamini, *Cinquecento*, pp. 377–9. G. Bertoni, "Nota su M. E. bibliofilo e cortigiano, *G.S.*, Vol. LXVI, pp. 281–3. D. Santoro, "Appunti su M. E.," *G.S.*, Vol. XV, pp. 402–13. R. Renier, "Per la cronologia e la composizione del libro di natura di Amore di M. E., *G.S.*, XIV, pp. 212–33.

Alberti, Platina, Ficino, Pico and his nephew Giovan Francesco, and Diacceto. He states the case against love with an endless string of examples taken from mythology and history, suggests remedies, and pronounces a hearty invective against women; and then, after making a long summary of the *Asolani,* he confutes with equal erudition all that he had previously said.

He then proceeds to definitions; and every term of the Neoplatonic vocabulary is discussed with minute but wearisome and empty precision "si che Dio, Angelo, anima, intelletto e intelligenza intronano la testa al paziente lettore lasciandola più vuota di prima."[1]

Love is described as "desiderio del bene," "desiderio di avere e usare e fruire quel che si crede bello anzi buono."[2] On the traces of Ficino, Equicola makes it the root of all desires and activities. "Essendo questo amore universale se non si dice ogni huomo amare avien che la cupidità è molteplice et corpo di molti capi, che secondo li effetti muta nome ... ma quella cupidità per la quale semo tirati a generare e parturire nel bello dicemo amore."[3]

All the affections have their origin in self-love which leads us to desire those things that seem to us useful and pleasant and the final aim of all human endeavour is "voluttà."[4] This in its completest form is divine love, but it may be known, though imperfectly, through terrestrial love and through "quello che del veder e conversar si diletta ne si eleva alla purità celeste ne si deprime o descende alla spurcitia del coito ma resta in mezzo."[5]

Desire is said to be "solamente nelle cose non havute, amore

---

[1] Savino, o.c., p. 56.
[2] O.c., Bk. II, Ch. 1, p. 74; Bk. II, Ch. 6, p. 136; II, Ch. 2, p. 99.
[3] O.c., Bk. II, Ch. 1, p. 74. Cf. Bk. III, Ch. 1, p. 155.
[4] Senza amicitie non si può stare e che sempre a nove ne preparemo ne è imposta necessità: percio che ne posseno essere fedelissimi fautori in aiutare nostre volontà a desiderati piaceri presenti, con certa speranza di posserli usare nel tempo che segue. O.c., Bk. II, 2, 91. Cf. Bk. VI, Ch. 1, pp. 364 et seq.
[5] O.c., Bk. II, Ch. 5, p. 132. For divine love see Bk. VI, Ch. 1, p. 411. Resta dunque quel esser beato che ama cosa ottima per ottima conosciuta, reamato quella fruisce senza noia, senza dubbio di mutazione, questo è solo Dio il quale è sempre e immutabile, da altri non depende, sempre proficuo amato sempre reama, dator unico di perfetta beatitudine.

nelle cose possedute e da possedere. . . ."[1] Beauty may be known through sight or hearing and awakes in us recollection of the Beauty that our souls have known in heaven.[2] The rest of the work is mainly occupied with extraneous matters. There are two lengthy chapters devoted to Venus and Cupid in which all the legends regarding them are collected, together with lists of all the names, symbols, and attributes that have been assigned to them by various races and religions.[3]

The fourth book, which deals with the senses, is a mass of medico-scientific detail, and includes, besides discourses on physiology, physiognomy, and palmistry, a discussion and condemnation of magic and astrology. In the fifth book Equicola treats of the qualities, moral, mental, and physical, that should mark the lover, and gives rules for dress and courtly behaviour and speaks of the significance of colours, precious stones, and so forth.[4]

The *Libro di natura d'Amore* enjoyed a wide diffusion and an ambiguous kind of popularity. It is rarely mentioned by the more serious writers of treatises, though it must have been known to most of them; and it must undoubtedly have been the treasure house of the compilers of books of games and emblems, paradoxes, and "motti," into which, as into a marsh, the tide of the "argomento d'amore" filtered away.[5] It was poor Equicola's fate to be shamelessly pillaged by his fellow authors, and in the century after his death to be hounded from Parnassus by the irrepressible Boccalini.[6]

His work has neither originality of thought nor literary grace to commend it, but it marks a further stage in what one might call the secularization of Neoplatonism. He inclines, so far as his

---

[1] O.c., Bk. II, Ch. 7, p. 141.   [2] O.c., Bk. II, Ch. 8, pp. 149 et seq.
[3] O.c., Bk. II, Ch. 3, p. 108; Ch. 4, p. 121.   [4] O.c., Bk. V, pp. 286, 314, 322.
[5] Among those who do acknowledge their debts are Nifo, *De Amore*, Leiden, 1641, p. 169. Betussi *Diaologo Amoroso*, Venice, 1543, p. 18 v. For an account of Equicola's popularity see Savino, o.c., Vol. X, pp. 99 et seq. Crane, who treats in great detail of the books of games, etc., does not discuss their relation to Equicola, but it seems fairly obvious.
[6] See T. Boccalini, *Ragguagli di Parnaso, Cent II, ragionamento XIV*, in "Scrittori d'Italia."

personal opinion can be disentangled from the mass of his erudition, towards a utilitarian view of love, and his introduction into his theme of so many extraneous and trivial matters set an example that his successors readily followed.

The *Cortigiano* of Baldassare Castiglione is not, strictly speaking, a "trattato d'amore"; it is an attempt "to form in words the perfect courtier," and the topic of love is incidental to that central aim.[1] In fact, it holds the same place in the economy of the book as it is there said to hold in the courtier's development. As the theme of ideal love is brought in as the crowning movement of the long and many-sided discussion of the courtier's qualities, rounding and concluding what has gone before, so the divine "furore" is regarded as the final perfecting of the man himself, a kind of supernatural grace in which his native virtues and acquired accomplishments find their consummation. It is a state to which, unless he is of quite exceptional temper, he can only hope to arrive in his mature years; it is as alien to the hot blood and fantastic mentality of youth as youthful love-making should be to reverend age.[2]

The argument follows the familiar lines. The description and praise of divine love are put into the mouth of Pietro Bembo, a delicate compliment to the author of the *Asolani* besides being

---

[1] Baldassare Castiglione (1478–1529), soldier, diplomatist, and man of letters, who spent his early years at the courts of the Sforza in Milan and of the Gonzaga in Mantua, and his later life in those of Leo X and Guidobaldo di Montefeltro, Duke of Urbino (1472–1508, m. 1486 Elizabetta Gonzaga). Castiglione was ambassador in England for the Duke of Urbino and Apostolic Nuncio at the Court of Charles V.

The *Cortigiano* was probably begun about 1514, but passed through many revisions, the final MS. being dated 1524 (see Cian's edition, Preface, p. vii). Even then Castiglione was not satisfied and was only provoked into publishing his work by the indiscretion of Vittoria Colonna, who had shown the MS. copy entrusted to her to many of her acquaintances. The first Aldine edition appeared in 1528. I have used the excellent critical edition of V. Cian, Florence, Sansoni, 1908. For Castiglione see also Savino, o.c., Vol. IX. Crane, o.c. E. Bottari, *B. Castiglione e il suo libro del Cortigiano*, Pisa, 1874. Walter Raleigh, Introduction to *The Book of the Courtier* from the Italian of Count Baldassare Castiglione: done into English by Sir Thomas Hoby, 1561, London, 1900.

[2] Ed. Cian, p. 414.

an acknowledgment of Castiglione's own indebtedness. Bembo's discourse is cast in dignified language, broken by interludes of what one might almost call elegant back-chat. There is the passage of humorous banter with Signor Morello over the propriety of an old man loving like a young one, and the discussion of the relative honesty of beautiful and ugly women.[1] They are a forecast of the "questions" that take up more and more space in later treatises; they are also a reminder of the nature of Castiglione's attitude to his subject.

He treats it with the kind of reverence that men show for an ideal that they admire, but of which they have no absolute conviction. Like many of his contemporaries he felt the attractiveness of the theory without being able to accept it wholeheartedly. He approaches it not as a philosopher nor as a poet, but as a high-minded and thoughtful man of the world who feels that his ideal will not quite square with life as he knows it. He would like it to be true, but he cannot believe in it sufficiently to give a completely personal touch to his treatment of it. So he repeats what he has read, and here and there compromises with human weakness. Divine love is hardly to be expected in the young; one must not ask humanity to rise above itself before it has had time to indulge its natural inclinations. Even lovers "more Platonico" may go so far as to kiss, since "l'amante razionale conosce che, ancora che la bocca sia parte del corpo, nientedimeno per quella si dà esito alle parole, che sono interpreti dell'anima, ed a quello intrinseco anelito che si chiama pur esso ancor anima; e perciò si diletta d'unir la sua bocca con quella della donna amata col bascio non per moversi a desiderio alcuno disonesto ma perchè sente che quello legame è un aprir l'adito alle anime che tratte dal desiderio l'una dell'altra si trasfondano alternamente ancor l'una nel corpo dell'altra e talmente si mescolino insieme che ognun di loro abbia due anime ed una sola di quelle due così composta regga quasi due corpi; onde il bascio si può più presto dire conguingimento d'anima che di corpo, perchè in quella ha tanta forza che la tira a se e le separa

[1] Ed. Cian, p. 419.

dal corpo . . . e però il divinamente innamorato Platone dice che basciando vennegli l'anima ai labri per uscir del corpo."[1]

It is, however, in the passages where he speaks of beauty that Castiglione is most eloquent. Like Bembo, his response to his philosophy is essentially aesthetic, but if Bembo's treatise is a work of ideal art, Castiglione's is one of applied art. The *Cortigiano* has a practical end in view, though it is also manifestly written to entertain. In his attempt to bring the Neoplatonic theorizings to earth and to give them a place in the life of his courtier, Castiglione gives one the impression that he was not sure of what to do with them. That love should be the desire for beauty he, with his strong feeling for comeliness in every manifestation of life, readily understands; and his words grow warmer at the thought of visible loveliness ". . . onde l'anima si diletta, e con una certa maravigla si spaventa e pur gode e quasi stupefatta insieme col piacere sente quel timore e riverenzia che alle cose sacre aver si sole e parle d'esser nel suo paradiso."[2]

He failed, and many others failed with him, in trying to identify the speculative love of the soul for its apprehensions of abstract truth, beauty, or righteousness with a kind of sentimental relation between the sexes that easily becomes unreal and was particularly unreal in the society around him. He can see as clearly as any the value of love as a social bond and a civilizing force, but the kind of ideal passion that sees in the beloved a symbol or an incarnation of some vaster power, and that inhabits a strange borderland of feeling between personal love and impersonal ecstasy, was something that he could not entirely grasp. It is perhaps a prerogative of youth and of great poets; but it is the inability fully to understand it that makes of even the final glorification of love a piece of finely modulated rhetoric rather than a personal vision.

"Qual sarà adunque O AMOR santissimo, lingua mortal che degnamente laudar ti possa? Tu bellissimo, bonissimo, sapientissimo,

[1] Ed. Cian, p. 424. Cf. A. Romei, *Discorsi divisi in sette giornate*, Venice, 1594, p. 56. [2] O.c., p. 425.

dalla unione della bellezza e bontà e sapienza divina derivi, ed in quella stai ed a quella per quella come in circulo ritorni. Tu dolcissimo vinculo del mondo, mezzo tra le cose celesti e le terrene, con benigno temperamento inclini le virtù superne al governo delle inferiori, e rivolgendo le menti de'mortali al suo principio con quello le congiungi. Tu di concordi unisci gli elementi, movi la natura a produrre e ciò che nasce alla succession della vita. Tu le cose separate aduni, alle imperfette dai la perfezione, alle dissimili la similitudine, alle inimiche l'amicizia, alla terra i frutti, al mar la tranquillità, al cielo il lume vitale. Tu padre sei de'veri piaceri, delle grazie, della pace della mansuetudine e benivolenzia, inimico della rustica ferità, della ignavia, in somma principio e fine d'ogni bene. E perchè abitar ti diletti il fior dei bei corpi e belle anime, e di là talor mostrarti un poco agli occhi ed alle menti di quelle che degni son di vederti, penso che or qui fra noi sia la tua stanzia. Però degnati Signor d'udir i nostri prieghi, infondi te stesso nei nostri cori e col splendor del tuo santissimo fuoco illumina le nostre tenebre, e come fidata guida in questo cieco labirinto mostraci il vero cammino. Correggi tu la falsità dei sensi, e dopo'l lungo vaneggiare donaci il vero e sodo bene; facci sentir quegli odori spirituali che vivifican le virtù dell'intelletto, ed udir l'armonia celeste talmente concordante, che in noi non abbia loco più alcuna discordia di passione; inebriaci tu a quel fonte inesausto di contentezza che sempre diletta e mai non sazia ed a chi beè delle sue vive e limpide acque dà gusto di vera beatitudine; purga tu coi raggi della tua luce gli occhi nostri dalla caliginosa ignoranzia, acciò che più non apprezzino bellezza mortale, e conoscano che le cose che prima veder loro parea non sono, e quelle che non vedeano veramente sono; accetta l'anime nostre che a te s'offeriscono in sacrificio; abbrusciale in quella viva fiamma che consuma ogni bruttezza materiale, acciò che in tutto separate dal corpo, con perpetuo e dolcissimo legame s'uniscano con la bellezza divina, e noi da noi stessi alienati, come veri amanti, nello amato possiamo trasformarci, e levandone da terra esser ammessi al convivio degli angeli dove pasciuti d'ambrosia e nèttare immortale, in ultimo moriamo di felicissima, e vital morte come già morirono quegli antichi padri l'anime dei quali tu con ardentissima virtù di contemplazione rapisti dal corpo e congiungesti con Dio."[1] Bembo and Castiglione are outstanding examples of a central truth about the "trattato"; namely, that its real value was not philosophical at all but artistic. Where its aesthetic qualities fail it becomes merely a savourless repetition of conventional motives as in the *De Pulchro* and *De Amore* of Agostino Nifo or the *Anthos* of Nicolò Vito di Gozze. The writers whose work still retains some vitality are either those who felt that the theme of Neoplatonic love was beautiful in itself and who could rise to a certain eloquence in expounding it; or those, a much larger number, who used it as a starting-point for exercises of literary virtuosity often only slightly related to the ostensible subject.

Works in the first category are few; perhaps between the *Cortigiano* and the stately dialogues of Tasso, which fall beyond our period, there is only one treatise that could unquestionably be placed in it and that is the little-known *Leonora* of Giuseppe Betussi.[2] It is, strictly speaking, a "Ragionamento sopra la Vera Bellezza," but the two topics of love and beauty were so inseparably connected that the one could never be treated without the other.

Like the third book of the *Asolani*, it gives one the impression

---

[1] O.c., p. 430.

[2] Giuseppe Betussi [*c.* 1515–*c.* 1573] began his literary life as a member of Pietro Aretino's circle in Venice and frequented the more bohemian literary society of that city.

The *Raverta* was first published in 1544 by Giolito, who produced other editions in 1545, 1549–50, 1562. It is reprinted in Daelli, *Bib. Rara*, Milan, 1864, Vol. XXX, and in Zonta, *Trattati d'Amore*. Zonta makes a careful version from the corrupt original texts [see his notes, p. 355]. The *Dialogo Amoroso di M. Giuseppe Betussi* in *Venezia al Segno del Pozzo*, 1543, 12no, is now very rare, but there is a copy in the British Museum and one in the Bodleian. Zonta reprints the *Leonora o Della Vera Bellezza* from the single little-known edition of 1557, in Lucca appresso Vincenzo Busdrago. For Betussi see Savino, o.c., Vol. X, pp. 162–264; Crane, o.c., pp. 130 et seq; Flamini, *Cinquecento*, p. 376. "Zonta," Note "Betussiane," *G.S.*, LII, pp. 321–66.

of a dream blending with some happy moment of memory to produce a graceful and finished little work of art. There is a touch of dream-like brilliance about the mere setting of the dialogue, a prospect of clear sunlight and rippling trees with the golden-haired Leonora della Croce sitting crowned with laurel in the midst of her little circle of knights and ladies. The dream is perhaps an intellectual luxury, and not one of the convictions that transform a life; but the enchantment of it has so far taken possession of the writer that in his praises of the ideal beauty and the love that follows it his words have a lightness and freshness that do not belong to any purely rhetorical artifice. It is with genuine exhilaration that he lingers on the familiar notes.

"Liberi ci ha fatto la natura ma sotto legge posti la ragione, la quale non è altro che un freno di se stessa...."

"E per meglio mostrarvi con l'occhio, con l'udito e con la mente noi ci facciamo conoscitori ed apprensori di quella, essendo la bellezza virtù incorporea e grazia incorporea la quale diletta l'anima colla cognizione di quella con l'occhio vedendo una bella immagine che ci rende forma ed esempio di Dio; e questo s'appartiene in quanto alla bellezza incorporale ed alla virtù visiva. Con l'udito sentendo il suon delle parole, la forza dei concetti e la dolce armonia della concordanza o del suono, o del canto trovato da primi padri nostri per magnificar Dio e render grazie immortali. Con la mente poi considerando la natura delle cose, ammirando le superiori e desiderando di divenir tali, quali ci pare convenire a chi ci ha creati e dato spirito divino e indegno da essere lasciato perdere in questo mare di miseria."[1]

It is rare, however, for the artistic merits of the "trattato" to be,

[1] *Leonora*, ed. Zonta, p. 336.
The topics of ideal love and beauty naturally passed into much of the vast feminist literature of the age, though without gaining in novelty by consequence. Besides the works of Trissino, Firenzuola, and Luigini mentioned above one might cite in this connection the *Dialoghi delle bellezze* of Niccolò Franco; Casale di Monferrato, Venice, 1542; and *La Donna di Corte Discorso di Ludovico Domenichi*. "Nel quale si ragiona dell'affabilita ed honesta creanza da dovere usare per Gentildonna d'Honore," in Lucca per il Busdrago, 1564, esp. f. 21, Origin of love.

as it were, intrinsic in the subject. Far more often the philosophical argument appears as something to be got over quickly, a conventional starting-point for the display of all manner of literary artifices, often pleasing in themselves. That even the writers felt the want of originality in their arguments is apparent in their continual efforts to give variety to a hackneyed theme. Sometimes the central thesis is stated in different terms, as in the *Infinità d'Amore* of Tullia d'Aragona, which sets out to debate the question "se si può amar con termini," but falls back upon all the familiar theories and definitions in the course of the discussion.[1] Sometimes the treatise takes the form of a critical exposition of philosophical love poems, like the *Lezioni* of Benedetto Varchi on poems of Petrarch, Michelangelo, and Giraldi Cinthio; or the *Sposizione d'un sonetto platonico fatto sopra il primo effetto d'amore* of Pompeo della Barba da Pescia.[2] Again, the main theme gives rise to endless questions, substantially the same in treatise after treatise: Which is the nobler, the lover or the beloved? Do men or women love more ardently? Do the ugly desire to be loved more than the beautiful? Is honour or the desire to please the beloved the greater stimulus to virtue? Why do those who have to conceal their love

[1] Tullia d'Aragona [*c.* 1509–1556], the famous courtesan, friend of Bernardo Tasso, Varchi, Molza, and Sperone Speroni, etc. Her life was spent mainly in Venice, Ferrara, and Rome. The *Infinità d'Amore* was first published in 1547, at Venice, by G. Giolito de' Ferrari, who also published the 2nd ed. of 1552. It was reprinted with a foreword by Camerini and a life of Tullia by Zilioli in Daelli's *Biblioteca Rara*, Milan, 1864, Vol. XXVI, and by Zonta in his *Trattati d'Amore del Cinquecento*, Bari, 1912. I have used this edition. On Tullia see Savino, o.c., Vol. X, pp. 264 et seq; G. Biagi, "Una etèra romana; Tullia d'Aragona," *N.A.*, 1886, p. 655. *Rime di T. d'A.*, ed. E. Celani, Bologna, 1891.

[2] The *Lezioni* were delivered in the Florentine Academy in 1553 and 1554 and published by Giunti in 1561. Varchi's chief fame rests, of course, upon his history of Florence and on his linguistic works. Pompeo della Barba's treatise has nothing original about it and seems to have been neglected even by the more exhaustive writers on the "Trattato d'Amore." I have not been able to discover any particulars about the author except that he collaborated with Antonio Buonagrazia in a translation of the *Heptaplus*, Pescia, 1555, and wrote a *Discorso filosofico sopra il Somnum Scipionis*, Venice, 1553. The *Sposizione* was published by Torrentino of Florence in 1549 and 1554.

love more vehemently than others?[1] These doubts in turn are either raised or illustrated by lyrics and "novelle" so that the "trattato" merges itself with these forms. The most conspicuous example of this disintegration is the *Raverta* of Betussi, where, after a preliminary discourse on love and on the conclusions reached by former writers, the major part of a long treatise is made up of miscellaneous verses, questions, and anecdotes. The lineal descendants of this type of writing are the books of games and paradoxes already mentioned. Other forms that derived from the main stream of Neoplatonism were the treatises on women, in which the endeavour to establish types of perfect beauty, and the usual definitions of love were interwoven with general precepts for feminine education and conduct, which developed steadily on purely moralistic lines in the period of the Catholic Reaction.[2]

The *Dialoghi d'Amore* of Leone Ebreo stand in another category.[3] They are a serious attempt to penetrate into the essence of

[1] For these questions see besides the *Asolani* and other treatises cited above, the *Dialogho d'Amore* of Ludovico Domenichi, Venice, 1562; *Paradossi* of Ortensio Lando, Lyons, 1543; *Lezioni* of Benedetto Varchi, Florence, Giunti, 1561.

[2] See Zonta, *Trattati del'Cinquecento sulla Donna*, Laterza Bari, 1913, for a brief but well-considered study of the general lines of the large feminist and anti-feminist literature of the age.

[3] Leone Ebreo [Giuda Abarbanel, c. 1465-15—] a Spanish Jew who took refuge in Italy from persecution in his native country. Was a personal friend of Pico between 1492 and 1494 and probably wrote the *Dialoghi d'Amore* about 1502, though the first sketch of them may have been made earlier. They were published posthumously in 1535. [See Saitta, "La Filosofia di L. E.," in *Filosofia Italiana e umanesimo*, Venice, 1928, pp. 88 et seq.] He also wrote a number of Hebrew elegies and a lost work on the harmony of the heavens, and was well known as a physician. The story of his conversion is almost certainly a legend.

The editions of *Dialoghi* are Rome, 1535 [cited here]; Venice, Aldus, 1541, 1545, 1549, 1552; Venice, Domenico Giglio, 1558; Venice, Giorgio dei Cavalli, 1565; Venice, N. Bevilacqua, 1572; Venice, Alberti, 1586, and another rare 16th cent. ed. without date or name of printer. The Latin translation was printed at Venice by Franciscus Senonensis, 1564. A modern reprint is that in *Scrittori d'Italia*, 1929. For Leone's life and writings see *Jewish Encyclopaedia*, Vol. VII, 1904, article "Leo Hebraeus," p. 683; S. Munk, *Notice sur Léon Hébreu in Melanges de Philosophie Juive et Arabe*, Paris, 1859, Appendix No. 4, pp.

Ficino's philosophy, and have none of the adventitious ornaments that characterize the courtly treatises. They contain real traces of original thought and their affinity with and influence on Spinoza have been noted more than once.[1] In spite of their essentially difficult character and the heaviness and prolixity of their style they were surprisingly popular. Ten Italian editions and a Latin version appeared in Italy alone between 1535 and 1586, while reprints and translations appeared in France and Spain; and they are mentioned in terms of the highest praise by subsequent writers on love such as Varchi, Betussi, Sperone Speroni, and Tullia d'Aragona.[2]

They revolve principally around two questions: the relation between love and knowledge as means of approaching reality, and the function of love in the universal harmony.

Leone begins by establishing the principle that right knowledge is essential to love and even to desire. We cannot desire what has no existence; in other words, nothing. Those things which are desired, though not in actual being, have a possible being whose nature we know and believe to be good, "... l'amore e'l desiderio sono de le cose che in qualche modo hanno essere reale e son conosciute sotto spetie di buone, eccetto che l'amore pare essere commune a molte cose buone possedute e non possedute ma'l desiderio è di quelle che non sono possedute."[3]

To the objection that one cannot love something that is alto-

---

522–8; Saitta, o.c.; Savino, o.c., Vol. X, pp. 102 et seq.; G. Gentile in *Studi nel Rin*, Ch. I; E. Solmi *Benedetto, Spinoza e L. E.*, Modena, 1903; B. Zimmels, *Leo Hebraeus*, Leipzig, 1886.

[1] E.g. by Solmi, Gentile, and Saitta.

[2] Varchi (*Ercolano*, Venice, 1575, p. 223), remarks on the lack of literary qualities in the *Dialoghi*, "Se i Dialoghi di L. E. dove si ragiona d'amore fossero vestiti come meriterebbero noi non avremmo da invidiare nè i latini nè i greci." In Tullia's dialogue he speaks with equal enthusiasm: "se bene in alcune cose e massimamente quando entra nelle cose della fede giudaica più tosto lo scuso che approvo" [ed. Zonta, p. 224]. Betussi, in the *Raverta*, refers to "l'opere di quello ebreo che si divinamente n'ha [di amore] scritto" [ed. Zonta, p. 4], and mentions them again in his *Dialogo Amoroso* [p. 18 verso, Venice, 1543].

[3] *Dialoghi d'Amore*, ed. c, p. 8, Dial. I.

gether lacking, Leone draws a distinction between "amore reale," which is the love of something definitely known, and "amor immaginato," which may be felt for "tutte le cose desiderate per l'essere che hanno nel imaginazione del quale essere immaginato nasce un certo amore il suggetto del quale non è le cosa proprio reale che si desidera per non havere essere in realtà ma solo il concetto di quella cosa pigliatà da suo essere commune e di tal amore il suo suggetto è improprio, per che non è vero amore che gli manca il suggetto reale, ma è solamente simulato e imaginato, perchè il desiderio di tal cosa è spogliato di vero amore."[1] So some things may be both loved and desired, such as truth, wisdom, "e una persona degna quando non l'haviamo." Others, such as all good things we possess, are loved but not desired; and some are desired and not loved, "com'è la sanità e i figluoli quando ci mancano e l'altre cose che non hanno essere reale."[2] Love and desire may be felt for three classes of objects: the useful, the delightful, and the honest, and here Leone gives an acute analysis of the love of possessions which creates new and insatiable desires, and of the love of pleasures which exhausts itself and creates disgust by its own satisfaction, and finally of the love of virtue and wisdom, which is the highest activity of man. Virtue with regard to the lower loves consists in mediocrity, that is, in liberality or temperance as opposed to either form of excess, but no love of the honest can be excessive. It is characteristic of the age that Leone should write in praise of bodily health as a thing both useful, delightful, and honest, but he strikes an unaccustomed note in his treatment of fame and glory.

"Debbesi lodare la virtù honesta, ma non si debbe operare la virtù per essere lodato, e se bene li lodatori fanno crescere la virtù, scemeria più presto quando essa lode fusse la fine perchè si facesse...."[3]

One is reminded of the parallel that has already been suggested between Leone and Spinoza by this attempt to define a happiness not dependent on riches, fame, or lust, and by a suggestion of the

[1] O.c., p. 9, Dial. I. [2] O.c., p. 10, Dial. I. [3] O.c., p. 16, Dial. I.

moral disinterestedness that made beatitude not the reward of virtue but virtue itself. From these general categories the treatise proceeds to consider human friendship and divine love. Some friendships are based on utility or pleasure and cease to be when their occasion is removed, "ma la vera amicitia humana è quella che è causa del honesto e vincolo della virtù per che tal vincolo è indissolubile e genera amicizia ferma e interamente perfetta. . . . La causa di tale unione e colligatione è la reciproca virtù o sapientia di gli amici la quale per la sua spiritualità e alienatione da materia e astratione delle conditioni corporee rimuove la diversità da le persone all'individuazione corporale, e genera negl'amici una propria essentia mentale conservata con sapere e con un amore e volontà comune . . . e in ultimo dico questo che l'amicitia honesta fa d'una persona due e di due una."[1]

What Leone seems here to suggest is that the human spirit is one, and that the separate individualities of men are accidents of their earthly being, while the higher levels of spirituality are the common possession of the whole race, though only a rare few transcend their personal limitations to participate in that universal being. Such a theory is borne out by his representation of the relation between the divine mind and the human in which "l'anima intellettiva" is described as a ray of the divine light given to man to make him rational, immortal, and happy. We know and love according to the capacity of our own minds, and not according to the greatness of God, in whom all wisdom and all virtue are concentrated; and true felicity consists not simply in knowledge or even in love which is the result of knowledge, but in the complete conversion of the human mind into the divine (nel atto coppulativo de l'intima unità cognitione e divina che è la somma perfettione dell'intelletto creato, a quello è l'ultimo atto e beato fine nel quale più presto si truova divino che humano . . .).[2]

In this state the mind is raised above itself so that we see it to be "ragione e parte divina" and there remains in us no impression of defect, but an entire satisfaction and fruition of joy. To know

[1] O.c., p. 17, Dial. I.   [2] O.c., p. 22, Dial. I.

the divine mind is to know all things in a single vision not under the limitations of time and space, but perfectly and simultaneously. The human mind is infinite potentiality, but it is illumined by God (intelletto attuale che illumina il nostro possibile), so that every act of knowledge is really a divine manifestation. All forms of things are infused into the human mind, which is the image of the divine in whom all things exist "... non solamente per ragione d'intelletto ma ancor causalmente come in prima e assoluta causa."[1] The mind, therefore, when it knows itself, comes to know all things in itself, and so is brought to the true "conoscenza unitiva" of the divine mind, of which it is, in fact, an effluence. Leone does not completely identify the human mind with the divine, but relates the two so intimately that he is well on the way to a clearcut theory of immanence.

The same is true of his treatment of the universe as a product of spirit.

In writing of love as a cosmic force he takes up the argument already treated by Ficino in the *Symposium*, but comes nearer to a thorough-going pantheism in his conclusions. Of the three kinds of love, natural, sensitive, and rational, the first exists by itself in bodies that are not sensitive, that is to say in the elements, metals, stones, and parts of the earth, all of which have a natural inclination to fulfil their own ends, which is natural appetite or love. Sensitive love is found in animals who instinctively seek what is beneficent to themselves and fly from what is harmful. Rational love is the prerogative of man, but coexists in him alongside with the two lower forms. If it is asked how creatures incapable of knowledge can love, the writer replies that although they have no power of knowledge in themselves they are guided to their ends by nature or the World Soul, as the arrow is guided not by its own intelligence but by the intelligence of the archer. Natural forces are called gods "per la loro grandezza, notitia, opera e principalità che hanno in questo mondo inferiore, ancor perchè credevano essere ogni uno di questi governato per virtù spirituale participativa

[1] O.c., p. 26, Dial. I.

de l'intellettual divinità" or, as Plato maintained, because the real essences and forms of things are incorporeal principles or ideas in which visible objects participate.[1] And as Saturn and Mars are among the gods: "Così ancor fra le idee Platoniche ci sono alcun principio di bene e di virtù, e altri che son principii di male et di vitii, per che l'universo ha bisogno de l'uno e dell'altro per la sua conservazione, secondo il quale bisogno ogni male è bene, che tutto quel che bisogna a l'essere de l'universo è certamente buono, poi che l'essentia di quello è buona. Si che il male e la corruzione son così necessarij a l'essere del mondo come il bene e la generazione che l'uno dispone l'altro ed è via di quello."[2] The apology for evil as a necessary concomitant of the universal order is made with a frankness that leaves even Ficino in the shade. It is a conclusion that a pure monistic scheme cannot logically escape, though it offers a somewhat unstable basis for practical morality and results at length in an optimism more ugly and unsatisfying in its unreality than the completest pessimism. Its final development is always to evade or deny the darkest facts of our consciousness and perhaps it is sounder and more honest philosophy to accept those facts in all their bitterness, even if it means admitting that the problem they present is insoluble.

Leone's account of the relations of God and matter further illustrate the pantheistic quality of his thought. The primal matter is co-existent with God from eternity, and although it may be objected that, since God produces all things, matter must also have been produced by Him, matter or chaos is called the companion of God ". . . per essere produtto esso Chaos ab eterno e trovarsi sempre mai in compagnia di Dio, ma per essere compagna del creatore nella creazione e produtione di tutte le cose e sua consorte ne la loro generatione poi che quello è stato immediate produtto di Dio e l'altre cose tutte sono state produtte di Dio e da quel Chaos o sia materia, esso Chaos con ragione si può chiamare compagna di Dio, ma per questo non manca che essa sia ab

---

[1] O.c., p. 31, Dial. II.   [2] O.c., p. 31, Dial. II.

eterno produtta di Dio, si come Eva essendo produtta da Adamo gli fu compagna e consorte e tutti gli altri huomini nati da tutti due."[1]

Love, being, goodness, and beauty are more truly and essentially existent in the intellectual world than in the material and are conferred upon matter by the spirit, which loves its own effects in the material world and wishes to remedy their deficiencies, so perfecting both itself and them. Love leads every part of the cosmos to fulfil its proper function in the universal harmony, and consequently morality appears to be not so much an individual affair as a universal power.

"Tu hai altra volta inteso da me, O Sofia, che tutto l'universo è uno individuo cioè come una persona e ogn'uno di questi corporali et spirituali, eterni e corruttibili è membro e parte di questo grande individuo essendo tutto e ciascuna de le sue parti produtta da Dio per uno fine comune nel tutto, insieme con uno fine proprio, in ogn'una de le parti, seguita che tanto il tutto e le parti sono perfette e felici quanto rettamente e interamente conseguono gl'offitij ai quali sono indirizati dal sommo opifice."[2]

Such a view meant a vindication and a glorification of every aspect of nature which only Leone's Hebrew faith prevented from becoming an unqualified pantheism. God and nature remain distinct in his thought, but are so intimately connected that the distinction is more verbal than actual. He shows a notable affinity in this respect with Leonardo da Vinci for whom nature was the perfect revelation of the divine and the sure source of wisdom.

The *Dialoghi d'Amore* had numerous admirers, but it cannot be said that they added anything to their original. One fact, however, emerges. In all the treatise writers who profess indebtedness to Leone Ebreo the justification of nature and the rehabilitation of the body assume a greater boldness than before; and this is especially true of the literary group that included Benedetto Varchi, Sperone Speroni, Tullia d'Aragona, and Betussi.

[1] O.c., p. 34, Dial. II. [2] O.c., p. 72, Dial. II.

Varchi, although he makes the usual divisions of love into celestial, human, and terrestrial, insists upon the essential unity of the three:

"Et ultimamente è di sapere che tutti gli amori essendo naturali sono buoni come havemo detto di sopra e diremo di sotto; ma il non sapergli usare gli fa rei."[1] Sperone Speroni, whose treatise has the touch of eighteenth-century common sense that makes him always so curious an anachronism, defends the body as a shield set between the soul and the heavenly splendour to prevent the former being consumed like Semele. "TULLIA: Dunque son mala cosa le nostre membra quando per lor cagione il piacer nostro amoroso in noia e danno ci si converte. MOLZA: Anzi, alla nostra imperfezione son buona cosa le nostre membra; essendo quelle tra amore e noi quasi un solecchio il qual levando gran parte del suo soverchio splendore, il rimanente ci fa possenti di sostenere; altrimenti all'apparir del suo lume la nostra debole umanità alla maniera di Semele quando da Giove in proprio forma fu visitata, cenere e polve diventerebbe."[2] The emphasis on this point was due, no doubt, to a more or less conscious desire to find some ideal possibilities in every aspect of humanity, but it proceeded also from a sense of the unreality of "amore umano," that ambiguous middle term between speculative and sensual love which was often only a specious veil for immorality. That the writers often wrote of this figment neither believing in it themselves nor expecting to be believed, seems obvious. The lively *Infinita d'Amore* of Tullia d'Aragona shows how little serious the treatment of the argument had become. Varchi and Tullia dispute subtly about the philosophy of love, not because it affects them deeply, but because they have read their authorities and are pleased to exercise their "dear wit and gay rhetoric that has so well been taught her dazzling fence."

[1] Varchi, *Lezione*, p. 15, Florence, 1561.
[2] Sperone Speroni, *Dialogo di Amore*, written 1528, was published in *Dialoghi*, Venice, Giolito, 1542, and ran through many editions. Quotation is taken from *Opera*, Venice, 1740, 5 vols., Vol. I, p. 17. Cf. Betussi, *Raverta*, ed. Zonta, in *Trattati d'Amore del 1500*, Bari, 1912, p. 37, p. 140. Tullia d'Aragona, *Infinità d'Amore*, in same volume, p. 226.

A touch of pertness runs through the dialogue; it passes in an atmosphere of flirtation and compliment and the gravest matters are lightly dismissed. At one point the discourse turns upon whether the same being may be at once more worthy and less worthy than itself if viewed from different angles. Varchi sets out to prove that God loves Himself and is, therefore, both lover and beloved, and so must be of greater dignity as beloved than as lover. Tullia, who has been made to give this information by a series of Socratic questions, protests that such an example is not fair when one is talking of human things, and demands another.

"VARCHI: Che pensate voi che sia più degna cosa o l'essere padre o l'esser figluolo?

"TULLIA: L'esser padre: ma per l'amor di Dio non entriamo nella Trinità."[1]

There is here a frivolity of spirit as remote from the artistic dignity of Bembo as it is from the earnestness of Ficino, and the dialogue recalls more than once the hollowness of the writer's professions and the gulf that yawned between theory and practice in the society she frequented. Certainly in that age of quick wits and light loves the weaknesses of the Neoplatonic position could not fail to make themselves felt, even to their own supporters. Bandello and Firenzuola both paid tribute to the fashionable philosophy almost in the same breath with which they told, with evident enjoyment, some of their most unedifying tales, and Pietro Aretino satirized the fashion sharply in *Il Filosofo*, while a host of "Arti d'Amore" depicted, with much efficacy, loves the reverse of philosophical.

These have often a tang of actuality that the other treatises lack. In spite of the skill that sometimes went to the writing of it, the "trattato d'amore" as a whole leaves an impression of emptiness. Its historical interest is considerable, and its artistic merits by no means negligible in so far as its details are concerned; but the highest artistic excellence lay beyond the reach even of its best

---

[1] *Infinità d'Amore*, p. 229.

exponents. There could be no perfect fusion of matter and manner where the matter was only an affair of conventional or at best of intellectual acceptance. Yet the fact that the "trattato" flourished as it did shows that it appealed to something in the consciousness of the age. It was primarily a confirmation of its aesthetic enthusiasms, the creed of a society that found its chief satisfaction in beauty; and it pleased the fundamental optimism that liked to flatter itself with the thought of an ideal aim in human passions, even when practice did not conform to theory.

TRANSLATIONS

Page 182. *Soleva, says Varchi* . . .
Messer Marsilio, says Varchi, being far advanced in years, was wont, when reading with his disciples, to say: "I go away, but though I depart I leave you another in my stead," meaning Messer Francesco, who was surnamed il Pagonazzo.

Page 182. . . . *desiderium perfruendae* . . .
. . . the desire of enjoying and imitating beauty in the beautiful as it says in the *Symposium*.

Page 183. *Ex quo mundus* . . .
Whence the intelligible world is everywhere made beautiful.

Page 185. *Con la colorita freschezza* . . .
with the fresh hues of the morning rose.

Page 186. *Che hanno alla sempiteraità* . . .
Who think upon eternity.

Page 186. *nel mezzo delle sue* . . .
in the midst of his fullest joys sighs not after some other thing.

Page 186. *Ma perciò che egli* . . .
But because it (the soul) dwells for diverse years shut up in this prison of our members, so that as long as we remain children it beholds no light, and later, beset by the host of youthful lusts and losing itself among terrestrial loves, may forget things divine, the sun each day, and the stars each night, and the moon at diverse times appearing, recall it after their fashion. For what is their appearing but an eternal voice that cries to us,

"Oh, fools that vainly dream! Ye blind ones, busied with these your false beauties, like Narcissus ye feed yourselves on vain desire, and perceive not that these are but shadows of the true beauty that ye forsake. Your souls are eternal; why then do ye make them drunken with fleeting loveliness? Behold us, goodly creatures that we are, and think how beautiful must be the one of whom we are but ministers."

Page 188. . . . *si che Dio* . . .
. . . so that God, angel, soul, intellect, and intelligence are dinned into the head of the long-suffering reader, leaving it emptier than before.

Page 188. *desiderio di avere e usare* . . .
the desire to have and use and enjoy that which is believed to be beautiful, or rather good.

Page 188. *Essendo questo amore* . . .
Since this love is universal, though every man is not said to love, it follows that desire is manifold and a body with many heads, which changes its name according to its effects . . . but that desire by which we are drawn to beget and bring forth beauty we call love.

Page 188. *quello che del veder* . . .
That which delights in beholding and conversing and neither uplifts itself to celestial purity, nor debases itself by descending to the foulness of copulation, but abides in the midst.

Page 188. *solamente nelle cose* . . .
only for those things that we have not, love for things possessed or to be possessed.

Page 191. *l'amante razionale* . . .
the rational lover knows that, though the mouth is indeed part of the body, none the less it is through it that we give egress to words, which are the interpreters of the soul, and to that indwelling breath that is called soul also; and for this cause he delights to unite his mouth in a kiss with that of the beloved lady, not in order to provoke in himself any lewd desire, but because he feels that that union opens up a passage for their souls which, drawn by desire for one another, diffuse themselves each into the other's body, and so mingle together that each has two souls, and a single soul, thus composed of two, sustains, as it were, two bodies; whence a kiss may be called a union of souls rather than of bodies, since it has such power over the soul that it draws it forth and separates it from the body . . . and therefore the divinely enamoured Plato says that in kissing his soul came to his lips that it might go forth from the body.

Page 192. . . . *onde l'anima si diletta* . . .

. . . because of which the soul rejoices, and is afraid with a kind of amazement, and yet exults, and like one bewildered, feels, together with delight, the awe and reverence that we are wont to feel for sacred things, and believes itself to be in its own paradise.

Page 192. *Qual sarà adunque O AMOR* . . .

What mortal tongue then, O most sacred Love, shall be capable of praising thee worthily? Thou, most beautiful, most righteous, most wise, springest from the union of the divine beauty and righteousness and wisdom, and abidest in it, and through it, as in a circle, returnest unto it again. Thou most dear bond of the world, mediator between things celestial and terrene, with benign persuasion, thou inclinest the supernal virtues to the government of the lesser ones, and by turning the minds of mortals back to their first cause, unitest them with it once more. Thou makest the elements to accord together, thou urgest nature to bring forth, and whatsoever is born to perpetuate life. Thou gatherest together things separated, thou givest perfection to the imperfect, likeness to the unlike, friendliness to the unfriendly, fruits to the earth, calm to the sea, vital fire to the heavens. Thou art the father of all true delights and of all graces, of peace, of mercy, of benevolence; the foe of barbarous cruelty, and of cowardice, and, in brief, the beginning and ending of all good. And because thou delightest to dwell in the flower of fair bodies and fair souls, and sometimes from thence to reveal thyself awhile to the eyes and minds of those who are worthy to behold thee, I think that now thou hast thy dwelling here among us. Deign therefore to hear our prayers, infuse thyself into our hearts and lighten our darkness with the splendour of thy most holy fire, and, like a trusty guide, show us the right path through this blind labyrinth. Correct the deceitfulness of the senses, and after our long erring give us the true and stable and good; make us perceive the spiritual fragrances that enkindle the powers of the intellect, and hear the celestial harmony so readily that no discord of passion may henceforth find place in us; intoxicate us at that inexhaustible fountain of content that ever delights and never satiates, but gives to him who drinks of its pure and living waters a savour of true blessedness; purge our eyes of cloudy ignorance with the beams of thy light, so that they may no longer prize mortal beauty, and may know that those things which they formerly seemed to see, are not, and that those which they see not, truly are; accept our souls that present themselves as a sacrifice unto thee; burn them in the living flame that consumes every material blemish, so that, wholly separated from the body, they may unite themselves with the divine beauty in a most sweet, perpetual bond, and that we, like true lovers, lost to ourselves, may transform ourselves into the beloved, and, uplifting ourselves from the earth, may be admitted to the banquet of the angels, where, nourished with immortal nectar and ambrosia, we may finally die a most joyous and vital death, as did those ancient fathers whose souls thou didst ravish from their bodies and unite unto God by most ardent zeal of contemplation.

Page 195. *Liberi ci ha fatto la natura* . . .

Nature has made us free, but reason has placed us under a law, that is under her own restraint. . . . And, that this may be more clearly manifest to you, know that we come to apprehend and know beauty through the eye, the ear, and the mind, since beauty is an incorporeal virtue and grace the knowledge of which delights the soul. With the eye we see a fair image that presents unto us a form or type of God; and thus it is with regard to incorporeal beauty and the power of vision. With the ear we hear the sound of words, the force of ideas, and the sweet harmony of concord whether in music or in song, devised by our first parents to glorify God and offer immortal thanks. With the mind we consider the nature of things, admiring those above us, and longing to become like them and such as to be worthy of Him who has created us and given us a divine spirit that ought not to be left to perish in this ocean of misery.

Page 196. *se si può amar con termini* . . .

Whether it be possible to love within limits.

Page 198. . . . *l'amore e'l desiderio* . . .

. . . love and desire are concerned with things which have real being of a sort, and are known by their species to be good, but while love seems to be common to many good things possessed and unpossessed, desire is only for those things that are not possessed.

Page 199. . . . *tutte le cose desiderate* . . .

. . . all things desired on account of the being which they have in imagination, from which imagined being proceeds a kind of love whose object is not the particular thing that we desire, since that has no actual being, but only the idea [concetto] of this thing derived from its generic being, and the object of such love is not particular, and therefore it is not real love if a real object be lacking to it, but only a thing simulated or imagined, for desire of such a thing is devoid of real love.

Page 199. *e una persona degna* . . .

and a worthy person whom we do not possess.

Page 199. *Com'è la sanità* . . .

As are health and children when we lack them, and such other things as have no actual being.

Page 199. *Debbesi lodare* . . .

Honest virtue should be praised but one must not act virtuously in order to be belauded, and albeit such as praise cause virtue to increase, it would yet faster decline if praise were the end for which it was practised.

Page 200. *ma la vera amicitia* . . .

but true human friendship is that which is a source of honour and bond of virtue for such a bond is indissoluble and begets a friendship stable and wholly perfect. . . . The cause of such union and intimacy is the reciprocal virtue and wisdom of the friends, which by its spiritual character and separateness from matter and freedom from corporeal conditions, removes the diversity of persons from corporeal individuality, and generates in the friends a common mental essence sustained by wisdom and by their common love and volition . . . and finally I say that virtuous friendship makes one person of two and two persons of one.

Page 200. (*nel atto coppulativo* . . .)

(in the copulative act of the inmost unity and divine knowledge, which is the highest perfection of the created intellect and the ultimate act and blessed consummation in which it finds itself rather divine than human.)

Page 201. (*intelletto attuale* . . .)

(active intellect that illumines our potentiality.)

Page 201. . . . *non solamente per ragione* . . .

. . . not only as regards the intellect but also causally as in their primal and absolute cause.

Page 201. *per la loro grandezza* . . .

because of the greatness, fame, activity, and dominion that they possess in this lower world, and also because each one of them was thought to be governed by a spiritual power that partook of the divine intelligence.

Page 202. *Cosi ancor fra le idee* . . .

Thus, too, among the Platonic ideas, there are some which are principles of good and of virtue, and others which are principles of evil and of vice, because the universe has need both of the one and of the other for its preservation, and in so far as this need is concerned every evil is good, for everything that is needful to the continuance of the universe is good undoubtedly, since its essence is good. Therefore evil and corruption are as necessary to the existence of the world as goodness and generation, for the one leads to the other and is a predisposing cause of it.

THE "TRATTATO D'AMORE"

Page 202. . . . *per essere produtto* . . .

. . . because this same Chaos is produced from all eternity and finds itself ever in company with God, and because it was the companion of the Creator in the creation and production of all things and His consort in their generation—since it was itself produced directly by God and all other things were produced by God and Chaos, that is to say, matter— therefore may Chaos be called the companion of God, although it was from all eternity brought forth by Him, as Eve, when she was brought forth from Adam, became his companion and helpmeet and all other men were born of those twain.

Page 203. *Tu hai altra volta inteso* . . .

Thou hast formerly learned of me, O Sofia, that the universe is an individual, that is as it were a person; and every one of these corporeal and spiritual, eternal and corruptible things is a member and part of this great individual, the whole and every part being created by God for a common purpose in the whole as well as for a particular purpose in each one of the members; whence it follows that both the whole and the parts are perfect and happy in so far as they rightly and entirely pursue the ends towards which they are directed by the supreme artificer.

Page 204. *Et ultimamente* . . .

And finally be it known that all these loves, being natural, are good, as we have said above and will say hereafter; but ignorance of their right use makes them evil.

Page 204. *Dunque son mala cosa* . . .

TULLIA: Then must our members be evil, since by reason of them our amorous delight turns to weariness and hurtfulness.

MOLZA: Nay then, but our members are kind to imperfectness, being as it were a shield between us and love, the which, by dimming some part of his exceeding lustre, makes us capable of sustaining the rest; otherwise at the appearing of his light our frail humanity would be consumed to dust and ashes after the manner of Semele when she was visited by Jove in his own proper shape.

Page 205. *Che pensate voi* . . .

VARCHI: Which do you think is more honourable—to be a father or to be a son?

TULLIA: To be a father; but for the love of heaven do not let us begin on the Trinity.

CHAPTER VII

NEOPLATONISM AND THE ARTS

THE diffusion of Neoplatonism in the sixteenth century was so enormous that it is not possible to estimate its direct influence on the artists of the age with anything approaching certainty. There was no need for an artist to be a learned man for him to be acquainted with its main doctrines, which were available in scores of treatises and hundreds of lyrics, besides being continually debated in the intellectual society of the day. The connection between artists and men of letters was much closer than it had been in the previous century, and the interest of men of letters in the arts was of the keenest. The letters of Castiglione, of Annibale Caro, of Pietro Aretino, for example, show this interest in all its intensity, sometimes in the form of general reflections and appreciation, sometimes in that of practical advice. The artist, instead of being a more excellent type of craftsman, with his "bottega" and his own fairly limited circle, was the friend of Popes and Princes, an integral part of learned and courtly society.

It may truly be said that Neoplatonism was inherent in the whole intellectual background of the time, but here it has seemed most satisfactory to study its effects on those artists who provide some definite evidence of having been affected by it. This does not mean that its influence ceased with them; it was transmitted indirectly to their scholars and admirers, and may often have been the result not of imitation but of conscious principle in many who have left no record of their ideas.

Neoplatonism seems to have reacted on the arts principally in two ways: by its theory of ideal beauty and by that of the universality of man.

The problem of Beauty has tormented thinkers since the time of Plato and actively torments them still. Nor have their speculations been simply academic and without effect on the practice of the arts. The general principles of the theorists, if not the subtleties of their arguments, pass into common knowledge and play their part in shaping artistic development. It is naturally true that a painter at work on a picture is not quite identical with the same man theorizing about his art. He is not in cold blood trying to illustrate his generalizations, but is passing through an intimate experience in which not the intellect alone but the emotions, the imagination, and the senses have their place. The finished work is the result of many causes, personal, cultural, imaginative, even physiological, and it is not possible to say with rigid precision where one ends and another begins. Still it is generally true that any genuine belief about the nature of reality or of beauty will colour the expression of the more instinctive and unconscious elements. If an artist believes that beauty is inherent in a greater or lesser degree in the objects of the external world, he will probably give much attention to the study and representation of that world, especially of those objects in it which are generally accepted as beautiful. If, on the contrary, he holds, like Blake, that beauty is a revelation of a spiritual world independent of "the vegetable universe," or if he accepts the view that the outer world is a creation of the human mind and beauty simply an intenser mode of mental experience, he may neglect the art of representation and indulge his own vision or fancy to an unlimited extent.

Endless variations, both of belief and practice and endless possibilities for either good or bad art, lie between the views thus roughly summarized. When any of them are followed out to an extreme conclusion the artistic results are apt to be depressing. If the beauty of a work of art is held to lie in the subject depicted, one may reach the state in which any portrait of a pretty girl is looked upon as a good picture. On the other hand, if beauty resides solely in the expression of the individual fantasies of the artist, the way is obviously open for mere charlatanism or eccentricity to proclaim itself as genuine vision. Beauty for the Neoplatonists was a transcendent grace existing eternal and unchangeable and independent of its earthly epiphanies. This faith in a supra-sensible beauty, common to sounds, bodies, and souls, might, other things being equal, have led to a revival of the visionary art of the Middle Ages.[1]

Such a revival was, however, impossible in a world that had seen the artistic developments of the thirteenth, fourteenth, and fifteenth centuries. The break with primitive ideals that begins in the Pisani and continues through Cimabue and Giotto and Orcagna to the art of the quattrocento was too complete to be repaired.[2]

Even Fra Angelico, in whom the mediaeval spirit has a late and exquisite representative, could not quite withdraw himself from the new trend of feeling. The wonderful *Deposition* in San Marco is a perfect devotional picture, but the figures in it are human beings, studied in all their varieties of type and emotion, and not the symbols of an ecclesiastical tradition.

It would be too much to call the artists of the fifteenth century realists.[3] The word has come to have an ugly connotation, and

[1] As Saitta [*Marsilio Ficino*, pp. 235 et seq.] points out, Ficino's theory, which he derived directly from the Vth *Ennead* of Plotinus, contained in germ the idea that beauty is purely a creation of the mind. But although traces of such a belief may be found in Ficino's successors the general tone of the treatise writers does not suggest that his thought was understood in this sense. Beauty is always the eternal and supersensible idea in which mundane things participate; and the continual endeavour to set up positive canons of beauty shows an unmistakable belief that it was an objective essence that could, with sufficient ingenuity, be defined.

Michelangelo and Raphael show signs of having interpreted Ficino's words in a subjective sense. The former in his sonnets speaks of the beauty that was given to him at his birth "per fido esemplo alla mia vocazione" and of love which is "un concetto di bellezza immaginata o vista dentro al core." Raphael, in a famous letter to Castiglione, speaks of the lack of beautiful models and says that failing them, "io mi servo di certa idea che mi viene alla mente." [Leone Zanetti, *Lettere e disegni di Raffaello*, Bologna, 1924, p. 18. This letter, which is unlike R.'s other letters in style, may have been a rehandling of his ideas by a literary friend. Still "Raphael made a century of sonnets."]

[2] The break seems to begin even before the Pisani. Some of the reliefs on the churches of Pistoia and Lucca, which date from the eleventh and twelfth centuries, show, for all their stiffness and crudeness, a feeling for the human form naturalistically considered.

[3] Though examples of extreme realism, such as Donatello's *Magdalene* [Baptistery, Florence] and Zuccone [on Giotto's Tower] or the strawberry-nosed old man in Ghirlandajo's picture in the Louvre, exist.

NEOPLATONISM AND THE ARTS

they have nothing as a group, of the minute and painstaking realism of the Flemings. Yet their works suggest transcripts from the world around them, which they view with a vision singularly clear and unblurred. Humanity is their chief preoccupation, but it is a humanity simply and directly considered, moving on the familiar earth in the clear light of day. Man is never portrayed as more than man. If they regard him as divine they reveal him to be so simply in being perfectly human. Within their limitations they reach an expressiveness that few artists before or since have attained. To a study never too extensive or pedantic of the monumental and passionless art of Greece they brought a new depth and sweetness of emotion, a sense of homely pieties and of familiar things faithfully presented yet rendered moving by the love with which they have been studied and set forth. In a sense they are more classical than the more learned artists who succeeded them, for they have more of the directness and lack of exaggeration that belong properly to the classics. In the *Annunciation* by Andrea della Robbia in the Innocenti of Florence, and the still lovelier *Visitation* in San Giovanni Fuorcivitas at Pistoja; in the tomb of Ilaria del Caretto at Lucca; in the singing boys of Donatello, and the doors of the Florentine Baptistery; and the *Pietà* of Giovanni Bellini at Rimini, classical influence seems to be not so much the result of deliberate study as a remote ancestral beauty surprisingly reborn in the latest of its line.

It was perhaps inevitable that mere developments of technical resources, the desire to exploit to the full the possibilities of the advances in the study of anatomy and nature, of antique art, of perspective and chiaroscuro, should have tended to break up the serenity and simplicity of quattrocento art and to lead to the more elaborate virtuosity of the next century. Still, with any genuine artist technical developments do not take place entirely "in vacuo"; they are always in some measure the result of an inward movement. The means of expression grow and change because there are new ideas to be expressed; and through the exercise of art fresh ideas are brought into being. The difference between fifteenth- and sixteenth-century art was a psychological as well as a technical one, and it was in effecting that change that Neoplatonism was largely instrumental.

The one artist of the fifteenth century in whom the Neoplatonic doctrine of beauty may have had somewhat the effect of a return to mediaeval ideals is Botticelli. The view has not much direct evidence to support it; but when one remembers the marked change that came over his art after its first naturalistic period, it seems not improbable that the belief in a beauty not dependent on proportion of parts and pleasing colour or even on mere bodily comeliness as that is ordinarily understood, should have helped to release those elements in him that are now regarded as peculiarly Botticellian.[1] The hypothesis must be advanced with due caution, for even in his least mature works there are manifest signs of a personal idiosyncrasy that would never have remained faithful to the tradition of the Pollajuoli and Verrochio or even to that of Fra Filippo Lippi in which he had been brought up. In the *Fortezza* and the *Judith* there are already many of his characteristic mannerisms; the delicate and perhaps slightly affected movements, the fluttering draperies, the facial type with its dreamy and remote expression, the elaborately implicated lines of hair or foliage. It was natural to him to see in terms of linear harmony rather than of sculpturesque form or of subtle chiaroscuro and to this peculiarity of visual perception much of the quality of his

[1] It was his "aria virile" that impressed itself on his contemporaries. The masculine draughtsmanship that he learned in youth from the Pollajuoli and the influence of Andrea del Castagno is quite as marked, especially in some of his early paintings, as the dainty and ornate workmanship of Fra Filippo. If one compares the portrait of a man holding a medal in the Uffizzi (*c.* 1477) or even the magnificent portrait of a youth in the National Gallery (1482) with the *Birth of Venus* (1486) or the *Mystic Nativity* (1500, also in the National Gallery) one cannot mistake the revolutionary change that came over his art. His achievement as a naturalistic painter was remarkable, but in later life he came to rely more and more upon vision and imagination and less upon the representation of natural objects, as that was understood by his Florentine contemporaries.

NEOPLATONISM AND THE ARTS

work is due.[1] Still it remains true that, while few artists have had a more entirely personal manner, few have been more dependent on literary inspiration; and the "otherworldliness" of Neoplatonism may conceivably have produced an atmosphere in which the strange sensitive plant of his genius could expand. Positive proof of his association with the Academy is, however, not to be had; he cannot well have been ignorant of its views, but there is nothing to show how far he accepted them or was interested by them. The literary sources of his pictures have been most minutely and carefully studied, but the only evidence they provide is of a highly controversial kind.

He owed much to Poliziano's verse, though it is not known whether he had much personal association with the poet. The Lorenzo for whom some of his most important works—the *Primavera*, the *Birth of Venus*, the *Pallas and Centaur*—were executed was not the Magnifico, but Lorenzo di Pierfrancesco de' Medici, his uncle.[2] Of a connection with any other member of the Academy, unless perhaps Landino or Alberti, no definite trace exists. The picture of Botticelli's personal character that emerges from the lives by Vasari and L'Anonimo Gaddiano is that of a man somewhat dreamy and unpractical, devoted to his art, but generally content with the society of his fellow artists and of his own rather humble family circle. There are, however, a few indications that point to his having had at all events some knowledge of Ficino's work.

The first is a suggestion only. Herbert Horne, in his discussion of the *Venus and Mars* of the National Gallery, where Mars is

---

[1] Yukio Yashiro, in his *Botticelli*, London, 1925, 3 vols., points out Botticelli's affinity in this respect with the Japanese artists. Such affinities are still more marked in the Sienese school where even the facial type is Oriental [see p.e. Lippo Memmi's *Annunciation*, Uffizzi, Florence; A. Lorenzetti, *St. Dorothea*, Pinacoteca, Siena] and Botticelli must certainly have been acquainted with examples of Sienese art whose inspiration may have helped him to develop the manner of his later paintings.

[2] Herbert Horne, *Botticelli*, London, 1908, pp. 50 et seq. This exhaustive study deals most minutely with the literary sources of Botticelli's pictures.

represented lying asleep, while Venus watches him, and a trio of tiny cupids try to carry away his armour, writes:

"In the Museum at South Kensington is a relief in 'gesso' [1859, No. 5887] somewhat earlier in date than Botticelli's picture, representing Venus lying naked on one side and Mars asleep on the other.... The arrangement and attitudes of the figures of the God and Goddess closely recall Botticelli's painting, but in spirit and treatment they are very different. It would seem, then, that we here have evidence of some version of this subject current at the time in the Florentine 'botteghe,' according to which Mars is represented sleeping while Venus wakes; a conception which remains unexplained by the verses of Lorenzo il Magnifico on the 'Amori di Venere e Marte' and such other contemporary allusions to the antique myth as are known to me."[1]

Botticelli's picture was probably painted about 1485. Ficino's *Convito* had been begun more than twenty years earlier, and the manuscript of the Italian translation had been available since 1474–5. In the eighth chapter of the fifth oration there is the following passage: "Et se Venere prossimamente vi si aggiunge, benchè ella non impedisca la magnanimità da Marte concessa niente dimeno raffrena il vizio della iracundia. Dove pare che faccendo Marte più clemente lo domi: ma Marte non doma mai Venere. Marte ancora seguita Venere, Venere non seguita Marte."[2]

This passage is suggestive but not, of course, conclusive, as Botticelli might quite well have had an earlier painting or sculpture and not Ficino's words in mind when he painted the picture.

There is also the possibility that in painting the *Primavera* and the *Birth of Venus* he was giving his version of the myth of the two Venuses; the *Primavera* representing Venus Genitrix, the life-giving power of nature, and the other picture Venus Urania.

[1] Horne, o.c., p. 141.
[2] Ficino, *Convivio*, Italian trans., Florence, 1544, p. 113. This parallel has not to my knowledge been pointed out, but in the huge literature of Renaissance art it may well have been noticed by some writer unknown to me.

Yet it is not so much in mere symbolism as in something more subtle and evanescent that Botticelli's debt to Neoplatonism might be traced. With an exquisite perception of sensuous loveliness there was deeply rooted in him the desire for a beauty not wholly of this world that found its final appeasement in the religious ardour of Savonarola. It seems at least probable that belief in beauty as a "non so che divino" was a determining factor in his abandonment of the art of naturalistic representation for that of imaginative vision.

In the *Birth of Venus* or the allegory of Spring or the *Pallas and Centaur* the quality that he seeks to express cannot be called precisely religious; yet the sentiment in these pictues is not really far removed from that of the *Madonna of the Magnificat* or the *Madonna with Five Saints* in the Uffizzi. The same face may serve for Venus and for Mary, not, as in some later painters, because devotional feeling has been lost in classical reminiscence, but because the painter has apprehended through the pagan legend and the Christian story the light of a spiritual world that all nations and ages have desired. Therefore, the goddess of heavenly love and the Virgin Mother, daughter of her Son, may share in the same ethereal grace and wear the same expression of wistfulness, as of two beings who have come to bless the earth, but in so doing have forsaken their true home.

Nor is it only in his human figures that his love of a remote spiritual beauty shows itself. He could impart to any thing he drew some of the same dream-like quality. His flowers, exquisitely natural, yet suggest that they are no growths of mortal soil. The crown of woven beams above the head of the *Madonna of the Magnificat* seems as much an efflorescence of the spirit as does the pensive melancholy of her face. He delighted in drawing all objects responsive to the power of the wind—trees, grasses, water, hair, filmy draperies. They combined to satisfy his passion for linear beauty and his ideal longings, by presenting him with a refinement of sensuous loveliness, that yet seemed to partake of the unearthly and mysterious force that created it. His works are full of this wind-born movement which shivers through the outer world and communicates itself to the dancing figures that look almost as if they were poised for flight. It appears as a gentle tremor rustling the warm grove of the *Primavera*, as a powerful impulse in the *Birth of Venus*, as the freshness of eternal spring in the drawings for the last cantos of the *Purgatorio* and the first of the *Paradiso*, as the horror of doom in the *Mystic Crucifixion*. The same aerial life possesses the Graces of the *Primavera* or the Tornabuoni frescoes, the *Pallas*, the *Venus Anadiomene*, the dancing angels who form a living garland of "sempiterne rose" about the *Coronation of the Virgin*. Swift light movement has always been pre-eminent among symbols of spiritual life and, above all, of spiritual joy; and it is largely through his mastery in portraying it that Botticelli achieved so extraordinary a success as an illustrator of Dante. The illustrations for Landino's edition of the *Divina Commedia* (1481) were executed by Baccio Baldini after designs by Botticelli. The series of drawings from Botticelli's own hand that is now scattered between Berlin and the Vatican, was intended for a manuscript copy of the poem and was undertaken probably before 1496 for Lorenzo di Pierfrancesco de' Medici, but never completed. Both series bear witness to a most minute and faithful study of the text. They differ from other attempts at illustrating the *Commedia* by their satisfying treatment of the *Paradiso*. The difficulty of treating it pictorially is so great that it is not surprising that most artists do so with little success. The most widely known illustrations of Dante are Doré's, and one might safely wager that nine persons out of ten would think first of the *Inferno* at the mention of his name. The drawings of Luca Signorelli show the same bias; so, one one may well surmise, would Michelangelo's "lost" illustrations have done. Even Blake, for all his visionary power, seems often chaotic and almost heavy beside the delicate precision and flame-like intensity of Botticelli. He was by temperament attuned to the mood of the *Paradiso*, but he moved also in an atmosphere that favoured the better understanding of it. Different ages and individuals have emphasized now this and now that aspect of the

Commedia—its artistry, its human insight, its philosophy, its ethical or religious teaching, its political significance, real or imagined, its command of the macabre and the terrible; but to Landino, the Neoplatonist commentator, the final glory of the poem was the ecstatic end of the soul's quest, the unparalleled revelation of the beauty that "eye hath not seen nor ear heard." The whole tremendous structure had been raised in order to point men to those spiritual heights where the fullness of liberty and joy is one with the reign of universal law. It was here that the true meaning and value of the poem lay. It was not surprising if between the rapture of the poet and the enthusiasm of the commentator Botticelli's imagination took wing. His drawings repeat, though within narrower limits, the triumph won by Dante himself in the third *Cantica*; they give to the most abstract ideas and the most rarefied of human emotions a form of unforgettable loveliness. Much of the external symbolism of the poem has been omitted, and the few drawings in which the background has been elaborated show what riches have been lost by this incompleteness.[1] Yet in the central point of each illustration, the figures of Dante and Beatrice, the painter's genius wonderfully seconds the poet's, and with the most surprising inventive subtlety conveys through those two forms, many times repeated, the emotional variations of the poem. Paradise is around the pair, but it is also within them; every phase of joy and awe, aspiration, worship, and ecstasy, is instantly translated into the movement of their bodies which are only the transparent veils of their spirits. The spare, almost ascetic quality of the line suggests something incorporeal, while its exquisite pliancy faithfully interprets the movements of thought that agitate these aerial forms.

All but a final quintessence of beauty seems to have been refined away; and this unearthly quality grows more marked as Dante and Beatrice, passing upward through the spheres, are transformed

---

[1] For instance, the picture of the heavenly hierarchies (Canto XXVIII) or that of the angels flitting among the flowers of the "mirabil primavera" (Canto XXX).

from glory into glory. One follows the upward flight of souls that have shed the passions and bonds of material life and found their true essence which is pure as the divine element in which it dwells. It is the heavenly quest of the Neoplatonists made visible; one of the clearest transcripts of mystic ecstasy ever achieved by any figurative art.

Still the prevailing standard of Renaissance Art was the imitation of nature. It was a classical ideal that was already well established in Italy by the fourteenth century. Dante, in the description of the bas-reliefs in the first circle of Purgatory; Petrarch, in his sonnet on Laura's portrait by Simone Memmi; Boccaccio, in the fifth novel of the sixth day of the *Decameron*; all agree in praising the perfection with which natural objects have been reproduced and their opinions mark the cleavage with the visionary art of the Middle Ages that had already come into being. In later writers, such as Castiglione, Dolce, or Vasari, the imitation of nature is considered as the true aim of the artist and exactitude of imitation the canon of achievement. "E veramente, chi non estima questa arte, parmi che molto sia dalla ragione alieno; chè la machina del mondo, che noi veggiamo coll'amplo cielo di chiare stelle tanto splendido, e nel mezzo la terra dai mari cinta, di monti, valli e fiumi variata, e di si diversi alberi e vaghi fiori e d'erbe ornata, dir si pò che una nobile e gran pittura sia, per man della natura e di Dio composta; la qual chi pò imitare parmi esser di gran laude degno: ne a questo pervenir si pò senza la cognizion di molte cose, come ben sa chi lo prova."[1] Yet, although the ideal was an ancient one, it received a peculiar colour that was wholly characteristic of its age. It became a further application of the belief that man is an earthly god who rivals and disputes with nature, and even excels her by adding to her the qualities of his own mind.[2] His universality appears in his

[1] Castiglione, *Il Cortigiano*, ed. Cian, p. 107. Cf. Ludovico Dolce, *Dialogo della pittura* (ed. Milan, Daelli, 1863, p. 9), where one of the speakers, Pietro Aretino, says "la pittura non essere altro che imitazione di natura." Vasari, *Vite degli più eccellenti pittori e scultori*, Florence, 1878, 9 vols., Vol. I, pp. 430–47.

[2] *Il pittore disputa e garreggia colla natura.* Leonardo da Vinci, *Literary Works*, ed. J. P. Richter, 2 vols., London, 1882, Vol. I, p. 332.

power of concentrating all the manifestations of the cosmos in himself, and of creating new worlds by his own intellect and imagination.

To the humanists of the first period the art in which the universal powers of the mind are chiefly displayed is poetry. It embraces all arts, and in rhyme and number, and with diverse ornaments tells of all that men have done or known or contemplated and of "cose eccelse e dal fonte della divinità attinte occultamente scrive."[1] Landino, in the preface to his *Dante*, quotes the arguments advanced by Plato in the *Ion* or the *Phaedrus* to prove that poetry is a divine activity, and then proceeds: "Et i Greci dicono poeta da questo verbo 'piin' il quale è mezzo tra il creare, che è proprio di Dio quando di niente produce in essere alcuna cosa, e fare che è de gli huomini in ciascuna arte, quando di materia e di forma compongono. Perciochè quantunque il figmento del poeta non sia al tutto diniente, pure si parte dal fare e al creare molto si appressa. Et è Iddio sommo poeta e il mondo suo poema."[2]

It would be untrue to say that the plastic arts were despised during the first period of humanism, but in comparison with poetry they were accorded generally an inferior status. They were regarded as more allied to the work of the goldsmith or the household craftsman than to the liberal arts, as the most perfect of manual crafts but not as serious rivals to the creations of pure intellect. Painting and sculpture are localized and limited, capable only of depicting the outward show of things, whereas poetry knows no limits and can portray all the unseen world of man's spirit. Some knowledge of the arts should, however, form part of a liberal education for the pleasure it affords and because it prevents its possessor from being swindled by dealers in paintings and other works of art.[3]

[1] Cristoforo Landino, Preface to *Commentary on Dante*, edition printed at Venice, 1578 (Giovanbattista Marchio Sessa e fratelli), p. 2.
[2] Landino, o.c.
[3] For this first point of view see Maffeo Vegio, *De Educatione Liberorum*, Bk. III, Ch. IV, p. 861.

In Leon Battista Alberti, who was at once artist and thinker, the claims of painting are set forth with a new and proud self-consciousness. His treatise, *Della Pittura*, is one of the most interesting works of Renaissance art criticism. It consists largely of advice upon purely technical problems of colour, proportion, and perspective, but it is notable also for a sharp criticism of mediaeval art on account of its use of the gold background and of its indifference to naturalistic representation. Alberti is fascinated by the study of chiaroscuro, and believes the exact and varied reproduction of natural objects to be the supreme function of the artist. He advises the study of the poets, so that the painter may be well supplied with subjects for his paintings and himself gives a description of the Calumny of Apelles, as described by Lucian, which was subsequently interpreted by Botticelli. Painting, for him, should fulfil all the functions of poetry and, indeed, of dramatic poetry. He gives elaborate suggestions for the proper treatment of dramatic scenes in which the gestures and facial expressions of men reveal their mental states. Above all, he insists that the painter who is a true master of his Art will see his works adored by other men and will find himself regarded almost as a god.[1]

With Leonardo da Vinci the pre-eminence of painting among the arts is still more clearly asserted. It is for him a "muta poesia," including everything that poetry can describe, but appealing to the most spiritual of the senses, sight.[2] The carved or painted image will always draw the wonder and worship of men in a way that mere words cannot do. Painting may be called mechanical because

---

[1] L. B. Alberti, *Opere volgari*, ed. Bonucci, Florence, 5 vols., 18—, Vol. IV, p. 41, *Della Pittura*, but one may set beside this such a treatise as that of Cennino Cennini on painting or that of Ghiberti on sculpture ["Commentario" Cicognara. *Storia della Scultura*, Prato, 1823, Vol. IV, pp. 172–208] and the care with which such an educator as Vittorino had promising pupils trained in the practice of the arts, accomplishments which Castiglione thought proper even to his perfect courtier (o.c., p. 106).

[2] The belief that sight is the most perfect of the senses is, of course, a commonplace with the Neoplatonists. See esp. Ficino, *Com. in Symposium*, *Opera*, Vol. II, Oraz. V, Ch. III, p. 1335. Also *De Lumine*, *Opera*, Vol. I, pp. 976–86.

it is executed by the hand, but "If you condemn painting, which is the only imitator of all visible works of nature, you will certainly despise a subtle invention which brings philosophy and subtle speculation to the consideration of the nature of all forms—seas and plains, trees, animals, plants, and flowers—which are surrounded by light and shade. And this is true knowledge and legitimate issue of nature; for painting is born of nature, or, to speak more correctly, we will say it is the grandchild of nature, for all visible things are produced by nature and these her children have given birth to painting. Hence we may justly call it the grandchild of nature and related to God (parente di Dio)."[1]

In the actual practice of art the conception of the universality of man expressed itself either in an attempt to depict a god-like humanity, or in the endeavour of the artist himself to be universal. The pre-eminent exponent of the first ideal is Michelangelo on whom Ficino's Neoplatonism had a life-long influence. As is well known, he spent his youth as a member of Lorenzo's household, and his poems prove how deeply that influence had permeated into his consciousness, and how genuine was his affinity with it. They are addressed ostensibly to his friends, Cavalieri and Vittoria Colonna, and were certainly partly inspired by these personal relations, but the love of which they are fundamentally the expression is the love of the beauty, remote, limitless, and unattainable, in which Michelangelo the mystic was fain to lose himself. Yet his art exacted of him that he should translate that infinity into terms of the finite. It was no longer possible for him, as it had been for the Byzantine artists, to suggest the Absolute by a tide of golden light on which the fragile forms of humanity are sustained. He, too, though with difficulty, had accepted the limits of the world. He could only strive to make man himself the image of the divine; to suggest by the outward form the infinity within. But it is an infinity cramped and tormented, ill at ease under earthly conditions. Michelangelo might share his contemporaries' belief that man was a terrestrial god, but not their contented

[1] Leonardo, o.c., Vol. I, p. 326. The translation is Richter's.

acceptance of his mortal state. For him the god was in exile, the ruler of the earth and yet a stranger on it.

The sense of strain and dissatisfaction in his work is apparent even in his earliest classical efforts and grows steadily more marked in the works of his maturity. No doubt it was partly due to interest in purely technical aspects of his art and the desire to experiment to the full with the resources at his command; and partly to something innately violent and restless in his imagination. If one sets his *Battle of the Centaurs and the Lapithae* beside one of the Graeco-Roman reliefs that it so closely resembles one sees at once that there is present in it a force that will not long remain within the restraints of classic form. Whenever he had lived he would have been a supremely original artist, but he would not have been precisely the same artist, and in the double character of Florentine Neoplatonism, in its mingling of mystical doctrines with its picture of a glorious humanity, he received precisely the ideas most capable of becoming an ardent faith in his mind and of colouring his imaginative life.

In man he saw the incarnation, at once magnificent and imperfect, of the beauty that haunted his thoughts and could never be either fully seen in the world or perfectly revealed in his art.

> Amor, la tua beltà non è mortale
> Nessun volto fra noi è che parreggi
> L'immagine del cor.[1]

Man is not merely the lesser universe; he is for Michelangelo the only one. No other artist of the age was so exclusively preoccupied with the human form to the almost total neglect of all other natural things. He had none of the passion for decorative detail of the Florentine quattrocentisti, none of the sensitive appreciation of nature that distinguishes Leonardo. It is true that the painters of the sixteenth century were possessed, in some cases one might say obsessed, with the beauty of the body. After the asceticism of the Middle Ages there is a period of revelling in the physical that

[1] *Poesie*, ed. K. Frey, Berlin, 1897, No. LXII.

ranges from the glowing vitality of the great Venetians to the frigid carnality of Sebastiano del Piombo or Vasari.[1] Michelangelo's feeling for the object of his worship was more subtle. Probably, as the changing rhythm of his poems shows, he both loved and hated it. Only through some "leggiadro e mortal velo" did spiritual beauty reveal itself to him; yet the vehicle of enlightenment was also the prison from which the divine principle must break before entering into its birthright.

Still the body was the language of the soul, the only one over which Michelangelo had complete command. It does not seem too extravagant to suggest that the intensely dramatic and psychological character of Renaissance art owed its origin in some degree to the Neoplatonic belief that the body was actually the creation and outward expression of the soul, partaking of its beauties and deformities and clearly mirroring its passions. From Ficino onwards there are few of the treatise-writers or poets who do not make some mention of the theory.

"Vengo a dire che se l'anima vorrà levarsi al cielo onde è stata tolta e di dove fu la sua partenza . . . verrà a purificare e a fare più bello il corpo che non lo ha formato la natura, dando a lui nuovo lume e nuovo senso. Ma se poi vorrà accostarsi alla lascivia ed alla imperfezione di questa spoglia ella verrà a farsi deforme e mancante ed egli a rimanere laido e contaminato."[2]

In fact, Michelangelo used this very argument to defend himself against critics who said that the Virgin in the Pietà of St. Peter's had been portrayed as too young, saying that pure women retain their youth far longer than those less virtuous; and that he had intended to symbolize the perfect chastity of Mary by the immortal youthfulness he had conferred upon her. In the stormier art of his later years—the Medici tombs, the Sistine roof, the

---

[1] Vasari and del Piombo were, of course, Michelangelo's disciples and much of the idealization of the body in Renaissance art was due to his influence, p.e. in the work of Tintoretto or the later Raphael.
[2] Leonora of Giusseppe Betussi in Zonta, *Trattati d'amore del Cinquecento*, Bari, 1912, p. 36.

Last Judgment—the human body has become the image of the tragic mystery of the world which is the mystery of man. He is the true "nexus et colligatio" of the physical and the spiritual, which are in him marvellously tempered together but everlastingly at war. The problem and the struggle have confronted men in all ages, but Michelangelo's vision of them was informed by his early training. Had he been a mediaeval artist he could not so have glorified man; had he been a modern he might not have felt so overwhelmingly the need to transcend the limits of humanity and find a reality beyond them.

To deal with his glorification of man in detail would require a complete analysis of his works, for his whole imaginary world is peopled by a race of giants; but if one considers the figure of Adam in the scene of the creation of man on the roof of the Sistine Chapel, the sight of this being almost as vast and as regal as the Ancient of Days who is touching him into life, but young and half-drowsy, and full of unused powers, brings the words of Pico irresistibly to mind ". . . nec certam sedem, nec propriam faciem, nec munus ullus peculiare tibi dedimus, O Adam, ut quam sedem, quam faciem, quae munera tute optaveris ea pro voto, pro tua sententia habeas et possideas. . . . Poteris in inferiora quae sunt bruta degenerare. Poteris in superiora quae sunt divina ex tui animi sententia regenerari."[1]

That Michelangelo intended a deliberate illustration of this idea cannot be said with certainty; but one can hardly doubt that such a conception was present in his mind even if only half-consciously, when he drew the first man as a creature of god-like potentialities lying between the earth from which he has been formed and the God whose image he is to bear.

Yet the longing to escape out of the littleness of earthly existence is as clearly reflected in his art as any sense of human grandeur. There is the very ecstasy of flight in the study for a *Resurrection*, now in the British Museum, in which the lovely form of the Christ floats upward through the grey air of morning with a sense

[1] Pico, *De Hominis Dignitate, Opera*, p. 314.

of utter detachment from the earth where the startled guards are falling back from the broken tomb. There is the same aspiration, resolving itself into a tragic peace, in the long lines of the *Dying Slave* of the Louvre. It reappears in the tortured movements of those other slaves of the Florentine Academia, struggling out of themselves as much as out of the imprisoning stone, and becomes a terrible resignation in the figures of the Medici tombs, in the *Dawn* "haggard as the sleepless" and the *Night* whose only desire is not to wake. These figures, carved in a moment of intense personal bitterness and despair, might be said to represent the defeat of the God-like spirit by its earthly burden, though even in its abasement it is immortal if only with an immortality of woe.

The influence of Michelangelo is marked in the works of Raphael's later period and particularly in the same tendency to enlarge and exaggerate the human form. The towering figure of Adam in the *Dispute of the Sacrament* or the Plato in the *School of Athens* show unmistakable traces of Michelangelo's manner both in the facial types and in the vastness of their proportions. There is, however, no trace in them of Michelangelo's unrest. They have the assurance, the serenity, the sense of complete and harmonious life, possibly even of a slightly self-satisfied life, that runs through the most enthusiastic passages of the Neoplatonists. The huge syntheses of human culture that Raphael attempted in the *Stanze of the Vatican* are themselves an interpretation of the universality of man. The *Stanza della Segnatura* displays in a kind of luminous allegory the Florentine ideal of the essential unity of all truth. Philosophy and poetry find their consummation in theology, but the poets and philosophers are no less noble than the doctors of the Church and only a little inferior to the glorified saints, since all are animated by the diverse operations of one spirit.

Although Leonardo da Vinci, like Michelangelo, spent his early days in Florence it does not appear that he ever had any such close connections either with the Medici or the Academy as had his fellow artist. He was very far from being an unlearned man, but he seems to have been much less dependent on literary inspiration than the majority of his contemporaries, regarding as he did the direct study of nature as the one essential knowledge for the painter. Yet his note-books, fragmentary though they are, show a tendency of thought genuinely akin to that of the Neoplatonists.

For him the infinity of man is treated psychologically rather than symbolically. His imagination, instead of expanding itself on the idealized and god-like forms of Michelangelo and the later Raphael, works inward to the infinite subtleties of the human heart. When Pater wrote of *La Gioconda's* beauty as one into which "the soul with all its maladies had passed," he possibly overemphasized the significance of this particular portrait, but his words were true of Leonardo's art as a whole.[1] The painter's mind, he says, should be a mirror in which all nature is reflected, and should have nature's impartiality, reflecting alike things beautiful or repellent.[2] So, in treating humanity, Leonardo seems to have achieved something of that "love of good and ill" that Keats set himself to attain, that poetic character which "has as much delight in conceiving an Iago as an Imogen." The scientific and artistic powers of his mind found their unity in that lofty tolerance of his that refused to hate because hatred was a flaw in understanding. His pursuit of truth, as he perceives it, is so ardent that knowledge and love cannot be forced apart in his consciousness; "love is more fervent as knowledge is more certain."[3] The only thing that the wise man dare abhor is falsehood, since "To lie is so vile that even if it were in speaking well of godly things it would take off something from God's grace, and Truth is so excellent that if it praises but small things they become noble."[4] Whether it is a conscious echo of the Neoplatonists or not, he gives with his own strange felicity of phrase, a definition of his own artistic experience that might have come directly from their works.

"The lover is moved by the beloved object as the senses are by the sensible object and they unite and become one and the same

---

[1] Pater's famous essay is in his volume *The Renaissance*, London, 1873.
[2] Leonardo, o.c., Vol. I, p. 253.
[3] Ibid., Vol. II, p. 302.
[4] Ibid., Vol. II, p. 292.

thing. The work is the first thing born of this union; if the thing loved is base the lover becomes base. . . . When that which loves is united to the thing loved it can rest there, when the burden is laid down it finds rest there."[1]

He himself was the universal lover and the realm of nature his beloved. Life had for him such a peculiar sacredness that he considered those who destroyed it as unfit to have it.

In his search for truth he felt that nothing was to be refused. It was his custom always to carry with him a sketch-book in which he could hastily note every object that caught his vigilant eyes. There he drew not merely the startlingly beautiful but the startlingly ugly. Few artists have left lovelier studies of childhood than those scattered among his drawings or carried to a higher perfection in the *Virgin and Child and St. Anne* or the *Madonna of the Rocks.*

Few have felt the appeal of a certain type of delicate and enigmatic femininity as strongly as he. In the faintly ironical and yet serene beauty of his smiling heads he too may have tried to fix the "non so che" of ideal beauty in a strange quintessence of brooding dreams and intellectual detachment. Yet he was as ready to fill sheets of drawings with caricatures and monstrosities as with the most gracious forms; as capable of depicting the sexlessness of the Bacchus—St. John with its suggestion of refined and subtle corruption, as the sexlessness of the Christ of the *Last Supper*, in whose face the imperfections of humanity seem to be transcended in a tranquillity not of mortal experience. They are studies at once revealing and mysterious, like the most penetrating intuitions of the great poets. But although Leonardo spent the utmost diligence on his studies of human beings, he differs from his contemporaries in giving man a less exclusive pre-eminence. On the contrary, he regards him as a part, though a most noble part, of a harmony which is essentially of the same nature as himself. To put it metaphorically, his approach to nature is psychological also. He was as intent on penetrating into the soul of "inanimate"

[1] Leonardo, o.c., Vol. II, p. 299.

things as into the secrets of the human heart. He pursues truth through nature with the same mingling of scientific exactitude and perceptive love as he brings to his studies of humanity, lingering with precise care over the outward semblance only that he may pierce to the principle of reality behind it. Not only in the most carefully finished of his backgrounds, but in the slightest of his unfinished drawings (as in the broken phraseology of his notebooks) there is some mysterious quality for which the hackneyed word "magic" seems the only adequate description. The most trivial natural objects seem, under his pencil, to acquire an independent vitality, to reveal secrets of a being that the normal eye had not suspected, just as a clump of grasses by Dürer or even one of Piranesi's warped and stunted trees can suggest an eerie and witch-like life that has nothing to do with the human world. It is, if one will, Leonardo's own strange spirit that informs his studies of nature and gives them their enchanted life.

> O Lady, we receive but what we give
> And in our life alone does nature live,
> Ours is her wedding garment, ours her shroud.

Yet it seems clearly a case in which his conscious philosophy helped to direct his genius. His belief in a soul in nature was so intense that he found a soul in her, even if it was his own. He was one who might have echoed Campanella's fiery defence of the worlds that others despised as dead matter—"so have they mind and God"; and his works come nearer than pages of argument to convincing one of a truth in his belief. When one has studied for a while the sheet of flower drawings in the Academy at Venice one has a curious feeling of having looked more closely at the "Idea" of a violet as that might exist in the mind of its maker. The *Landscape in Rain*, now at Windsor, illustrates in a slight though masterly way some of Leonardo's general remarks on the study of aerial perspective, yet it conveys a sense of being more than a mere exercise in light and shade. Leonardo has fixed not simply the falling of water through darkened air, but the spirit of the storm, which has become a living entity, much as the gale on the heath in *Lear* or the wind that swung the fir branches against the windows of *Wuthering Heights* have become actors in the drama, messengers of powers outside and yet akin to the souls of man.

The function of the natural background in his works is an active rather than a passive one. It gathers up and emphasizes the emotions of the human figures instead of acting as a simple framework for them. The majority of earlier painters had treated nature as a mass of decorative detail or as a stable setting for the variety of human passion. One can study the first method in the frescoes of the Riccardi Chapel and the second in Perugino whose serene Umbrian landscapes glow, equally luminous and still, behind the secure happiness of a Madonna and Child or the agony of a Crucifixion. Perhaps that eccentric master, Piero di Cosimo, who, it may be noted, flourished side by side with the Academy, came nearer than anyone else to Leonardo's peculiar apprehension of the kinship between man and his environment. Piero's animals, real or fabulous, and his surprising landscapes give the sense of being possessed by some uncanny intelligence that is conveyed with infinitely greater imaginative power and stylistic beauty by Leonardo's studies of nature. But where Piero rendered the sympathies that run through man and nature with a touch of fantastic and at times of slightly sinister playfulness, Leonardo perceives in them a similar spiritual and at the same time scientific problem. He tries to discover the fundamental facts that determine the outward appearance, the modelling of the bones in man and beast, the stratification of the rocks, the laws that control the elements—but he is not content with the simple repetition of the facts, and appears always to feel in them some significance beyond themselves. Man and the external world, for all the subtlety that he brings to their portrayal, are enigmas for which he offers no solution. "Abeunt omnia in mysterium" might be inscribed on most of his works; and perhaps in their quality of potent, yet indefinite, suggestion lies a large part of their greatness.

In the Uffizzi *Annunciation* a feeling of mystery but of peaceful and happy mystery broods in the placid oval faces of the angel and the Madonna, and is repeated in the prospect of clear greenish sky and dark trees that opens behind them. So in the "Monna Lisa" all the strangeness and the vaguely sinister implications of the sitter's expression have passed into the weird landscape with its pointed blue-green rocks, and treacherous sea, lying calm between spikes and shoals on which the unwary navigator must be thrown by the currents that move beneath the still surface. One surmises behind the tranquil dimpled face a spirit evasive and self-contained, but capable, like that ocean, of sudden impulses of cruelty, and of tortuous wiles that are only another aspect of the fine-spun dreaming in which it can lose itself in its happier hours. In *The Virgin of the Rocks* the darkness of the background seemed to Rossetti to symbolize "the shadow of the end," the menace of sorrow and death hanging over the *Madonna and Child*, but symbolism so direct is perhaps hardly characteristic of Leonardo. Light plays on the faces of the group in the foreground and melts from them into the rich gloom beyond, with some suggestion, it may be, of the emergence of the human spirit from its dim surroundings into the light of its own consciousness. But the light is no less inexplicable than the darkness, and the smile that hovers about those delicate lips baffles and fascinates the onlooker as completely as does the shadowy distance.

Man's pre-eminence continues; but it is no great step from Leonardo's treatment of nature to a cult of landscape for its own sake. The Neoplatonists' radiant faith in the dignity of man was destined to meet with many buffetings in the long-drawn sufferings of Italy after the hey-day of the Renaissance; science and philosophy alike began to stress more emphatically the incalculable extent and power of nature. Some record of the change has been fixed in the dark studies of Salvator Rosa, where nature fills the canvas, and man, if he appears at all, is a tiny, lonely figure, overwhelmed by her unfriendly vastness.

With the passing of the great days of the Renaissance, Neoplatonism probably contributed something to that decline of the arts which reached its climax in the seventeenth century.

The belief in a progress in art by which the disciple comes almost automatically to excel his master, combines in many Renaissance writers with belief in an objective beauty which is finally identified with the work of some particular artist. For Vasari the ideal was realized by Michelangelo; for Dolce and Aretino by Titian; for Castiglione by Raphael. In Vasari especially one hears the cry that art can go no further and that the young painter must set himself to copy the perfection attained by his forerunners.

In a sense the cry was true. Renaissance art had reached so spectacular a development that even in the happiest circumstances some falling off might have been expected. Many of its masterpieces contain a hint of the full ripeness that precedes decay, of virtuosity that might rapidly deteriorate into mannerism. By the middle of the sixteenth century calamity on calamity had fallen on Italy, shattering the splendid dreams of the humanists, and leaving to their heirs a bitterness of disillusionment only to be measured by the height of those earlier aspirations. In every phase of life, political, intellectual, moral, and religious, external authorities sought to impose their discipline upon a society which felt no corresponding change of heart, but was, none the less, obliged to accept their rule. The whole atmosphere of post-Renaissance Italy is alive with the dissidence between men's outward actions and professions and their essential state of mind. The intricacies of this conflict give the period as a whole its painful fascination, but they also explain the unsatisfactory character of so much of its literature and art. The collapse of the splendour of the Renaissance left to the Italians the monuments of a cultural development unequalled in Europe, while it stifled the vital force by which that development had been reached. The old spirit of eager curiosity, of boundless faith in man, and unrestrained delight in every manifestation of life, was broken. The new misery of disappointed hopes and present distress could not safely be given utterance. The intellectual energy of Italy was, indeed, never wholly quenched, but burned on in the speculations of isolated scholars and scientists The national tragedy denied articulate speech, found a voice in music; but the other arts ceased in the main to be a faithful expression of life; and became only a refuge from it.

The grandiose manner of the Renaissance remained; faith in universal harmony and in the soaring human spirit was gone. Poets, painters, and sculptors repeating and exaggerating the stylistic idiom of their predecessors, were using a language which had become empty of content.

In the figurative arts this is peculiarly true of the numerous imitators of Michelangelo and Raphael. The epigoni of the former, including Vasari, who was quick to follow his own advice, tended generally to confound mere size and display with sublimity. Studies of over-developed bodies in restless motion aped the master's tormented visions; till instead of the sufferings and exultations of a race of demi-gods, one finds in the ultimate decadence of the style the weary reiteration of flesh that fills the frescoes of Verrio at Hampton Court and kindred productions. Some of the mountains of marble that cumber the Papal tombs in St. Peter's illustrate the yet more devastating effects of the same cult upon later generations of sculptors.

Raphael's imitators also seized eagerly upon the obvious characteristics of his art—its sweetness, placidity, and fluency—but were far less apt to grasp its underlying elements of thoughtfulness and strength. That smooth and luminous ideal world where all conflicts are reconciled and all discords harmonized was the embodiment of a vision that was lost irretrievably. Its serenity and formal perfection could only decline into an artistic counterpart of the cloying prettiness of Arcadia. Its sweetness, divorced from its power, was translated into that sentimental religiosity of the secento of which Carlo Dolci's works are a crowning example.

The foregoing remarks must obviously be qualified for any just estimate of late Renaissance and post-Renaissance painting. Long after the other schools of Italy had begun to decline the Venetians maintained a vigorous life and those other schools, even in their decadence, produced a proportion of work which was meritorious if not of the highest order. Still the corrosive acid of "secentismo" was at work, and found ready victims in the imitators of Michelangelo and Raphael. The qualities of those artists were precisely those which the special weakness of the new age could most readily pervert. In the one case energy was turned into sensationalism and false magnificence; in the other sweetness and formal grace became a facile prettiness and sentimentalism.

No doubt it would have needed exceptional genius or independence for artists reared in the shadow of the two giants to have abstained from imitation; but it is also true that the theoretic basis on which they worked encouraged them to go on imitating. Contemporary theorists trained in the Neoplatonic tradition, assured them that the absolute beauty had been captured and might be reproduced by the clever copyist; and it might well have taxed a far more morally vigorous generation to have neglected so broad and easy a road to immortality.

TRANSLATIONS

Page 218. *Et se Venere* . . .

And if Venus presently draw nigh, although she diminish not the valour conferred by Mars none the less she restrains the vice of wrathfulness. Whence it appears that by rendering Mars more merciful she rules him; but Mars never rules Venus. Mars, moreover, follows Venus, Venus follows not Mars.

Page 222. *E veramente, chi non estima* . . .

And truly he who honours not this art seems to me far estranged from reason; for this universal frame that we behold, with the wide heavens so resplendent with bright stars and in the midst the earth girt with the sea, varied with mountains, valleys, and rivers and adorned with such diverse trees and fair flowers and grasses, may be called a noble and great painting executed by the hand of nature and of God; the which if any man can imitate he seems to me worthy of high praise, nor can any man thither attain without the knowledge of many things, as he knows well who has attempted it.

Page 223. cose eccelse . . .

and writes in parables [occultamente] of things most excellent drawn from the divine fountain head.

Page 223. Et i Greci . . .

And the Greeks say "poet" from the verb "piin," which is mid-way between creating, which is peculiar to God when out of nothing He bringeth anything forth into being, and making, which pertaineth to men when in any art they compose with matter and form. For which cause albeit the feigning of the poet is not wholly of nought, yet it departeth from making and draweth near unto creating. And God is a master poet and the world His poem.

Page 226. Amor, la tua beltà . . .

Oh, Love, not mortal is thy loveliness.
There's not a face among us to come nigh
The image in the heart . . .

Page 227. Vengo a dire . . .

I would say now that if the soul will lift up herself unto heaven whence she was taken and from whence she took her flight, she will purify the body and make it more beautiful than ever nature formed it, giving it new lustre and new senses. But if instead she choose to yield herself unto luxuriousness and to the imperfections of this frame, she will become deformed and impoverished, while it (the body) will remain uncomely and defiled.

Page 228. . . . nec certam sedem . . .

. . . nor settled place nor proper form nor any peculiar gift did we give thee, O Adam, that what place, what form, and what gifts soever thou wouldst freely choose, these by thy will and purpose thou shouldst hold and possess. . . . Thou mayst abase thyself to things inferior, that is, unto the brutes. Thou mayest, by thy soul's decision, be born again unto the things above which are divine.

CHAPTER VIII

THE LYRIC: MICHELANGELO

THE influence of Petrarch, which was strong in the "trattato d'amore," was still more dominant in the huge lyric literature of the sixteenth century. The fashionable idolatry of the "Rime" was so blind that it reacted disastrously on weaker talents, and was generally rather a hindrance than an inspiration, even to the most gifted. Practically every man of letters had to his credit a few sonnets and "canzoni" in which he lamented the cruelty or celebrated the loveliness of some golden-haired and rose-cheeked lady whose beauty was a sweet torment and a guide to Paradise. Both content and phraseology rapidly became almost entirely conventional and although the Ficinian stream mingled with the Petrarchan one, it served as a rule only to supply further rhetorical artifices.

Most of the treatise writers already discussed further embodied their theories in verse, and what is true of the "trattato" is also broadly true of the lyric. That is to say, that the philosophical elements are rarely realized with sufficient intensity to make them an integral part of the poem; they remain as a dead weight on the poet's thought. It is only, as a rule, on the all too rare occasions when the poets abandon both Petrarch and the Neoplatonists and allow some common emotion to speak for itself, that the lyric of the age comes to life. It is in the domestic sentiment of Francesco Coppetta de'Beccuti, in the unhappy passion of Gaspara Stampa, even in the relish with which Il Lasca or Berni can commend an adversary to the good offices of the hangman, and not in the chilly correctness of Bembo or Varchi that one must look for genuine merit.

Again, as in the "trattato," Neoplatonism finds its best expression in writers like Tansillo, whose sense of beauty is powerful enough to give some reality to their interpretation of ideal love or in Vittoria Colonna, where it mingles with profound devotional feeling, and gives sincerity to her vision of the soul's struggles in its earthly captivity and to her aspirations towards the glories of heaven.

But between the age of Poliziano and Lorenzo and that of Tasso and Campanella only a few names detach themselves from the vast crowd of writers to whom the composition of lyrics seems to have been neither a necessity nor an art, but a disease.

It was left for Michelangelo to inform the Petrarchan-Neoplatonic lyric with something of the fire and vigour that distinguishes his art. With all his formal imperfections he towers above the more polished versifiers who surrounded him. They wrote fluently and too often had nothing to say; he used a language of which he was often scarcely master, but it is unmistakably genius trying to speak. The philosophical ideas which were with them for the most part conventional assumed with him a character at once imaginative and passionate. Certain fundamental conceptions of Neoplatonism harmonized with the natural temper of his mind; they enriched his imagination, but they never choked it. He nowhere attempted any merely academic exposition of his tenets. It was only in certain crises of the spirit, when he was struggling for expression that Ficino's thought came to him, answering and confirming his own with all the force of a belief that the awakening mind once hailed as possible and that maturer experience now approves as true. The framework of his philosophy came from his training, but its value from his own exultations and agonies.[1]

The question of his sources is not very complex. He owed much undoubtedly to a youth spent in immediate contact with the Florentine Academy. Nothing in his life is more remarkable than the way in which his mind absorbed and transmuted the elements

---

[1] The general outlines of Michelangelo's life are sufficiently well known for no detailed references to be needed. My remarks are based principally on the lives by Condivi, Symonds, Romain Rolland, A. Venturi, and C. Ricci, and on the *Letters* (ed. Frey, Berlin, 1875].

of his amazing education, unless it is the persistence with which those early influences coloured his thought to the last without impairing its originality. The one really debatable point is how far he had any direct knowledge of Plato or the Alexandrian philosophers; and though the answer is not absolutely certain it does not seem to admit of much doubt. There is no evidence that he knew Greek, unless one chooses to read into his early connection with Poliziano more than the recorded facts will warrant. His general culture, his Biblical studies, and his life-long association with the learned men of Florence and Rome point probably to some knowledge of Latin; but the fact that he never, even in writing to Popes and foreign princes, wrote in any language but Italian suggests that his Latin scholarship was not profound. It is quite possible that he had read all Ficino's version of the *Dialogues*; it is equally possible that he knew only such works of the Florentine philosophers, whether original or translated, as were available in the vulgar tongue, this knowledge being, of course, vivified for him by his personal relations with the authors. The philosophical elements of his poems are the current ones popularized in Ficino's *Symposium*, Benci's *Pimandro*, the joint work of Pico and Benivieni, and the *Libri d'amore* of Diacceto; and foreshadowed in Dante, Petrarch, and the "stil novisti." Michelangelo treated these elements freshly because he combined them with strong personal emotion, but one need not look beyond the books here mentioned to find his formal themes. His philosophic culture may conceivably have been wider than this, but his poems suggest not so much any ordered study as a passionate grasp on a few basic ideas.

These ideas were so intimately woven into the general pattern of his life and thought that one cannot ignore the connection even in an analysis that aims at isolating a particular strain in his work. His poems are a kind of spiritual autobiography that links up the chronicle of fact, as recorded by Condivi, with the movements of the inner world that was bodied forth in the vault of the Sistine and the Medici tombs. If, on the one hand, his verse touches on actual, homely, and even grotesque details of his external life, it reaches out, on the other, towards the infinite being and supersensuous beauty that were the furthest goals of his desire.[1]

The poems, with few exceptions, fall into several fairly well-defined groups. There are a number of early love poems, addressed to an unknown lady, Petrarchan in style, but far more vigorous than the bulk of sixteenth-century lyrics; and a series, much later in date but of very similar character, addressed to "una donna altiera." From these the poems dedicated to the beloved friend Cavalieri and to Vittoria Colonna

> Anima e cor della mia fragil vita
> Alta donna e gradita

detach themselves by subtler and intenser qualities of beauty.

[1] The poems have had a curious history. They were never published in Michelangelo's lifetime, though once, in 1546, he contemplated publication and actually went to the length of preparing a volume. The project was abandoned, however, and the poems remained in MS. until 1623, when Michelangelo Buonarotti the Younger, the poet's great-nephew, brought out an edition. Unfortunately, it was rendered almost worthless by the well-meant activities of the editor. The poems as they stood were too passionate and too rugged for an age of moral prudery and literary pedantry. The younger Buonarotti suppressed the fact that many of them had been written for the poet's men friends and smoothed away their characteristic obscurities in order to bring them into harmony with the fashionable Petrarchism. The revision was undertaken in a sincere desire to protect a great man's memory from slander and contempt; but the consequences for Michelangelo's poetic reputation were highly mischievous and lasted for more than two centuries. It was not until 1863 that Guasti restored the text to something like its original state, though his edition was by no means complete and failed in not making clear the distinction between poems belonging to different cycles. In consequence critics like Thomas, Niccolò de Sanctis, and Amico-Mantia, assumed that they were all inspired by Vittoria Colonna, and spent much ingenuity in devising romantic love stories and fitting the poems into them.

At length, in 1897, Karl Frey published an edition containing not only all known complete poems, but also the many fragments scattered over Michelangelo's manuscripts. Frey endeavoured to establish as far as possible the dates of composition and the names of the persons to whom the poems were addressed, and his edition remains the most accurate both as to text and as to the history of the poems. It is quoted throughout this chapter.

The small group of religious sonnets was written in old age. Besides these, there are the fifty short poems on the death of Cecchino de'Bracci; a few sonnets to del Riccio, Vasari, and other friends, and a number of miscellaneous poems, burlesque, political, and personal.

This is not the place for any but the most cursory reference to their purely literary merits. Poetry was not Michelangelo's native idiom. His verse seems often not so much a finished achievement as the toil and ferment from which achievement might ultimately spring. Yet it has at times a piercing beauty such as scarcely reappears in Italian before Leopardi. There are lines and passages and whole poems that burn with an unearthly incandescence as if the poet's mere difficulty in speaking at all had somehow charged his words with an additional significance. He was inevitably influenced by Petrarch in matters of literary form, but although he sometimes lapsed into mannerisms and conceits, he kept singularly free from the conventional motives of Petrarchism. The external incidents—meetings, partings, quarrels, salutations—and the descriptions of physical beauty that figure so largely in contemporary poets scarcely appear at all in his work. He concentrates almost exclusively on inward experience and allows himself only a little sparse imagery taken from the sculptor's art, frost and fire and the darkness of the night. In this naked poetry of passion and intellect Neoplatonism found an authentic voice. Michelangelo never tried to use its phraseology as a veil for emotions of a different order; and aspects of his philosophy that had not a strong personal appeal for him he left alone.

His acceptance of it rested on a real psychological basis. When one considers his art and his life one finds them dominated by two forces, the instinct of creation and the instinct of flight, opposing and yet complementary phrases of a single overwhelming instinct of worship. It was the conflict between the mystic and the artist, between the ascetic and the child of the Renaissance that made Michelangelo's life a torment and his art a glory. As the impulse towards creation lessened, the impulse of flight grew stronger, but they existed always side by side.[1] His religious fervour is as much a part of the visionary quality of his mind as any image that he fixed on stone or canvas. No man could ever have said with more truth: "My soul and body crieth out, yea for the living God." It is one of the ironies of history that he, with his thirst for the timeless and the absolute should have been gifted with genius in the most concrete of the arts. His desire to flee the world was no empty formula; it was a crying reality. Yet it was no less necessary to him to translate his rapture into plastic form and so to limit and imprison the very infinity he worshipped. The language of Neoplatonism becomes convincing on his lips because it corresponded closely with his own artistic and religious experience. Love for

> . . . un concetto di bellezza.
> Immaginata o vista dentro al core,[2]

really produced in him some such dilation of the soul as a religious mystic feels in an act of prayer, and this ecstasy always far exceeded in perfection either whatever visible object first called it into being or any attempt to embody it in art. The apprehension of beauty in the external world passed into that state of enlightenment in which the mind, before it has formed any definite imaginative conception seems to possess beauty as a universal power. It is only after this experience that it proceeds to the precise ordering

---

[1] It would be a mistake to suppose that the religious sonnets written between 1547 and 1560 represent a kind of death-bed repentance. They express sentiments that were always strong in Michelangelo though they only became dominant in the latter years of his life. One might quote in support of this view his known attachment to Savonarola, the evidence of the letters which are full of religious feeling, and the emotion that prompted such an early work as the Pietà of St. Peter's and such an early fragment as the following [No. XXV in Frey's edition. Written before 1524]:—

> Vivo al peccato, a me morendo vivo;
> Vita già mia non son ma del peccato
> Mie ben dal ciel mie mal da me m'è dato
> Dal mie sciolte voler di ch'io son privo.

[2] No. LX. Between 1533 and 1536.

of its thoughts and then to an urgent need for expression. In his longing at once to lose himself and identify himself with that unseen beauty, and to realize it, however imperfectly, in his art, Michelangelo might have seen in his own soul an image of the "doppia Venere." His passion is rooted in an eternal paradox. Visible things must be loved since they alone can recall the vision of pure beauty, but to see that vision and try to reveal it to men is to know that matter is forever at enmity with the spirit. There is a sense in which every work of art is a betrayal; for Michelangelo the betrayal must have been bitter in proportion to the force of his genius. Moreover, in his moral life the austerity of his faith lent to the opposition of the material and the spiritual a terrible solemnity. He felt himself bound to live in this world as the vowed citizen of another, but again and again saw himself false to that obligation. In the weariness of his later years even the art to which he had dedicated himself as to a divine mission seemed to him only one of the "favole del mondo" by which he had been led astray. But it is precisely his sense of the tragic dichotomy of the human spirit that gives nerves and sinews to his poetry. His despair and sorrow spring from the deep consciousness of infirmity and his rare moments of joy have the authenticity of things won perilously out of the toil and heat of the fight.

> Come fiamma più cresce più contesa
> Dal vento ogni virtù che'l ciel esalta,
> Tanto più splende quanto è più offesa.[1]

The early poems and the cycle of the "donna altiera" may mostly be eliminated. They show at least that "amor profano" was no more a literary figment with him than "Amor sacro"

> Come può esser ch'io non sia più mio?
> O Dio, o Dio, o Dio!
> Chi m'à tolto a me stesso?

---

[1] No. CV, ed. cit.

is the voice of a prisoner twisting in his bonds, just as the line

> Chi mi diffenderà dal tuo bel volto?[1]

suggests the breathlessness of panic.

In these agonized and humiliated cries there is no trace of a philosophic attitude that Michelangelo was too sincere to feign.

It is in the poems addressed to Cavalieri and Vittoria Colonna that one must look for Neoplatonic elements, thrilling and passionate in the poems for Cavalieri, more grave and devout in those directed to Vittoria.[2] Michelangelo's love for these two most cherished of his friends was deep and sincere and was subject at times to human doubts and difficulties; but in both cases the personal relationship was a starting-point for something more subtle, for the awakening of all the idealizing and abstracting faculties of the poet's mind. Cavalieri and Vittoria were objects on whom his limitless capacity for adoration could spend itself, symbols through whom he continually apprehended something greater than themselves. They are beings of flesh and blood and yet as truly expressions of ideal beauty as the *Thinker* or the *Delphic Sybil*.

[1] Nos. VI, V. Between 1504 and 1511. The poem, No. XXXII, quoted later is one of the few exceptions.

[2] The friendship with Tommaso Cavalieri began in Rome about 1532. Cavalieri was young, gifted, and exceptionally beautiful, and Michelangelo's attachment to him had from the beginning something of the enthusiasm of a cult. It seems to have frightened Cavalieri. He was a man of high character and never abused his great influence with his friend, but he remained somewhat aloof, troubled by the vehemence of the passion he had stirred. The sense of distance and insecurity in their relations may well have accentuated the ecstatic and impersonal note in Michelangelo's verse just as it produced his complaints against "Che non ha morte e morte altrui procaccia." That his connection with Vittoria Colonna was a love affair in the ordinary sense few now believe. It seems to have been quite truly a "Platonic friendship" rooted in common intellectual interests and in the deep religious faith that time was strengthening in both the friends. It was marked on Vittoria's side by something protective and maternal and on Michelangelo's by a loving veneration that exalted Vittoria both before and after her death into "a thing enskyed and sainted."

THE LYRIC: MICHELANGELO

The phases of such a relationship are difficult to follow, since they fluctuate continually between the personal and the impersonal, the idea at times taking flesh and colour from the individual, the individual fading at others almost wholly into the idea. One may trace this same interplay of personal tenderness and ideal rapture in the love of Dante for Beatrice, where the maiden of the *Vita Nuova* moves in an unearthly light and even in Paradise the blessed spirit has not quite renounced her womanhood; or again in the *Canti* of Leopardi, where Silvia and Nerina pass like fading incarnations of the glory, at once more unapproachable and more immediate to the soul, that is celebrated in *Alla sua Donna*. Michelangelo's love for Cavalieri and Vittoria was not like the *Amor Divino* of Benivieni, a sentiment wholly abstract and philosophical; it had solid roots of genuine human affection. Neither was it, like the loves of the contemporary Petrarchisti, a polite convention or a very mundane passion masquerading as a philosophic one. It served to bring Michelangelo into contact with the unseen power he served. There was room in it for fear and misery and dejection and for the loneliness of one who has outlived those who are most dear to him and sees life stretching before him to old age without their companionship.[1] Yet the personal drama is played against a background of immortal light that brightens at times until all individual presences are annihilated in it. Love becomes the infinite desire for an infinite being; and the language of human passion only the imperfect symbolism through which it tries to speak of its transfiguration.[2]

Love and death; the eternity of ideal Beauty and the caducity of its earthly manifestations; loss and unappeased desire; those are the fundamental notes of Michelangelo's poetry. Two isolated

---

[1] E.g. No. CIX, 18, To Cavalieri, 1546, or the fragment of an elegy on the death of Vittoria Colonna, 1547, No. XCIX.
[2] No. CXXVI.
        L'acceso amor donde vien l'alma sciolta
        S'è calamita al suo simil ardore
        Com' or purgata in fuoco a Dio si torna.

lines, dating from about 1526, might have been written as the text and epitome of the Neoplatonic poems to come.

> Non posso or non veder, dentro a chi muore
> Tuo luce eterna senza gran disio.[1]

The eternal light shines in perishable things and moves man to desire the glory of heaven; but it is only through visible beauty that he can learn to desire it

> Tardi ama il cor quel che l'occhio non vede.[2]

The eyes enamoured of beauty and the soul eager for salvation are, indeed, set upon different aspects of the same reality; both seek the divine image as far as that may be known in human conditions.

> Gli occhi miei, vaghi delle cose belle
> E l'alma insieme della sua salute
> Non ànno altra virtute
> C'ascende al ciel che mirar tutte quelle.

> Dalle più alte stelle
> Discende uno splendore
> Che'l desir tira a quelle
> Nè altro à il gentil core
> Che l'innamori e arda e che'l consigli
> C'un volto che ne gli occhi lor somigli.[3]

Earthly beauty is only evil if it is allowed to distract the soul from its upward pilgrimage. It may be loved and rightly loved, as the type of the pure incorporeal beauty of the spiritual world; but to love it for itself alone is to invite disillusion.

Love "suggetta al variar d'un bel viso" is "fallace speme," but so vital is spiritual affection to Michelangelo that he claims it as the very reason for which God created the world, a force that change and death are powerless to affect.

[1] No. XXX.
[2] No. CIX, 104. The madrigal from which this line is taken and all other poems grouped under the number CIX formed part of the proposed edition of 1546.   [3] No. CIX, 99. Perhaps addressed to Cavalieri.

> Ben può talor col mie ardente desio
> Salir la speme e non esser fallace,
> Che s'ogni nostro affetto al ciel dispiace
> A che fin fatto arrebbe il mondo Iddio?
> Qual più giusta cagion dell'amart'io
> È che dar gloria a quell'eterna pace
> Onde pende il divin che di te piace
> E c'ogni cor gentil fa casto e pio?
>
> Fallace speme à sol l'amor che muore
> Con la beltà, c'ogni momento scema
> Ond'è suggetta al variar d'un bel viso.
> Dolce è ben quella in un pudico core
> Che per cangiar di scorza o d'ora strema
> Non manca, e qui caparra il paradiso.[1]

Beauty, then, is an incorporeal essence "immaginata o vista dentro al core," but it is also something that the whole creation groans and travails to produce. Nature appears to the poet as a fellow artist toiling through years of failure and experiment to attain perfection. After a slow and laborious evolution some miracle of beauty is born to startle mankind, but hardly has it appeared when it must vanish from the earth. Indeed, in this, Nature is less fortunate than man, for his creations of paint and stone may last for generations, while her masterpieces endure only for the little period of human life or human youth. And as the artist only touches his highest achievement within a short time of his death, so the coming of perfect beauty must foretell the end of the world.

> Negli anni molti e nelle molte pruove
> Cercando il saggio al buon concetto arriva
> D'un immagine viva
> Vicino a morte in pietra alpestra e dura;
> C'all' alte cose nuove
> Tardi si viene e poco poi si dura.
> Similmente natura
> Di tempo in tempo d'uno in altro volto

---

[1] No. CIX, 101. To Cavalieri.

> S'al sommo errando di bellezza è giunta
> Nel tuo divino, è vecchio e de' perire
> Onde la tema molto
> Con la beltà congiunta
> Di strano cibo pasce il gran desire;
> Ne'so pensar ne dire
> Qual nuova o giovi più, visto'l tuo' spetto
> O'l fin dell' universo o'l gran diletto.[1]

Yet in the cold light of reflection one sees clearly enough that the world goes on, indifferent, while the beloved's beauty perishes from day to day, and must soon be gathered back into the darkness. In spite of his philosophy, the fact confronted Michelangelo as a tragic problem. No man perhaps ever made of the human body so eloquent a language, and no one can have felt more keenly the bitterness of its decay. One must remember that if one is to feel the full force of his poems. The romantic feeling for Nature that was latent in Neoplatonism and found voice in the verse of Campanella left him untouched; he was won by the grace of individual human beings, a more personal and painful thing. The Nature worshipper may feel that his goddess has some permanence, at least in relation to himself, but the lover never knows from day to day what catastrophe may overtake his love. Michelangelo, though he believed in the incorporeal nature of beauty, was drawn to its mortal forms through the very sense that they were doomed. Even in his old age "la stagion rinverde per un bel volto" and he feels in looking on it the still potent stimulus that urges him upward. If at one moment he exclaims "L'arte e la morte non van bene insieme," at another he asks:

> La forza d'un bel viso a che mi sprona ?
> C'altro non è c'al mondo mi diletti:
> Ascender vivo fra gli spirti eletti
> Per grazia tal c'ogni altra par men buona,
> Se ben col fattor l'opra si consuona
> Che colpa vuol giustizia ch'io n'aspetti
> S'i amo anz'ardo e per divin concetti
> Onoro e stimo ogni gentil persona ? . . .[2]

---

[1] No. CIX, 50, To V. C.   [2] No. CXLI. Printed among poems of 1550-4.

Yet beauty dies in the person of the beloved, and the lover asks, wistfully: Can this mortal put on Immortality? In one poem Michelangelo seeks an answer in the Platonic doctrine of reincarnation. The beloved's beauty may grow less with the lapse of time, but cannot die. All that it loses is stored up by Nature, and will in some future day become incarnate again.

> Sol perchè tue bellezze al mondo sieno
> Eterne al tempo che le dona e fura
> Credo se ne ripligli la natura
> Tutto quel ch'ogni giorno a te vien meno
> E serbi al parto d'un più largo seno
> Con miglior sorte e con più strema cura
> Per riformar di nuovo una figura
> C'abbi'l tuo volto angelico e sereno.[1]

This thought moves him again to wonder whether the beauty that he sees has already existed in the world, and now returns, as it were, from the gathered memory of the race; or if it is "news from a foreign country," a report or a dream that touches the heart and leaves it burning with strange dissatisfaction, or a beam of the first light striking down through the worlds?

> Non so se s'è la desiata luce
> Del suo primo fattor che l'alma sente
> O se dalla memoria della gente
> Alcun altra belta nel cor traluce,
> O se fama o se sogno alcun produce
> Agli occhi manifesto, al cor presente
> Di se lasciando un non so che cocente
> Ch'è forse or quel ch'a pianger mi conduce.
> Quel ch'i sento e ch'i cerco e che mi guidi
> Meco non è, ne so ben veder dove
> Trovar mel possa, e par c'altri mel mostri
> Questo Signor m'avvien, po' chi'i vi vidi
> C'un dolce e amaro, un si e no si muove
> Certo saranno stati gli occhi vostri.[2]

---

[1] No. CIX, 46. To V. C.
[2] No. LXXV. To Cavalieri, 1542-6.

The answer to these doubts is implicit in the questions themselves. Beauty is "l'immortal forma" the divine idea that vivifies base matter and moulds it into its own likeness. The "leggiadro e mortal velo" is lovable not for itself, but for the reflected radiance that shines from it.

> Per ritornar là donde venne fora
> L'immortal forma al tuo carcer terreno
> Venne com'angel, di pietà si pieno
> Che sana ogn'intelletto e'l mondo onora.
> Questo sol m'arde e questo m'innamora
> Non pur di fuora il tuo volto sereno:
> C'amor non gia di cosa che vien meno
> Tien ferma speme in cui virtù dimora.
>
> Nè altro avvien di cose altere e nuove
> In cui si preme la natura, el cielo
> E c'a lor parto largo s'apparechia.
> Nè Dio, sua grazia, mi si mostra altrove
> Più chèn alcun leggiadro e mortal velo
> E quel sol amo perch'in lui si specchia.[1]

Love that is awakened by the beauty of created things belongs, like the human soul itself, to a middle world, neither good nor evil, mortal nor immortal, but capable of becoming any of these things. It is evil and mortal if it cleaves to the garment of flesh alone; but may grow to be immortal and glorious if it realizes that the real object of its desire is not in the material world at all.[2]

The lover who has apprehended this truth has received his initiation into the heavenly calling and set foot on the first rung of the ladder of perfection. From the physical contemplation of his beloved's beauty he passes on to consider the spiritualized image that he has formed in his mind; and the possession of this image gives him a new nobility in his own eyes.

> I'mi son caro assai più ch'i non soglio;
> Poi ch'i t'ebbi nel cor, più di me vaglio
> Come pietra, c'aggiuntovi l'intaglio
> E di più pregio che'l suo primo scoglio.

---

[1] No. CIX, 105.   [2] No. CXXVIII. Cavalieri? 1547–50.

THE LYRIC: MICHELANGELO

> O come scritta o pinta carta o foglio
> Più si riguarda d'ogni straccio o taglio
> Tal di me fo, da po'ch'i fu bersaglio,
> Segnato dal tuo viso, e non mi doglio.
>
> Sicur con tale stampa in ogni loco
> Vo, come quel c'à incanti o arme seco
> C'ogni periglio gli fan venir meno.[1]

Here for a moment a doubt crosses his mind. Can his perception have any objective reality? Is not the beauty that he worships simply an emanation from his own mind?

> Dimmi di grazia, Amor se gli occhi miei
> Veggono'l ver della beltà, ch'aspiro
> O s'io l'ò' dentro allor che dov'io miro
> Veggio scolpito el viso di costei.
> Tu'l de saper, po'che tu vien con lei
> A torm'ogni mie pace, ond'io m'adiro;
> Nè vorre' manco un minimo sospiro
> Nè men ardente foco chiederei:—[2]

Love resolves his doubt by saying that beauty is indeed inherent in the loved object, but is purified and perfected when it passes through the eyes into the soul.

> La beltà che tu vedi e ben da quella
> Ma cresce, poi ch'a miglior loco sale
> Se per gli occhi mortali all'alma corre.
> Quivi si fa divina, onesta e bella
> Com'a se simil vuol cosa immortale.
> Questa e non quella a gli occhi tuoi precorre.[3]

So the lover, contemplating the beloved image, loses himself; but lives again in the person of the beloved whenever his passion is reciprocated. There was perhaps no more overworked motive in the Neoplatonic repertoire, but Michelangelo infused it with

---

[1] No. CIX, 95.
[2] No. XXXII, To an unknown lady, 1529-30.   [3] Ibid.

a force so new and so overpowering that one seems to be hearing it for the first time. "Veggio co' be' vostri occhi" has been claimed as the finest lyric of sixteenth-century Italy and perhaps the claim is not altogether extravagant; at least it is an amazing instance of how genius can take even a hackneyed theme and vitalize it afresh.

> Veggio co' be' vostri occhi un dolce lume
> Che co' mie ciechi già veder non posso
> Porto co' vostro piedi un pondo addosso
> Che de' miei zoppi non è lor costume.
> Volo con le vostr'ale e senza piume
> Col vostro ingegno al ciel sempre son mosso.
> Dal vostro arbitrio son pallido e rosso
> Freddo al sol, caldo alle più fredde brume.
>
> Nel voler vostro è sol la voglia mia
> I miei pensier nel vostro cor si fanno
> Nel vostro fiato son le mie parole.
> Come luna de se sol par ch'io sia
> Che gli occhi nostri il ciel veder non sanno
> Se non quel tanto che n'accende il sole.[1]

In the poems addressed to Luigi del Riccio on the death of Cecchino de' Bracci, Michelangelo carries the idea a stage further. In order to make a portrait of the dead youth it will suffice to paint his friend.

> Dunche Luigi a far l'unica forma
> Di Cecchin, di ch'i parlo in pietra viva
> Eterna, or ch'è gia terra qui tra noi,
> Se l'un nel'altro amato si trasforma
> Po'che sanz essa l'arte non arriva
> Convien che per far lui ritragga voi.[2]

Again he speaks of how the dead friend survives in the living,

[1] No. CIX, 19, Cavalieri.   [2] No. LXXIII, 15, 1544.

> Qui vuol mie sorte c'anzi tempo i dorma
> Nè son già morto: e ben c'albergo cangi
> Resto in te vivo, c'or mi vedi e piangi
> Se l'un nel altro amante si trasforma.[1]

and the living anticipates his immortality by mounting heavenward with the enfranchised spirit of his beloved. In a late madrigal the poet thinks of Vittoria Colonna, now among "Coloro che morte accresce e'l tempo non offende," and feels himself so present with her that he prays that he may not again sink back into himself and be lost in the illusions and passions of life.

While either of the lovers remains in the body perfect freedom and perfect love are impossible. In life

> . . . un anima in due corpi è fatta eterna
> Ambo levando al ciel e con pari ale.[2]

but it is only when the mortal barriers are broken that the two spirits can love without constraint and know each other with immediate intuition.

> S'i amo sol di te, Signor mie caro
> Quel che di te più ami non ti solegni
> Che l'un del altro spirto s'innamora
> Quel che nel tuo bel volto bramo e'mparo
> E mal compreso è dagl'umani ingegni
> Chi'l vuol saper convien che prima mora.[3]

On earth the lover finds himself an exile, and his vision is darkened again and again by envy or grief or some other passion that perturbs the life of man. Michelangelo, in one of the madrigals of his sad later years, turns questioning to the souls of the blessed and asks them if they at least have passed beyond these torments. He hears their answer

> La nostra eterna quiete
> Fuor d'ogni tempo è priva
> D'invidia amando e d'angosciosi pianti

---

[1] No. LXXIII, 16.   [2] No. XLIV, To Cavalieri, c. 1533.
[3] No. XLV, To Cavalieri.

and breaks out into the irrepressible cry of one homesick and heartsick for his native country.

> Se'l ciel è degli amanti
> Amico, e'l mondo ingrato
> Amando, a che son nato?[1]

Life in the lower world is evil, and its prolongation only loads the soul with new sins, obscuring its inherent glory and making it forgetful of whence it came. It was not strange that Michelangelo, lingering on to old age through recurring disillusionment and the loss of friends and the fiery miseries of his conscience, should have felt it was well with those who died young.

> Condotto da molti anni all'ultima ore
> Tardi conosco, o mondo, i tuoi diletti
> La pace che non ai, altrui prometti
> E quel riposo c'anzi al nascer muore.
> La vergogna e'l timore
> Degli anni c'or prescrive
> Il ciel, non mi rinnova
> Che'l vecchio e dolce errore
> Nel qual chi troppo vive
> L'anim'ancide e nulla al corpo giova.
> Il dico e so per pruova
> Di me che'n ciel quel solo a miglior sorte
> Ch'ebbe al suo parto più presso la morte.[2]

What, then, is this life of beatitude? It is before all to be free of human limitations, of the brutish insensibility of matter, of the hardness of men, of the blindness and fickleness of one's own heart. It is to be lifted above the inexorable flight of time into the unbroken peace of God;

> Beata l'alma ove non corre tempo
> Per te s'è fatta a contemplare Dio.[3]

---

[1] No. CIX, 35.   [2] No. CIX, 34.
[3] No. LIX, 1533-6. Fragment belonging possibly to Cavalieri cycle.

THE LYRIC: MICHELANGELO

Or, as Michelangelo wrote so touchingly of his dead father, it is to be oneself a god no longer troubled by our tragic mutations of life and will.

> Tu sei del morir morto e fatto divo
> Ne temi or più cangiar vita ne voglia
> Che quasi senza invidia non lo scrivo.[1]

The friendships formed on earth between virtuous souls continue and grow stronger, since what each loved in the other exists now in its pure state, free from all the impediments of material life. The soul, being itself god-like, can love only what is eternal and of equal dignity with itself.

> Non vider gli occhi miei cosa mortale
> Allor che ne'bei vostri intera pace
> Trovai, ma dentro ov'ogni mal dispiace
> Chi d'amor l'alma a se simil m'assale:
> E se creata a Dio non fusse uguale
> Altro che'l bel di fuor ch'a gli occhi piace
> Più non vorria: ma perchè è si fallace
> Trascende nella forma universale:
>
> Io dico ch'a chi vive quel che muore
> Quetar non può disir, nè par s'aspetti
> L'eterno al tempo, ove altri cangi il pelo.
> Voglia sfrenata il senso è, non amore
> Che l'alma uccide, e'l nostro fa perfetti
> Gli amici qui, ma più per morte in cielo.[2]

Through the language of this sonnet, so ardent yet touched with such a strange impersonal quality, one may perhaps surprise the dominant truth of Michelangelo's Neoplatonism and the belief in which his troubled spirit could sometimes find solace. It was not this or that particular beauty that he ultimately desired, but Beauty herself. One might put it in other terms and say that he was worshipping his own inspiration, the mysterious force that could neither be bidden nor gainsaid, but whose coming

[1] No. LVIII, In morte del Padre, 1534.   [2] No. LXXIX, Cavalieri.

transformed the world for him and urged him on to a frenzy of creation. He shared the impulse common to poets in all ages to celebrate the mistress of his spirit, whether as a being of remote and unearthly majesty or as a presence moving outcast and unacknowledged among men.

> Calling the lapsèd soul
> And weeping in the evening dew.[1]

In her Michelangelo could see the justification of his long life of toil and disappointment. He was from birth her predestinate servant and she had been set before him as the sure hope of his calling.

> Per fido esemplo alla mia vocazione
> Nel parto mi fu data la bellezza
> Che d'ambo l'arti m'è lucerna e specchio.
> S'altro si pensa è falsa opinione.
> Questo sol occhio porta a quella altezza
> Ch'a pingere e scolpir qui m'apparecchio.
> Se giudizii temerarii e sciocchi
> Al senso tiran la beltà che muove
> E porta al ciel ogni intelletto sano
> Dal mortal al divin non vanno gli occhi
> Infermi e fermi sempre pur là dove
> Ascender senza grazia è pensier vano.[2]

An answer has been made to the problem of the decay of beauty. The outward forms wither away; the Idea, whose presence made them lovable, remains unchanged and may still be found and worshipped by the questing soul. Whether Michelangelo regarded the Idea of Beauty as identical with God or, more Platonically, as an entity having a separate existence in the eternal world, it is difficult to determine. In the following sonnet he seems to support the first view, but such a fragment as "Amor, la tua beltà non è mortale" suggests the second. He approached the question as

[1] Cf. Shelley, *Ode to Intellectual Beauty*. Du Bellay, *Si notre vie est moins qu'une journée*. Leopardi, *Alla sua donna*. Baudelaire, *A la très chère, a la très belle*. W. B. Yeats, *The Rose of the World*.
[2] No. XCIV, 1541-4.

a poet and not as a metaphysician, and it may well be that its dogmatic solution was indifferent to him. What did concern him was the conception of Beauty as the pledge of the divine in the material and as the archetype that nature and the artist were at one in following.

> Veggio nel tuo bel volto, Signor mio
> Quel che narrar mal puossi in questa vita
> L'anima della carne ancor vestita
> Con esso è gia più volte ascese a Dio
> E se'l vulgo, malvagio, isciocco e rio
> Di quel che sente altrui segna e addita
> Non è l'intensa voglia men gradita
> L'amor la fede a l'onesto desio
>
> A quel pietoso fonté onde siam tutti
> S'assembra ogni beltà: che qua si vede
> Più ch'altra cosa alle persone accorte.
> Nè altro saggio abbiam nè altri frutti
> Del cielo in terra: e chi v'ama con fede
> Trascende a Dio e fa dolce la morte.[1]

Because it draws from "quel pietoso fonte onde siam tutti" beauty comes always to the soul as a reminiscence of its native place. Sometimes it seems to be almost a reproach, a voice from the lost state of innocence, speaking to one on whom time and error have done their utmost, and then the poet's words tremble away in humble penitence.

> Per qual mordace lima
> Discresce e manca ognor tua stanca spoglia
> Anima inferma or quando sie ti scioglia
> Da quella il tempo e torni ov'eri in cielo
> Candida e lieta prima
> Deposto il periglioso e mortal velo?
> C'ancor ch'i cangi il pelo
> Per gli ultimi anni e corti

---

[1] No. LXIV, To Cavalieri.

> Cangiar non posso il vecchio mio antico uso.
> Che con più giorni più mi sforza e preme.
> Amor a te non celo
> Ch'i porto invidia ai morti;
> Sbigottito e confuso
> Si di se meco l'alma trema e teme
> Signor nell'ore streme
> Stendi ver me le tue pietose braccia
> Tom 'a me stesso e fammi un che piaccia.[1]

Again, when the radiance shines on him from the beloved's eyes, he feels himself drawn back to them, as to the heaven in which his love began. But there is nothing in the rapture he feels of the common love of the heart and senses; there seems, indeed, to be very little even of the personal contact of two minds. It is rather a rarified and intellectualized passion of the spirit for the highest it can apprehend, and though the beloved's beauty may bring the ideal to to mind it becomes itself absorbed into the splendour it evokes.

> La vita del mio amor non è'l cor mio
> Ch'amor di quel ch'i t'amo è senza core
> Dove cosa mortale, piena d'errore
> Esser non può giammai, nè pensier rio.
> Amor nel dipartir l'alma da Dio
> Me fe' sanz'occhio e te luc'e splendore
> Ne può non revederl'in quel che more
> Di te per nostro mal mie gran disio.
>
> Come dal foco 'l cald'esser diviso
> Non può, dal bell'etern'ogni mie stima.
> Ch'esalta, ond'ella vien, chi più'l somiglia
> Poi ch'ai negli occhi tutto' l paradiso
> Per ritornar la dov'io t'amai prima
> Ricorro ardendo sotto alle tue ciglia.[2]

No individual object, however rare or perfect, can express the Idea as that makes itself known within the soul. The artist in

[1] No. LXXXVII.
[2] No XCII. Uncertain whether addressed to Cavalieri or V. C.

THE LYRIC: MICHELANGELO

his moments of achievement or the lover in his rare intervals of peace may dream for a while that he has attained his goal; but there comes always an inexorable voice saying: "This is not your rest," and he knows that he has tried to stay himself with a shadow.

> Amor la tua belta non è mortale
> Nessun volto fra noi e che pareggi
> L'immagine del cor, che'nfiammi e reggi
> Con altro foco e muovi con altr'ale.[1]

The central passion of Michelangelo's life was one that he could not satisfy and that he well knew must remain unsatisfied. Yet now and then his very restlessness seemed to him precious, as the earnest of a joy that the soul, contented and at ease among earthly limitations, could never even imagine.

> E se'l primo suo colpo fu mortale
> Seco un messo, di par venne d'Amore
> Che mi disse: Ama, anz'ardi, che chi muore
> Non à da gire al ciel nel mondo altr'ale.
>
> I son colui che ne'prim anni tuoi
> Gli occhi tuoi infermi volsi alla beltate
> Che dalla terra al ciel vivo conduce.[2]

One is tempted to say that if the Academy had done no more than supply him with a language it would have justified its existence.

TRANSLATIONS

Page 244. . . . *un concetto di bellezza* . . .
    . . . an idea of loveliness
    Imagined or beheld within the heart.

Page 245. Come fiamma più cresce . . .
    As flame that by a contrary wind is blown
    Increases, so more clear the more offended
    Shines out the virtue heaven makes its own.

---

[1] No. LXII, c. 1533-6.   [2] No. LXI, 1533-6.

Page 245. Come può esser . . .
>How comes it that I am mine own no more?
>Ah God, ah God, ah God!
>Who robs me of myself?

Page 246. Chi mi diffenderà . . .
Who shall defend me from thy lovely face?

Page 248. Non posso or non veder . . .
>Nor can I now behold in mortal things
>Thy light eternal without strong desire.

Page 248. Tardi ama il cor . . .
The heart is slow to love what's hid from sight.

Page 248. Gli occhi miei . . .
>Mine eyes that are enamoured of things fair
>And this my soul that for salvation cries
>May never heavenward rise
>Unless the sight of beauty lift them there.
>Down from the loftiest star
>A splendour falls on earth,
>And draws desire afar
>To that which gave it birth.
>So love and heavenly fire and counsel wise
>The noble heart finds most in star-like eyes.

Page 249. Ben può talor . . .
>Perhaps this hope's not all misfortunate
>   That soars with my enkindled ardour now;
>For to what end did God the world create
>   If all affections heaven disallow?
>Or what should be my end in loving thee
>   But that eternal peace to glorify,
>Which lent thee heavenly grace men joy to see
>   And makes true hearts devout and pure thereby?

>The love that dies with beauty's swift decay
>Alone shall find itself of hope bereaved,
>Suffering a lovely mien's inconstant sway.
>But sweet is love in blameless heart conceived
>That fails not for the outward form's decline
>Or death, but here gives pledge of life divine

Page 249. *Negli anni molti* . . .
  That wise man who, through labours manifold
  And length of years, toils at the rebel stone
  Shall see one form alone
  Perfect, in living grace, before he die;
  Since to high things untold
  Late we attain, and soon must bid good-bye.
  If Nature equally
  From age to age devising many a face
  Have beauty's absolute created here
  In yours most fair, she's old and must decay;
  And therefore does your grace
  Combine with potent fear
  With strangest food my hungry soul to stay,
  Nor can I deem or say
  Beholding you, which most shall harm or bless
  Creation's end, or so great happiness.

Page 250. *La forza d'un bel viso* . . .
  What power to spur me wields a lovely face?
  Since here on earth I find no like delight,
  This only moves me by unrivalled grace
  Living to soar above the heavenly height
  To join the souls elect; and if the creature
  Sort with its Maker, how should I offend
  High justice, if I love each heaven-born nature,
  Honour and prize each gracious soul as friend?

Page 251. *Sol perchè tue bellezze* . . .
  Still to preserve your loveliness on earth
   Eternal, I believe that nature hastes
  From time, who steals the charms he brought to birth,
   To garner all his slow defection wastes,
   And cherish it to bring it forth again
    With happier fate and more excelling power
   As one who shall return to dwell with men
    With your serene, angelic face for dower.

Page 251. *Non so se s'è* . . .
  I know not if it be the longed-for glory
   Of its creator that the soul perceives
  Or if from humankind's remembrance hoary
   Some other beauty there its twilight leaves,

    Or if it be a vision or a story
       Clear to the eyes or present to the heart
    That with its visitation transitory
       Leaves me to weep this unaccustomed smart.

    What now I feel and seek and take for guide.
       Is not mine own nor can I well discern
    Unless one show me, where it may abide.
       Bitter and sweet and yea and nay by turn
    Have moved me, friend, since first I looked on thee.
    Then surely in thine eyes that power must be.

Page 252. *Per ritornar là donde* . . .

    The immortal soul, aspiring to that height
       It stooped from, to your earthly prison came,
    An angel of compassions infinite
       To heal all hearts and bring our earth good fame.
    By it alone, not by your face serene
       Am I enflaméd and enamoured so
    For never love of passing thing could lean
       On hope so sure, or equal virtue show.

    So comes it when to crown her toils intent
    Nature brings forth new works and excellent;
    The heavens themselves such spacious births prepare.
    And God, by His own grace, I chiefly see
    In some fair vesture of humanity
    Which I love only for His image there.

Page 252. *I' mi son caro* . . .

    Now am I grown unto myself more dear
       More precious, since I held you in my heart,
    As carven stones that hold an image clear
       Excel the native rock from whence they start,
    Or as a parchment writ or painted on
       Is honoured more for every mark it bears,
    So, since your glances pierced me am I grown
       Branded with you, and heedless of all cares.

    Safely with such a mark through every place
       I go, as one that carries arms or spells
    That make all perils fade before his face.

THE LYRIC: MICHELANGELO

Page 253. Dimmi di grazia, Amor . . .
    Love, of thy pity, tell me if mine eyes
    Truly behold the beauty I adore,
    Or if it dwells in me, that evermore
    Where'er I look her imaged features rise
    Thou knowest; for with her thou dost devise
    To wreck my peace, whence I lament me sore,
    Yet wish this flame no milder than before
    Nor ask for any lessening of my sighs.

Page 253. La beltà che tu vedi . . .
    The beauty thou beholdest is indeed
    Hers, but increases as it mounts more high
    Through mortal eyes, and penetrates the soul.
    Pure, fair, and holy it becomes for need
    Of matching the soul's immortality.
    This and no other is thy vision's goal.

Page 254. Veggio co' bei vostr'occhi . . .
    With your fair eyes I see a tender light
    That with my blind ones I could never see,
    Upon your feet I bear a weight with me
    My halting steps could never move aright.
    I mount upon your wings, and take my flight
    With your swift mind to heaven's felicity;
    Grow flushed or pallid at your will's decree
    Cold in the sun, hot in most bitter night.

    In your disposing only is my will
    My very thoughts are fashioned in your heart
    And all my words compounded of your breath.
    I am that lonely moon, invisible
    To human eyes, save only for such part
    As the bright sun in heaven illumineth.

Page 254. Dunche Luigi . . .
    Therefore Luigi to portray the form
    Of Cecchin, whom I sing, in living stone
    And deathless, though he's earth beneath us here,
    If love can lovers each to each transform
    And art is powerless where no model's known,
    To picture him I'll make your portrait clear.

Page 255. *Qui vuol mie sorte* . . .
    Here, e'er my time, the fates have bid me sleep
    Yet not in death; though changed my mortal form
    I live in you who now behold and weep
    If love can lovers each to each transform.

Page 255. . . . *un anima in due corpi* . . .
    One soul is in two bodies made eternal
    Uplifting both to heaven on equal wings.

Page 255. *S'i amo sol di te* . . .
    If, dear my Lord, all that I love in thee
    Be what thyself most lovest be not wrath
    That soul of soul should thus enamoured grow.
    And human thought small understanding hath
    Of how thy fair face schools and kindles me;
    He first must die who this would rightly know.

Page 255. *La nostra eterna quiete.* . . .
    Our everlasting rest
    Beyond time's change is free
    From jealousy in love and anguished tears.

Page 256. *Se'l ciel è degli amanti* . . .
    If heaven to lovers be
    A friend and earth unkind
    Why loving was I born?

Page 256. *Condotto da molti anni* . . .
    Led by long years to my appointed hour
    Too late, O world, I know thy vain delight
    Thou offerest a peace not in thy power
    To give, and rest that never comes in sight.
    The terror and the shame
    Of years fast closing now.
    Only renew in me
    The old sweet treacherous flame
    Which if a man allow
    He profits not his flesh and slays his soul.
    I say, who know the whole
    Truth in myself: he is of heaven most blest
    Who nearest to his birth finds his last rest.

Page 256. Beata l'alma . . .
>Blessed the spirit where time fleets no more
>Through thee it has returned to look on God.

Page 257. Tu sei del morir morto . . .
>So thou art dead to death and god-like grown
>Nor longer fearest change in life or will.
>Scarce without envy can I make it known.

Page 257. Non vider gli occhi miei . . .
>No mortal creature did mine eyes behold
>>When in your own it found unbroken peace;
>But to the soul that no ill thing may hold
>>One like itself in love did bring such ease.
>And were it not in god-like image cast
>>More than the outward forms, the eyes' delight
>It would not seek, but since they cheat so fast
>>It soars to form eternal out of sight.

>Truly for man whatever turns to dust
>Quiets not longing; vainly we pursue
>Immortal things where all to change is given.
>Sense is not love but unrefrainèd lust
>That slays the soul; our love perfects anew
>Lovers on earth and, after death, in heaven.

Page 258. Per fido esemplo . . .
>To guide my labour with ensample clear
>Did heaven give me beauty at my birth
>To both my arts a mirror and a light.
>He errs who otherwise imagines here
>This eye of mine alone discerns the height
>That metes to all I carve or paint its worth.

>And if perverse and froward spirits use
>To sink in sense the beauty that should raise
>And heavenward bear each clear intelligence
>From mortal to divine the eyes refuse
>To pass, infirm and fixed for all their days,
>Since without grace none there ascends from hence.

Page 259. Veggio nel tuo bel volto . . .

    That, friend, which in thy gracious face I see
    Scarce in this present life may man express;
    The spirit, wearing yet its fleshly dress
    By this upborne has looked on deity.
    And though the throng, malign and brutish, free
    Its gibes and scoffs at what the few possess
    There fails no joy from this warm eagerness
    This chaste desire, this love, this fealty.

    For every beauty that we look on here
    Brings, to wise souls, in recollection clear
    The merciable fount whence all things flow;
    Nor other pledge nor other fruit have we
    Of heaven on earth. Who loves thee faithfully
    To God ascends, and makes death precious so.

Page 259. Per qual mordace lima . . .

    With what corroding pain
    Dwindles and hourly wastes thy weary flesh
    Sad soul? When shall the mesh
    Of time be loosed, and thou return to bliss
    Joyful and pure again
    Leaving the mortal body perilous,
    For though my winter is
    Come with these last short years
    I know not how to change my ancient use
    Which as time speeds, more goads and burdens me.
    Love be assured of this
    That I am envious
    Of dead men, such the terrors that confuse
    My soul within that in compunction cowers.
    Lord in my latest hours
    Throw wide for me Thy merciful embrace
    Unself me so, and fit me for Thy grace.

Page 260. La vita del mio amore . . .

    Not in my heart does my love's life abide
        For love with which I love thee needs no heart
    No thought of evil there may ever hide
        Nor any faulty mortal thing have part.

Love when the spirit left its heavenly place
    Made me sure-eyed and thee a light excelling,
That my strong love must needs for ever trace
    In what of thee must die, our woe compelling.
Inseparably close, as heat to fire,
To timeless beauty that has power to raise,
Fit souls to heaven, cleaves my whole desire
And since thou hast all heaven in thy gaze
I refuge take beneath thy brows, and burn
There where I loved thee first to make return.

Page 261. *Amor la tua beltà* . . .
    Oh, Love, not mortal is thy loveliness!
    There's not a face among us to come nigh
    The image in the heart which thou dost high
    Lift on strange wings, and with strange fire possess.

Page 261. *E se'l primo suo colpo* . . .
    Though mortal that first blow to me it brings
    A message, sent me on behalf of Love,
    That bids "Love on, flame on! For none can move
    From earth to heaven save upon such wings.

    "For I am he who in thy earliest years
    Turned thy frail eyes to look on loveliness
    That leads men living to the heavenly spheres."

CONCLUSION

From one point of view the period that has here been discussed might be called the incubation period of Italian Neoplatonism. Its main theories were widely diffused and repeated but little developed until the end of the sixteenth century, when they were expanded by the eager speculations of Campanella and Bruno. During this early period Neoplatonism held an important place in general culture, but although it was everywhere received with enthusiasm, it caused some confusion of mind. Ficino's teaching was in essence an idealization of the humanistic thought of the fifteenth century, but it appeared clothed with the outward semblance of the mystical philosophy of Alexandria, and its interpreters were not always capable of seeing where the difference lay. The Renaissance, without being the reversion to paganism that it has sometimes been called, had in the main lost touch with the mysticism of a Dionysius or an Origen. Some of its writers evolved a pantheistic mysticism of their own, but the variety and excitement of immediate human concerns were generally so powerful as to exclude any impulse towards "the flight of the alone to the Alone." Consequently much of the talk of heavenly love and ideal beauty rings false. The writers of lyrics and treatises too often tried to identify courtly trifling with the ascent of the mystic to his god, and the result is a great deal of particularly unpleasant insincerity.

None the less, Neoplatonism had a distinctive and valuable contribution to make to the art and literature of the age. It would not perhaps be untrue to call the elements it fostered Romantic. The term has been used to represent many things, from mere stage paraphernalia of daggers and broomsticks to that wholeness and sincerity of utterance and that refusal by the artist to allow any divorce between his intellect and the truths of his instinctive being that Mr. Middleton Murry has called true Romanticism. Here, however, the word may more conveniently stand for the explicit beliefs of those writers of the early nineteenth century who called themselves the Romantics, beliefs whose influence has persisted in various forms until our own time. A few of the most important may be traced under endless individual modifications, though it would require an elaborate analysis to treat them in adequate detail.

There is the sense that Nature is penetrated by spiritual forces and possesses a kind of conscious life which may be imagined as either friendly or hostile to man. There is the ardent championship of freedom as the most unchallengeable right and the most intimate need of the human soul, from which there follows a cult of the spontaneous rather than of the critical and reflective elements of personality, an exaltation of "the holiness of the heart's affections and the truth of Imagination." The enormous place held by love in Romantic literature is one manifestation of this belief. Another is the almost priest-like character attributed to the artist, and the claim that art as the faithful image of the spirit must be free to reflect and interpret every aspect of life. That claim is implicit in the most fanciful historical reconstructions, in the stagiest local colour, in the most jejune supernaturalism of the Romantics, as well as in the variety and richness of imagination and the emotional intensity of their best work. Finally there is the insistent longing for an ideal beauty and perfection, generally thought of as remote and sometimes as confessedly unattainable. The affinity between such views and the basic principles of Neoplatonism is obvious, but it may be interesting to suggest very briefly a few of the likenesses and differences in the treatment of them that mark the two periods.

Beliefs akin to those of the Neoplatonists underlie much of the Romantic attitude to Nature. The pantheistic feeling that has such diverse expressions in Pico and Leonardo, Campanella and Bruno, reappears in many writers of the nineteenth century and passes through analogous developments. Victor Hugo, who actually derived many of his ideas from the Hermetic writings and the *Cabala*, wrote apocalyptic poems whose thought is almost identical with that of the *Heptaplus* or the *Dialoghi* of Leone Ebreo. They describe a world animated by countless gradations of spiritual beings, the lower struggling continually to raise themselves while the higher lend compassionate aid to their struggles. At one end of the scale is God and at the other chaos, and between the two extremes are ranged angels and men, beasts, plants, and stones. Hugo holds moreover that the lower forms of life are penitential states into which guilty souls may bring themselves, and that man is the central grade of the hierarchy.

> L'homme qui plane et qui rampe, être crépusculaire
> En est le milieu. . . .
> L'ange y descend, la bête après la mort y monte. . . .
> Dieu mêle en votre race hommes infortunés
> Les demi-dieux punis aux monstres pardonnés.

For Hugo, and for many of the early nineteenth century poets, Nature is generally regarded as sympathetic towards man since she shares a life not essentially different from his own. The universe is a single organism in which the joy or suffering of the lowliest part reacts upon the whole.

> Robin redbreast in a cage
> Puts all heaven in a rage.

> The spirit of the worm beneath the sod
> In love and blessing blends itself with God.

But though Nature is sometimes depicted as sympathising with human suffering, she is more often credited with the enjoyment of a calm and a blessedness denied to man. Where humanity by some mysterious alienation has lost its birthright, she remains in close harmony with the supreme power of the universe and so offers to man a source of wisdom from which he cannot drink too deeply. Through the visible world he may seek and achieve contact with ultimate truth. As he loves and contemplates Nature and acquires further and further insight into her life, he finds himself lifted into a peace that transcends all merely personal pleasures or distresses. With some poets the very hope of immortality becomes an absorption of the individual soul into the soul of Nature. Adonais is indeed enthroned "where the eternal are," but he is also "made one with nature," a voice among her voices. Even where she is not regarded as definitely sympathetic, she offers a refuge in which a Childe Harold or an Alastor can console himself for the sufferings inflicted on him by the world. In her serenity there is strength, and in her storms a wild catharsis for the tormented spirit. Above all, in her beauty there is a power which, if it cannot make clear the mystery of man's fate, can at least reconcile him to it by showing him something in the world that appears to have abiding value and significance. The spell can bind even the pessimism of Leopardi and Vigny. They see in Nature only a harsh stepmother; and through the very anguish of disillusionment there breaks irresistibly the celebration of her loveliness.

With a later generation the feeling that Nature is an emanation from or symbol of the divine is often replaced by a belief in her as the only divinity. This is precisely the conclusion reached by a few of the later Neoplatonists; and it can hardly be accidental that in both cases the growth of this attitude coincided with scientific discoveries that threatened to disintegrate orthodox beliefs. Nature remains a source of wisdom, but she is no longer the shadow of heaven, the dim revelation of a spiritual world, but the mother and former of men. For Meredith, if she is less tender or less divine than she was for Wordsworth or Shelley, she is still not wholly indifferent but with "an eye to know her young" and a disposition eternally favourable to the strong and the courageous. In Swinburne's *Hertha* Nature worship becomes the cult of a kind of immanent "Life-force" at once good and evil, destroyer and creator:

> I the mark that is missed
> And the arrows that miss
> I the mouth that is kissed
> And the breath in the kiss.

The search and the sought and the seeker, the soul and the body that is.

Pantheism of this absolute kind ought perhaps to have moderated Swinburne's violent likes and dislikes, but unhappily no record exists of his reply to the man who pointed out to him the essential unity between himself and the Pope and the King of Naples that his theory implies.

There is considerably more divergence between the two groups in their estimate of man.

The Neoplatonists, filled with the sense of having liberated the human spirit from every hindrance to its free expansion, tended naturally to emphasize the greatness of his powers and the joy of their exercise. The Romantics, with scarcely less consciousness of human dignity, were intensely and painfully aware of the discrepancy between man's potential glory and the hard actualities of his wrongs, his sufferings, and his failings. The likenesses and differences between their respective points of view are nowhere more clearly epitomized than in their treatment of the artist. Both groups agree in claiming the creative faculty in man as the clearest evidence of his kinship with the divine. His activity, especially as it manifests itself in the arts, is "a repetition of the eternal act of creation in the mind of the infinite I AM." No limit can justly be set to his powers. "There is nothing that the human mind can conceive that it cannot also perform." The artist assumes a special function as the interpreter between humanity and the mysteries of the world around it and the kindred mysteries of its own soul. It is for him to bring every thought and passion, every vicissitude of life, every phenomenon of Nature into the empire of his spirit, and in so doing to reveal something of their essential character. In his work the eternal is apprehended through the temporal; the macrocosm is resolved into the microcosm.

> Hear the voice of the bard
> Who present, past and future sees,
> Whose ears have heard
> The Holy Word
> That walked among the ancient trees.

He holds, in fact, a position very like that of Ficino's philosopher, "a man in the presence of God, a god in the presence of men," or of Leonardo's painter who rivals nature in the variety of his works. The poets of the nineteenth century claimed for themselves a peculiar dignity as channels of revelation and "unacknowledged legislators of the world." The old pride of the Renaissance artist lives again in them, but their consciousness of superior power is often tempered by a sense of the isolation of the seer. His pre-eminence is a pre-eminence of suffering; in attaining the heights and depths of human experience he takes upon him a burden that sets him apart from the insensitive multitude which he has to guide and enlighten. If he is often haughty towards the world he humbles himself before the force that inspires him; his own sense of inadequacy is a measure of the tragic deficiencies of mankind. The effort of subduing the lower faculties of the soul to that higher truth is often an agonizing one; and in his attempts at resolving the conflict the poet sees in little "the giant agony of the world" and also the possibility, however dim, of its relief. His own experience shows him that it is somehow through this anguish that he attains inner harmony and artistic greatness; by some analogous process of suffering at once accepted and mastered must the race of man reach its perfection.

The Neoplatonists with the outstanding exception of Michelangelo show little comprehension of such an attitude. The postulate that suffering is the artist's necessary initiation into the higher regions of his art, and the only means by which any soul can arrive at true knowledge, awoke little response in them. They spoke often of the deaths and re-births through which the soul must pass, but though they might have felt the magic of a poem like *The Mistress of Vision* they would have shrunk from embracing the hard gospel of renunciation that Thompson preached. His ascetic strain had its root in his ardent catholicism, but the same identity between enlightenment and pain, the same sense that he who would find his life must lose it, dominates writers of an earlier generation who were not of the same faith.

> "None can usurp this height," replied the shade,
> "Save those to whom the miseries of the world
> Are miseries, and will not let them rest."
>
> Most wretched men. . . .
> Are cradled into poetry by wrong
> And learn in suffering what they teach in song.
>
> Knowledge by suffering entereth
> And life is perfected by death.

Belief in the value of suffering had yet as its corollary an intense compassion for those who suffer which brought into the Romantic conception of love an element rare among the Neoplatonists, though love is almost as central in the thought of the one group as it is in that of the other.

> All thoughts, all passions, all delights,
>   Whatever stirs this mortal frame
> These are but ministers of love
>   And feed his sacred flame;

but for the Romantics love is a redemptive power in a tormented world as much as the vital breath of a happy one. Their feeling for the dignity of man breaks into wrath and pity at the sight of human wrongs and degradations. The problem of evil has for them a terrible and universal poignancy, that intrudes between them and their dreams of ideal perfection. Questions of social justice pressed upon them, not as matters for academic discussion but as problems that could only be ignored by the sacrifice of precious truths.

> Quand on voile Lazare on efface Jésus.

Love alone can rescue man from whatever depths of abasement and reveal him anew as the image of God; and what is true of the individual soul is true also of society and of the whole creation. That thought underlies the often tangled philosophies of Blake and Victor Hugo, and lights up the last act of *Prometheus Unbound* with its vision of a world re-fashioned by the long patience of all-enduring love, so that the very stones rejoice and the deadliest fruits have ceased to yield poison. But such longing for "the general renewal of all things" is rare among the Neoplatonists, who generally either accepted the outer world with an optimism that scarcely desired to change it, or looked for a consummation of bliss wholly outside material conditions. At the same time the motive of ideal love appears in nineteenth-century literature in a form that would have seemed wholly familiar to Ficino or Michelangelo. The elusive quality in things that the Florentines had called the Idea of Beauty evokes in the Romantics a like passion of worship and a like anguish of desire. They pursue "the awful shadow of some unseen power," "the light that never was on land or sea," "the rainbow on life's weeping rain," as the Neoplatonists pursued their abstract "concetto di bellezza." For Wordsworth the pursuit is connected with the idea of pre-existence; our perceptions of the celestial light are "shadowy recollections" of an earlier and more blessed state. Other poets see the spiritual grace personified and invoke it as a conscious deity

> A la très chère, à la très belle
> Qui remplit mon cœur de clarté
> A l'ange, à l'idole immortelle
> Salut en immortalité.

Leopardi reproduces the very language of the Neoplatonists when he speaks of his imagined lady as the archetype that earthly beauties may resemble but never equal, and questions whether she may not be one of the "eterne idée."

Naturally poems that were addressed to a human beloved showed traces of the same mode of thought. The recognition of love as the highest activity of the spirit underlies the whole structure of Romantic literature and finds expression both in its highest achievements and in its worst sentimental excesses.

Love is considered as a mystical bond, manifest in time but having its origin and end in eternity. In *Evelyn Hope* the lovers are predestined for each other and inevitably bound to be united hereafter, although no word of love had passed between them in life. The idea of the lovers exchanging souls and living each in each inspires one of the most famous of the *Sonnets from the Portuguese* and a great part of *In Memoriam*, where the dead friend and the living still share one life. Side by side with this portrayal of a spiritual affection that sets time and separation and death itself at defiance, one finds the tendency, already marked in the Neoplatonists, of etherealizing the body till it partakes of the soul's beauty and cannot be thought of apart from it.

> I cannot tell what beauty is her dole
> Who cannot see her body for her soul
> As birds see not the casement for the sky.
>
> Thy soul I know not from thy body, nor
> Thee from myself, neither our love from God.

The whole Neoplatonic theory of love reappears in *Epipsychidion*, taking new life from the glow and bloom of Shelley's verse.

Indeed, the kinship of thought between the Neoplatonists and the Romantics that has here been lightly sketched was not accidental. Both were essentially seekers after liberty and fullness of life. The decline of mediaeval ideals in the one instance, and the "Age of common sense" in the other, had left a partial and narrow conception of human nature and a corresponding impoverishment of art and culture which the men of the new ages struggled to remove. In the revival and re-interpretation of Platonic and Neoplatonic doctrines they saw a creed that could at once inspire their endeavours and justify their claim that all experience, all knowledge, all life, were the rightful heritage of the human spirit, and that that spirit could by its own striving subdue the world to itself, and by love be made one with whatever ultimate good it can apprehend behind the shifting semblances that surround it.

APPENDIX

VERSE TRANSLATIONS TO CHAPTER V

Page 140. *Questo beato nel suo sancto sito* . . .
    This blessed One in His most holy place
    Was ever and is yet so liberal
    That unto others He accords His grace.
    So high is He above dominions all
    That all things He may benefit at will
    Without desire that evil should befall.

Page 140. *Intelligenza bisognò facesse* . . .
    Need was there He should make intelligence
    Immortal and with reason's light endued
    To whom the Eternal might Himself dispense.

Page 141. . . . *ad Dio non fur nemici* . . .
    . . . were not God's foes
    Nor yet fulfillers of the will divine
    But stood suspended between these and those.

Page 141. *Ad questo tutte per voler sapere* . . .
    God sends them here in number infinite
    That He may know whether those spirits want
    Or thickest darkness or the very light.
    So love in them doth liberty implant
    Concealed within their primal purity
    And unto each a body He doth grant
    And shows how low in sin it oft doth lie.

Page 142. *E se Paulo già vide "arcana Dei"* . . .
    And if in other ages Paul was shown
    "The hidden things of God," by grace it was
    Conceded to some end that so alone
    With holy doctrine he might bring to pass

> The Pharisees' defeat. Hell's spirits own
> No heavenly virtue, being false and base,
> But since to them secrets are oft displayed
> Great works they do by natural virtue's aid.
>
> And like to birds there wanders through the air
> Another order of malicious sprites
> Who neither faithful nor rebellious were;
> When the elect were numbered in the heights.
> I know not if't be fault in my Palmier
> Who seems from form to form to trace their flights
> Piercing the mind with pricks, when he would pass
> Euphorbius' soul into Pythagoras.
>
> And haply here the Tyanean errs
> Who says he lived once as a buccaneer
> And captured one yet viler, and avers
> That he entreated him with courteous cheer.

Page 143. *Sybilla "intendi" disse* . . .

> "Mark," said Sybilla, "how we come once more
> Unto the stream which doth the soul secure
> When it sets out on ways unknown before.
> Above this stream thou didst receive it pure,
> Clothed with such light that if it held it still
> It would possess the truths that aye endure.
> But how befalls it that it keeps so ill
> That truth which it in heaven did surely see
> E'er it oblivion drank of Lethe chill,
> Whose wave, once tasted, slays the memory
> Of truth once known, and makes it doubtful seem
> So that opinion reigns dividedly.
> This ignorance, like some bewildering dream
> It drinks, when, passing Lethe, it descends
> Not guessing how it sinks beyond that stream.
> In forest dark, a land unknown it wends,
> Alone, pursuing still a tortuous way
> And first, in wantonness it hellward tends.
> Then to return where its first dwelling lay
> Swiftly it takes the path which up this mount
> Leads to that bliss for which it yearns alway."

APPENDIX

Page 144. Eterno potere uno sempre e' solo . . .
Eternal power that dwells alone for aye
From whom alone and from whose word doth flow
Love ever burning in the heaven most high.
This to eternity engenders so
Life, by which all things live beneath the sun,
And ever lived all that we see or know.
This is an essence circumscribed of none,
That guides the world and in itself contains
All things, and from its bounds excludes not one.

Page 145. Et come e volle se e'creder pio . . .
Rightly we may believe that as He would
He framed space, time, and the creation's bound
In His desire without vicissitude
Which is begot in the abysm profound
Where the eternal power itself doth hide,
First pattern of whate'er on earth is found.
In which what through the world is scattered wide
Is verily, and thither must return
Wherever it may dwell or be described.

Page 145. Chi poi riceve l'adornato amore . . .
That being which receives the form of love
Infuses it in other creatures then,
Celestial witnesses your worth to prove.
Hence sparks of heavenly fire in you remain,
Given that nature to the sovereign good
May lead you, loosed from every error's chain

Page 145. Tutti gli spiriti in questi versi decti . . .
All souls that in these verses find a place
Of God's one city are the citizens
Created good, not all elect to grace.

Page 145. E volendo al suo centro pervenire . . .
And longing still its centre to draw nigh
Since it may not be one with Him, it well
Must seek its proper frame to unify.
This the great city is, wherein doth dwell
Whatever lives or feels or breathes or knows,

And what is praised on earth or damned in hell.
Infinite life around that structure flows,
Contains it all, and firm unites, and binds,
So that each part to each is drawn more close.

Page 146. *La vita sempre vixe nella mente* . . .
Life has forever lived within the mind
Which doth the universe in circle move.
True light it was, splendid and unconfined.
All good the Eternal raineth from above
Is in its essence charity divine
Since the Almighty Father lives by love.

Page 146. *Dota è la più solenne della mente* . . .
This is the loftiest gift the mind receives,
Given by grace to holy souls alone,
That more it sees than what the sense perceives.

Page 146. *Hor ombra di splendor* . . .
Now shadow of a splendour more than light.

Page 147. *Ad chi pensando, ad chi vien* . . .
Now He expected comes, now by surprise,
In weeds of pilgrim or of husbandman.
To one on earth, to one in paradise,
In mount or vale He shines, or desert's span
To some within the fane of conscience
Where He makes compact with the mind of man.

Page 157. *Sempre son questi ad dio tucti vicini* . . .
Ever are they to God Himself most near
Crowning the work Eternal Beauty wrought.
He chose and called them to His inmost sphere
Pure beauty with divine adornment fraught
Free from all tincture of external things. . . .

Page 147. *Tutto il visibil si contien nel mondo* . . .
The world doth all things visible display,
Nor were they, till through God they had their birth.
Lofty and deep He is, and so men say
That He who wrought a work of might and worth
Having beside Himself no archetype
In likeness of Himself did bring it forth.

APPENDIX

Page 148. *Et che ella vive già Platon non niegha* . . .
          Plato denies not that it lives indeed;
          All animals have life, and reason 'tis
          That what uniteth them of life has need.

Page 148. *Però qualunque voglia spirituale* . . .
          Therefore doth every spiritual will
          Come freely to the moment that divides
          The way of good from that which leads to ill.
          . . . To life doth the Eternal Father lead,
          Each as he lists pursues that other way,
          Closing his eyes to light that shines indeed.

Page 149. *Et quanto del piacer più s'abbandona* . . .
          And in so much as pleasures it forsakes
          So much the smoother seems its upward way;
          So much the less temptation overtakes.
          Often distractions in its path will stray
          In such wise that it may not scatheless go
          In love divine not wholly rapt away,
          Hence it befalls that oft it stumbles, so
          That hard the journey seems, and heaviness
          It is to leave desires unstayed; and though
          It be the good alone that nourishes
          The soul, the sense dissatisfied rebels
          And must be conquered for such faithlessness.
          More fair it grows when that revolt it quells
          Still upward on this mountain journeying
          Swifter as virtue to ascend impels.

Page 149. *Verso la terra più non volge voglia* . . .
          No more to earth it turns with longing then
          But that forgets, as on its downward flight
          It did that truth which must in heaven be ta'en.

Page 150. *Le buone cose fur da dio create* . . .
          All things of good report did God create
          To guide our souls to heaven and win them rest.
          All have their dwelling place beyond this gate
          And they are essences entirely blest
          Withdrawn from every contrary quality.
          Here present, yonder wholly manifest.

Page 150. *L'anime più fedeli e più devote* . . .
    Such souls as are most faithful and devout
    Can have no greater prize of happiness
    Then to have every passion winnowed out;
    And when this grace the soul may not possess
    Her fault it is in looking not to heaven
    For only thus she falls to sinfulness.

Page 150. *Quella ragion intendo che s'eterna* . . .
    Reason I mean which wins immortal worth.
    He, by whose will all that is seen or known
    Was made, with the first creature brought it forth.
    This reason with that all-directing one
    Make up in man the portion that excels
    Each other creature formed beneath the sun,
    And gives him sovereignty o'er all things else,
    Links him to God, and makes him worthy heaven. . . .

    And earnest of more honour yet is given
    By making man possessor of that good;
    In human stuff is placed celestial leaven
    Which comes to man out of the plenitude
    Of wisdom which for aye in God abides
    So that the twain are by one law subdued
    In such wise as omnipotence decides,
    And first in earth and heaven that law commands;
    Man, lest he sin, by this his conduct guides.
    Meetly one reason from that source expands,
    Through earth and heaven, and clasps the universe
    So that the whole is bound within its bands,
    From thence proceeds the law that's pure and terse
    In the first pattern, for in God it dwells
    And does to earth and man itself disperse.

Page 151. *Facta scienza delle cose umane* . . .
    Then, having knowledge gained of mortal things
    Despising them as vile it spurns them hence.

Page 151. *Già muor vivendo* . . .
    It dies yet living, and seeks otherwhere
    To live unchained and of itself content;
    And almost loosed out of the body's snare,
    Joys in itself, all other longings spent.

Page 152. *Nulla miseria humana* . . .
  No human frailty can dispose it more
  To do such things as are not loved in heaven.

Page 152. *Solo alla mente questo lume è dato* . . .
  Such light was given only to that mind
  Which with our soul descended from on high
  That there it might return with that combined
  And as the soul brought from divinity
  That mind, which is itself the life divine,
  By it alone it learned this course to try.

Page 152. *Eterna facta immobile e sicura* . . .
  Eternal made, and moveless and secure
  By this alone all virtues are received
  Such as in heaven they show unstained and pure. . . .
  The mind in heaven this justice doth behold
  In the excelling creatures manifest.

Page 153. *Et quando più nel sommo ben* . . .
  And when I most the highest contemplate
  So much the more my powers and genius fail
  The glories of that temple to relate
  There shone a light that reached creation's pale
  Diffused in all, so that all spirits are
  Illumined, each as its deserts avail.

Page 153. *Guardai in alto* . . .
  I looked aloft and far away descried
  Oh Architect of the Idea Divine!
  The light that mortal eyes may not abide.
  I saw a fair and glorious temple shine
  So that the more I gazed the stronger grew
  The will to gaze and make that vision mine.
  An ample sphere that showed not to the view
  Of what its substance or its life might be
  Whose ray did penetrate my vision through,
  Was in ten heavens divided verily;
  An axis through its centre passed; and two
  Poles linked and held either extremity.

Page 154. . . . *ogni seme congesto* . . .
  . . . every seed combined
  And every form that was or is to be

By the Creator shaped, is harboured here
And the sun's rays bring them maturity.

Page 154. *Quel motor infinito, eterno e pio* . . .
That mover deathless, holy, infinite
Depicts Himself in all created good;
God's shadow, and no other thing is it.

Page 154. *Giove mi par che in quel sua imago infundi* . . .
Methinks that Jove his image doth infuse
In this, which pure and all unmingled is,
Fertile of light and heat for others' use
It in itself nor shines nor burns; in this
There is no change, but ever in one way
Its pure form lives to all eternities.
This of our life is the unchanging stay
And such its vigour and its active might
That many natures dwell within its sway.
Light blends with it, though it contains no light
It girdles all, but is embraced of none
That is in any mortal vesture dight.

* * *

This is the veil and this the burning wall
Which doth all things below so bind and guide
That rightly to itself 'twould win them all.

* * *

This is the utmost and the nearest sphere
Which life and sense and spirit doth impart
To such as like Anteus are brought near
To earth. Here is the maker by whose art
And hand is pictured what is written clear
In the first heaven whence every work doth start.

Page 155. *Hor se la tua Lyra* . . .
Orpheus, had I thy lyre I now would sing
How elements and earth were by the Lord
Created, as a fixed and boundless thing.
Number and form and measure He conferred
On so fair temple that three persons seems
The wondrous and profound celestial Word.

APPENDIX

Page 155. *Vidi in ciascun suo cerchio* . . .
    In every cirque I saw a wingéd throng
    Of various souls. Here demi-gods appeared,
    There angels; yonder souls of heroes strong.
    Demons beheld I too, and therefore feared
    Their aspects, such a diverse host were they
    Part righteous-seeming, part with evil seared.
    One bringeth light to men, one takes away
    Light, and another kindles it within
    Pure bosoms where heroic minds hold sway.

Page 155. *L'intelligibil ciel sono e'miei throni* . . .
    The intellectual heavens are my throne;
    And all the spheres thou seest are the lyre
    From which the angels, moving, strike a tone.
    This world of sense, although it be a mire
    Of darkness, is my footstool, where I place
    My imprint to awaken man's desire.
    One like the other is; and both in grace
    Resemble what in thee I mark and write
    That thou my colours with thy brush may'st trace.

Page 156. *L'idea universal si trahe di pecto* . . .
    The universal mind sends forth a ray
    From its own breast that strikes and makes ascent
    And clasps the universe and is its stay.
    Within itself it holds all pleasures blent
    By heaven's gift; to this has Sovereign Jove
    And every other god his lustre lent.

Page 156. *Ben eran septe cieli* . . .
    Seven were these spheres indeed; but they were clear
    In such wise that each yielded to the sight
    Wherefore might none define their atmosphere.
    But striking grosser things their rays of light,
    Descending and returning to their fount,
    Of what they yonder see do here indite.

Page 156. *Nulla ociosa è quivi et nulla dorme* . . .
    Nothing is idle here and nothing sleeps
    But each is active and of mystery free
    No heavenly thing so clear God's likeness keeps.

* * *

Hence comes thy happy fortune, hence thy pain,
Hence the celestial fate to us descends;
This does thy life and this thy death ordain,
Among so many orbs heaven comprehends
None but for each man born some fate designs
And all earth shines where heaven's span extends.
Here are bright rays and lights, here each thing shines.
One more, one less; so every several star
A diverse kind of artifact combines.

Page 157. *Ne senza te ad te* . . .
Nor without thee to thee can any come
Thou art of thy own grace both end and way.

The heavens have power to move the acts of men
And mark their very imprint in your breast
So that they seem your spirits to constrain
Yet not by this are your free minds opprest
Which in their mortal precincts freely reign
In nowise subject to that power's behest.
For when the inward eye is whole and sane
It doth command the sense and overcome
The force the heavens pour on you in vain.

Page 157. *Cosi l'amante* . . .
So lives the lover in the loved one now,
Transforms himself to him, and is made one,
As love's clear seal declares upon his brow . . .

A joyful death which joins two lives in one
A joyful life which in that being fair
Wakes love and gives content's oblivion.

Page 158. *Salve dunque, sacrata e vera dea* . . .
Hail to thee therefore, goddess blest and true
Through whom all is that is; who quickened all
The lives thou dost in thy Idea renew.

Page 158. *Ciò che mai il cielo dal sacro seno scorse* . . .
Whatever heaven from its sacred breast
Of living light flung to the womb of earth
In this or that Idea is manifest.
As in a golden cloud are bodied forth
Infinite gems, each one of which doth hide

Immortal forms, within awaiting birth.
Hardly on earth are they to be described
And in a mortal vesture they enfold
Forms that in heaven are bare, to heaven allied.
I think there are not stars so manifold
As these ideas; and all are joined in one
Fairer than heaven, which heaven's height doth hold.
What here is nourished by moon or sun
After the forms celestial is designed
They from the fount where all has unison
There dwelleth all that is, for every mind
And every soul and life and truth is there
Harboured, and nothing out of it we find.
And if a free and lofty flight thou dare
Well shalt thou see that thou without Him art
And wast a dream, a shade, a cipher bare,
Save in so far as His designs impart
A form to thee, for He the pattern traced
Which, though the heavens revolve, shall ne'er depart.

* * *

Upon its ample vesture is enwrought
The image of the form divine, whereby
To rude and barren matter form is brought.

Page 159. *Questo è lo specchio* . . .
This is the glass and trump that calls the mind
To seek within herself thy loveliness,
And gazing on Thy shade is she enclined
Dying, Thee, life eternal, to possess.

Page 159. *Quivi una voce d'echo* . . .
To men on earth there comes an echoing voice
From out this place; but truly here in heaven
The muses' song makes every mind rejoice.

Page 160. *At divina cohors* . . .
Then the cohort divine and all the armies of heaven,
Some singing hymns of praise and some lightly wreathing their dances,
Bowing the while and circling, and chanting in marvellous order
Ever with sonorous voice singing the praise of the Lord.

Page 160. ... *vanos vitae mortalis honores* ...
　　... despise the empty honour of mortal
　　Life, and to follow virtue through labours unnumbered.

Page 160. *Quattuor in partes* ...
　　Here is the year no longer in fourfold seasons divided,
　　Here is eternal Spring; for no clouds darken the aether,
　　No rain moistens the skies, the fleet-foot hares, and the fallow
　　Deer and the timid sparrows in flowery meadows delighting
　　Forsake their fears.

Page 161. *Scire cupis superum* ...
　　Seek'st thou the essence to know of the monarch of regions supernal
　　God is Being that is without or end or beginning,
　　Simple, omnipotent He, unmoving though all things He moveth,
　　And such His countenance as no mortal man may behold.
　　He who by the word of His power made all things, by none is contained
　　And there was nothing created that God Himself did not frame.

Page 161. *Illic sublimes animas* ...
　　There certainly exalted souls abide
　　Whom nor dark day nor obscure night of ill
　　Constrained to sink to the foul bounds of Hell.
　　The Almighty Father by the mind divine
　　This creature with His glory hath adorned.

Page 162. *Simplex esse Deus* ...
　　Simple is God nor known to any man
　　In the excelling pureness of His mind
　　Where the beginning with the end subsists.
　　Into one whole He joins dispersèd things
　　And first established how created forms
　　Should come to birth; wherefore we say "Behold
　　Him who made earth and heaven and all that is . . ."
　　Nor canst thou any place ascribe to Him.
　　Nature is filled with Him, yet doth it not
　　Portray Him, who encircles heaven and earth
　　And the deep seas, and widely compasses
　　The world, but is in no place circumscribed.

APPENDIX

Page 162. . . . post corpora prima . . .
    . . . from the first bodies
    Thus ever into other forms they pass
    And are from these anew brought forth to life
    Till the long day with ripeness closes all.

Page 165. Marsilio questa tua filosofia . . .
    Marsilio, this philosophy of thine
    Is never heard upon the lips of men
    To whom at nones thou dost thy wares consign
    But forth it comes in foolishness again.
    What say'st? Who dost translate?
    —Plato—A plague on him and thee likewise
    Oh thou blasphemest to philosophise!
    Out on thee, out! For such a pack of lies
    Thou toldest at Careggi t'other day
    That, till thou'st read some more, hast nought to say.

Page 165. Bestia fuggita qua dalle maremme . . .
    Beast hither fled from the maremman plain
    Art not ashamed, vile traitor, at thy years
    Usurpéd gems and honour to obtain
    Filched from a sun that lights our human spheres?
        Haste to unstop thine ears
    For surely thou art the cicada's god.

Page 165. Costor che fan si gran disputazione . . .
    These folk who make so great an argument
    Of how the soul gets in and how it flies
    Or how within the peach the kernel lies
    Their studies on an empty husk have spent.
    Plato and Aristotle they present
    And hold that it reclines in peaceful-wise
    'Midst song and dance; and caper in such guise
    As fills one's brain with sheer bewilderment.
    The soul is like a pine seed in hot bread
    Or a pork collop in a cut loaf rolled.
    Who thinks not so has maggots in his head,
    And those who pledge for one an hundredfold
    Will pay us off with counterfeit instead.
        One lately to me said

Who's been in the next world and can't get back
That who would go should be a steeplejack.
They think they'll never lack
Fig-peckers and dressed ortolans to show
And nice sweet wine, and beds made up just so
And with the monks they go.
We'll off to Val di Buja you and I
Pandolf, nor hear them Hallelujah cry.

Page 169. *E non sarebbe* . . .

And Judas self would have escaped damnation'
Repenting, but he suffered hope to fail
Without which never man might see salvation;
Nor doth the word of Origen avail
To clear him nor the school of thought which says
That Judas shall be savéd in those days.

Page 169. *E poeti e filosofi e morali* . . .

Poets, philosophers and moralists
Know not indeed the things I tell you now,
But the presumptuousness of men insists
On knowing where the orders stand and how.
I was a seraph, foremost in their lists
But Gregory and Dionyse avow
Things that I never knew, for each doth err
Who would on earth be heaven's interpreter.

Page 170. . . . *non vengon costretti* . . .

. . . they are not bound
In water or in glass, but dwell in air
Showing deceit and falsehood everywhere.

In company they journey boasting then
That they have made what is not seem to be;
Some take delight in making fools of men,
Some find their pleasure in philosophy,
Some bring hid treasures to the light again,
Some tell false visions of futurity,
And thus to you a courteous tale I tell
For courtesy is present even in Hell.

Page 171. *Dicea Malagigi* . . .
    "Yet you have told me," Malagigi said,
    "One point which has perplexed me mightily
    That knowledge with the Son is limited;
    I cannot well discern how this may be."
    Said Astarotte: "You have wrongly read
    Your Bible and seem ignorant to me;
    For, questioned of that final day the Son
    Said that the Father knew of it alone.

    "Mark, Malagigi, while I offer you
    The definition that I now express,
    Then to your theologians turn anew.
    Three persons in one essence you confess
    Or in one substance, and even so we do
    And one Act, pure, of variableness
    For such in nature, of necessity
    The Being that ye all adore must be.

    "One mover of all movers great or small,
    One order, by which every order grows,
    One cause which is anterior to all,
    One power from which each other power arose,
    One source that is of sources principal,
    One fire by which each living splendour glows,
    One wisdom, giver of all wisdom's laws,
    One good of every other good the cause."

Page 171. *Sappi ch'ognun per la croce è salvato* . . .
    Know that all men are by the cross redeemed
    And haply after longest error all
    Shall with a single heart adore the truth
    And every soul find clemency and ruth.

    Suffice it that your faith alone is sure
    And the Blest Maid in heaven glorified,
    And that the gate shuts not while times endure
    But till the final day stands open wide
    And he who worships with a heart that's pure
    Shall find his sacrifice is sanctified.
    For ever dear to heaven is reverence
    With fear and worship and obedience.

And while the Romans kept with reverence due
To their devotions and their pious rites,
Though Mars and Jupiter and Juno drew
Their praise, and idols vain were their delights,
Such piety was good in heaven's view
Since man from beasts of earth it disunites;
So that they were exalted in their day
Of faith, and for neglect were cast away.

And even so, I say, those people trust
That worshipping the stars they worship well.
You know that justice grants unto the just
Reward and to the wicked sentence fell.
So none should think to be from mercy thrust
Who in observance of His laws doth dwell.
The mind it is that saves or damns each one
Who's not by too great ignorance undone.

Page 173. *Nota ch'egli è certo* . . .

Mark that he lives in ignorance obtuse,
Idle and crass, slothful and opposite
Who, deigning not his vision's power to use
Received in vain the gifts of soul and sight
And so for this can heaven find no excuse.
"He would not understand" the Psalmist cries
Of such a spirit headstrong and untaught
Who would not learn how virtue might be wrought.

Page 173. *Dimmi, rispose Malagigi, ancora* . . .

Then Malagigi answered, "Tell me more
Since you appear to me an angel wise
If that first mover whom we all adore
Knew in His secret thought your villainies
And saw their time and season long before;
Unjustly then it seems His sentence lies,
And ineffectual seems His charity
In damning you at your nativity."

But Astarotte, devilish in wrath
Exclaimed, "He held not Michael's self more dear
Than Lucifer, that righteous Sabaoth,
Nor Cain created less than Abel's peer;

APPENDIX

And if the one more pride than Nimrod hath
All unlike Gabriel the other's sneer;
He nor repents nor doth 'Hosanna' sing
Free will to each doth condemnation bring."

Page 174. *Altro certo offerir non ti possa ora* . . .
    The soul to Him that made it must belong,
    All else, as well you know, is bound to die;
    No more can I this diatribe prolong.
    Oh sovereign love, oh unknown courtesy!
    (That this is taken out of Petrarch's song
    You'll see folk still believe, and who knows why
    When so long since 'twas by Rinaldo said.
    But he's called thief who never stole a shred.)

BIBLIOGRAPHY OF CHIEF WORKS USED

AGLIO, P. [or Agli]. Poems. Magl., VII, 1025-31; Laur., LIV, 10, c. 97^r; Laur., LXV, 52, 16^t-21^t.

ALBERTI, L. B. Opera. Ed. M. Sessi. Venezia, 1534.
Opuscoli morali. Trans. C. Bartoli. Venezia, Franceschi, 1568.
Opere volgari. Ed. A. Bonucci. Florence, 1843-49, 5 vols.
Opera inedita et pauca separatim impressa. Ed. Mancini. Florence, Sansoni, 1890.
For La Hecatomfila and Deifira, see also Daelli. Bibliotheca rara. Vol. VI, Milan, 1863.

AMICO-MANTIA, A. L'amore et le rime de Michelangiolo. Messina, 1899.

ANGELI, D. Per un quadro eretico. Arch. St. dell'Arte, 1896.

APPEL, E. Leone Medicos lhere von Weltall uihr Verhaltniss zu greich u. zeit genössichen Aschauungen in Archiv. für Gesch. der phil., XX, 1907, pp. 287-403, 456-96.

ARAGONA, TULLIA D'. Infinità d'amore. [Venice, 1547] in Zonta, Trattati d'amore del Cinquecento and Daelli. Bibliotheca rara, Vol. XXIX, Milan, 1864.
Rime. Ed. Celani. Bologna, 1891.

ARENTINO, L. Dialogum ad P.P. Histrum. Ed. T. Klette. Griefswald, 1889.
Epistolarum libri VIII, ad fidem codd. MSS. suppleti et castigati et plusquam XXXVI epistolis quae in Editione quoque Fabriciana deerant locupletati, Rencensente Laurentianus Mehius. B. Paperini, Florence, 1741, 2 vols.
De studiis et literis. In Farrago aliquot Epigrammatum. Bâle, 1533 [ed. used in Trinity College, Dublin, without date].

ARGYROPOULOS, J. De Processione Spiritu Sancti, Typis factae Congregationis propagandae fidei. [In Graeciae Orthodoxiae, Tom. I, p. 400, ed. and trans. by Leo Allatius, Rome, 1652.]

BANDINI, A. M. Specimen Literaturae Florentinae saec., XV. Florence, 1751, 2 vols.

BARBA, P. DELLA. Sposizione d'un sonetto platonico fatto sopra il primo effetto d'amore. 1549 [ed. used. Florence, 1554.]

BARBA, P. DELLA, and BUONAGRAZIA, A. Translation of Heptaplus. Pescia, 1555.

BARGAGLI, SCIPIONE. Trattenimenti. Venice, 1587.

BARZELOTTI, G. Italia Mistica a Italia Pagana. N.A., Vols. XXXIII, XXXIV, III S., 1891.
BEMBO, PIETRO. Asolani. 1st ed., Venice, Aldus, 1505. In Ed. Prin. Opera, Venice, Hertzhauser, 1788. Ed. Sonzogno. Milan, 1880.
BENCI, T. Pimandro di M. Trismegisto. Florence, 1548, in 8vo.
BENETTI BRUNELLI, V. Leon Battista Alberti ed il rinnovamento pedagogico del' 400. Florence, 1925.
Le origione italiane della scuola umanistica. Rome, Milan, 1919.
BENIVIENI, G.
Canzone dell'amor divino, with commentary in 3 books by Pico in Pici Opera. Basle, 1572.
Canzoniere dell'amor divino, with author's commentary. Florence, 1500. [Opere, Giunti. Florence, 1519; Opere, Zoppino. Venice, 1522; Opere, De Gregori. Venice, 1524.]
A Platonick Discourse upon Love, written in Italian by John Picus Mirandula in Explication of a Sonnet by Hieronymo Benivieni. In Poems by T. Stanley, London, 1651. Reprinted with introduction by Edm. Gardner in The Humanist's Library, Merrymount Press, Boston, U.S.A., 1914.
Poem in praise of Dante, printed in ed. of D., pub. by Phil. Giunta, 1506.
BERENSON, B. The Drawings of the Florentine Painters. London, 1903.
The Florentine Painters of the Renaissance. London, 1896.
BERLINGHIERI, F. DI M. Poems. Magl., N. 20.
BESSARION, CARDINAL. In Calumniatorem Platonis. Venice, 1516.
Works—Migne, Patrologie Grecque, Vol. CLXI.
BETUSSI, G. Dialogo amoroso. Venice, 1543.
Il. Raverta [ed. G. Giolito. Venice, 1562.] In Zonta, Trattati d'amore del Cinquecento. Bari, 1912.
Leonora ragionamento supra la vera bellezza. Lucca, 1557. In Zonta, Tratti del Cinquecento sulla donna. Bari, 1913.
BEYER, H. W. Die Religion Michelangelos. Bonn, 1926.
BIAGI, G. Un'etera romana. T. d'Arragona. N.A., 1886, pp. 655–711.
BISTICCI, VESPASIANO DA. Vite di uomini illustri. Ed. L. Frati. Bologna, 1893, 3 vols.
BONGI, S. Annali di Gabriel Giolito de Ferrari, Vol. I, Lucca, 1895.
BOTTARI, E. Su Sperone Speroni. Cesena, 1875.
Matteo Palmieri. Lucca, Giusti, 1885.
B. Castiglione e il suo libro del Cortigiano. Pisa, 1874.

BOTTICELLI.
    I. Dani. B. e sua scuola. Florence, 1920.
    C. Diehl. Botticelli. Paris, 1906.
    E. Gebhardt. B. et son Epoque. Paris, 1907.
    Conte Gamba. Botticelli. Theime Becker Kunstler Lexicon.
    H. Horne. Sandro Botticelli. 1908.
    A. L. Frothingham. The True Meaning of the Pallas of B. American Journal of Archaeology, No. 4, 1908.
    G. Poggi. La Giostra Medicea e la Pallade. A proposito della Pallade. L'Arte, 1902.
    Laurence Binyon. The Art of Botticelli. London, 1913.
    Julia Cartwright. Sandro Botticelli. London, 1897.
    W. Pater. The Renaissance. London, 1873.
    A Venturi. B. and Dante. Lemonnier, Florence, 1922.
    A. Venturi. Botticelli. English trans., London, 1927.
    Yukio Yashiro. Sandro Botticelli. Medici Society, London, 1925, 3 vols.
    Jacobsen. Allegoria della Primavera di S.B. Arch. St. dell'Arte, 1892.
    B. Marrai. La Nascita di Venere e la Primavera. Arte e Storia, 1908.
    A. Venturi. La Primavera nelle Arti rappresentative. N.A., 1892.
    A. Warburg. S.B.'s Geburt der Venus und Frühling. 1893.
    J. Mesnil. B. les Pollajuoli et Verrocchio. Rivista d'Arte, III, 1905.
    J. P. Richter. Lectures on the N.G. London, 1898.
    A. Venturi. Per S.B. L'Arte, July–August, 1924.

BOTTIGLIONI. La lirica latina in Firenze nella 2ª metà del sec. XV.
    Annali della R. Scuola normale superiore di Pisa. XXV, pp. 9 et seq., 1913.

BOUTROUX, P. Problemi d'educazione e di morale. Florence, 1924.

BRACCESI, ALESSANDRO. Works.
    Liber amorum. MS. Laur., Cod. 40 and Cod. 41. Plut., VXI.

BUONINCONTRI, L. DI G. Astronomicon. Rome, 1484.
    De Rebus Caelestibus. Venice, 1526. [B.M. 11403 b 28.]
    [Rerum Naturalium. Urb. Lat. 703.]

BURCKHARDT, J. The History of the Civilization of the Italian Renaissance. London, 1929 (new English edition).

CARLINI, A. Del sistema filosofico Dantesco nella D.C. Bologna, 1902.

CARO, A. Opere. Milan, 1807, 8 vols.

CARTWRIGHT, J. A Heretical Picture. Magazine of Art. London, 1883.

CATTANI DI DIACETO, F. Works.
  Opera. Basle, 1564.
  Panegirico dell'Amore. Rome, 1526, in 4to.
  I tre libri d'amore di messer Fr. C. da Diaceto Filosofo et Gentil'Huomo Fiorentino, con un Panegirico dell'Amore et con la vita del detto Autore fatta da M. Benedetto Varchi. Venice, G. Giolito de'Ferrari, 1561.
CAPPONI, GINO. St. della republica di Firenze, Lib. V, Cap. 7.
CAVASSICCIO, B. Rime. Ed. V. Cian. Bologna, 1893.
CITTADINI, C. Rime Platoniche. 1585.
CENTORIE, A. L'Aura soave. Venice, 1551.
CESAREO, G. A. Gaspara Stampa, donna e poetessa. Naples, 1920.
CICOGNARA. Storia della Scultura, Vol. IV. Prato, 1823.
COLONNA, V. Sonetti publicati in occasione di nozze. (See Arch. St. It., N.S., Tom. XVI, Pt. II, p. 149.)
CONTI, A. Storia della Filosofia. Florence, 1864, Vol. II.
  Review of Pucinotti. Arch. St. It., Tom. II, Pt. II, p. 172. 1865.
CRANE, F. Italian Social Customs in the Sixteenth Century. Yale University Press, 1920.
CROCE, B. Estetica come scienza dell'espressione e linguistica generale. Milan, 1902.
DATI, L. Life of Matteo Palmieri. Cod. Laur., XL, 53.
DILTHEY, G. L'analisi dell'uomo e l'intuizione della natura dal rinascimento al sec. XVIII. 2 vols. Venice, 1926.
DOMENICHI, L. Dialoghi. Venice, G. Giolito de' Ferrari, 1562, 12mo.
  La Donna di Corte. Discorso di L. D. nel quale si ragiona dell'affabilità ed honesta creanza da doversi usare per Gentildonna d'Honore. In Lucca per il Busdrago, 1564, 4to, ff. 23.
DOMINICI, G. Lucula noctis. Ed. Coulon. Paris, 1908.
  Regola del governo famigliare. Ed. Salvi. Florence, 1860.
DONI, A. F. Disegno partito in più ragionamenti. Venezia, 1549.
DRESS, WALTER. Die mystik des Marsilio Ficino. Berlin, Gruyter, 1929.
EBREO, L.
  Dialoghi di Amore. c. 1502. 1st ed. Rome, 1535.
EMERTON, E. Humanism and Tyranny. [De Tyranno, p. 25 et seq.] Cambridge [Mass.], Harvard U.P., 1925.

EQUICOLA, MARIO. Works.
    Libro di natura d'amore. Venice, 1525. Ed. Giolito, Venice, 1554, Venice, 1563.
    Lives and Studies of.
        Flamini. Il Cinquecento, pp. 337–79. Milan.
        G. Bertoni. Nota su M.E. bibliofilo e cortigiano. G.S., LXVI, pp. 281–3.
        D. Santoro. Appunti su M.E. G.S., Vol. XV, pp. 402–13.
        R. Renier. Per la cronologia e la composizione del libro di natura di Amore di M.E. G.S., XIV, pp. 212–33. 1889.
FANO, A. S. Speroni. Saggio sulla vita e le opere. Padua, 1909.
FATTORI, E. Michelangelo e Dante. Firenze, 1875.
FERRI, L. Il cardinale N. da Cusa e la Filosofia della Religione. N.A., XX, 100. May 1872.
    Leonardo da V. scienziato e filosofo. N.A., XXII, 294, February 1873.
    L. da V. e l'idea del mondo nella Rinascenza. N.A., XXIII, 530, July 1873.
    L'Ac. Pl. di Firenze and le sue vicende. N.A., III, Vol. 34, 1891, pp. 226–44.
    M.F. e le cause della Rinascenza del Platonismo nel'400. Fil. DiSc. It. Roma, 1883.
FICINO, MARSILIO. Opera Omnia. Basle, 1573.
    Letters. Trans. Figliucci. Venice, 1564.
    Convivium. Trans. by C. Bartoli. Florence, 1544.
    Lives and Studies of.
        G. Saitta. La Filosofia di M.F. Messina, 1923.
        G. Saitta. L'educazione dell'umanesimo, Ch. XIV, p. 235. Venice, 1928.
        F. Gabotto. L'Epicureismo di M.F. Riv. di Filosofia Scientifica, 1891, Vol. X, 428.
        F. Pucinotti. Di M.F. e della Ac. Plat. nel sec. XV. Giachetti, Prato, 1865.
        A. Conti. Review of above. Arch. St. It., Tom. II, Pt. II, p. 172. 1865.
        F. Pucinotti. Della Filosofia di M.F., N.A., Vol. V, June 1867, p. 211.
        Walter Dress. Die mystik des M.F. Berlin, Gruyter, 1929.
        G. Capponi. St. della Rep. di Firenze. Barbera, 1875, Lib. V, Cap. 7.
        Life by G. Corsi, 1506. Prefaced to Vol. I of Opera. Basle, 1573.
        Ed. A. M. Bandini. Pisa Apud Augustinum Pizzorno, 1771.

FICINO, MARSILIO—(cont.)
L. Galeotti. Saggio intorno alla vita ed agli scritti di M.F. Arch St. It., N.S. 1859, Vol. IX, Pt. II, p. 29; Vol. X, Pt. I, p. 1.
L. Ferri. Di M.F. e delle cause della Rinascenza del Platonismo nel' 400. Fil. delle Scuole It., Vol. XXVIII, Rome, 1883.
L. Ferri. Ul. Platonismo di M.F. Fil. Sc. It., Vol. XXIX, p. 237. 1884.
E. Galli. La morale nelle lettere di M.F. Pavia, 1897.
E. Galli. Lo stato, la famiglia e l'educazione secondo le teorie di M.F. Pavia, 1899.
FILELFO, F. Epistolae. Basle, 1495.
Orationes cum aliis opusculis. Venice, 1496.
De morali disciplina. Venice, 1552.
FIORENTINO, F. I. Risorgimento Filosofico del'400. Naples, 1888.
Studi e ritratti della Rinascenza. Bari, 1911.
FIRENZUOLA. Della bellezza delle donne. Op. Milan, 1802, Vol. I.
FLAMINI, F. La lirica toscana del Rinascimento. Atti della R. Scuola normale di Pisa, 1891.
Il Cinquecento. Milan, Vallardi, 1879.
P. Aglio confilosofo di Marsilio Ficino. Pisa, 1893.
Gli imitatori di Dante. [In Studi di storia letteraria italiana e straniera.] Livorno Giusti, 1895.
Tansillo. Pisa, 1888.
FLAMINIO NOBILE. Trattato dell'Amore Humano. Lucca, 1567. Ed. Bologna. Pellegrino Bonardo, 1580. [Il Trattato dell'A.H. di F.N. con le postille autografe di T. Tasso pubblicato da Pier Desiderio Pasolini in occasione del Terzo Centenario della morte del poeta. Rome, 1895.]
FOLIGNO, C. Giornale Storico, 1926, Vol. LXXXVII, pp. 1 et seqq. Un Poema d'Imitazione Dantesca sul Savonarola.
FORNARI, V. Il convito di Dante. [In Dante e il suo secolo. Florence, 1865.]
FRANCO, N. Il Petrarchista. Vinegia, 1541.
Dialogo delle Bellezze. 1542. Eds. Casale di Monferrato in 4to, Venice in 8vo.
FRANCO, VERONICA. Terze Rime. Carabba, Lanciano, 1912.
GABOTTO, F. L. Valla e l'Epicureismo nel'400. Riv. di Fil. Scientifica, 1889.
L'Epicureismo di M. Ficino. Riv. di Fil. Scientifica, 1889, Vol. VIII.
GALLI, E. Lo stato, la famiglia l'educazione secondo le teorie di M.F. Pavia, 1899.
La morale nelle lettere di M. Ficino. Pavia, 1897.
GAMBARA, V. Rime e lettere. Brescia, 1759.

GARDNER, E. Dante and the Mystics. London, 1913.
GARSIA, A. Il magnifico e la Rinascita. Florence, 1923.
GEBHARDT, E. Les origines de la Renaissance en Italie. Paris, 1879.
GEIGER, L. Rinascimento ed Umanesimo. (It. trans. D. Valbusa, revised by G. Zippel. Florence, 1899–1901, 2 vols.)
GELLI, G. B. Capricci del Bottaio. 1549.
GENTILE, G. La Filosofia. [Storia dei Generi Letterarii. Milan, in course of publication.]
Problemi della Scholastica. Laterza, Bari, 1923.
G. Bruno ed il concetto dell'uomo nel Rinascimento. Florence, 1920.
Studii nel Rinascimento. Florence, 1925.
GERINI, G. B. Gli scrittori pedagogici italiani del secolo 15°. Turin, 1898.
GILSON, E. La Philosophie au moyen âge. Paris, 1925.
Giornale Storico della letteratura italiana. Passim (G.S.).
GOTTIFREDI, B. Specchio d'Amore. Florence, 1547.
GRAF, A. Attraverso il' 500. Turin, 1888.
GRUYER, G. Les illustrations des écrits de J. Savonarole publiés en Italie au XV et au XVI siècles et les paroles de S. sur l'art. Paris, 1879.
GUARINO, B. De Ordine Docendi e Studendi. [In Woodward, Vittorino da Feltre, p. 159.]
HALDANE, R. B. The Philosophy of Humanism. London, 1922.
HARRISON, JOHN SMITH. Platonism in English Poetry of XVIth and XVIIth Cents. Columbia U.P., New York, 1903.
HETTNER, HERMANN. Italienische Studien. Braunschweig, 1879.
HOFFDING, H. History of Mod. Philosophy, Vol. I, Bk I. English trans. London, 1900.
Jewish Encyclopedia, Vol. VII, 1904. Leo Hebrauus, p. 683.
LANDINO, C. Commentary on Dante, 1480. 1st ed. Florence. Niccolò di Lorenzo della magna. August 1481.
Commentary on Dante. Pietro Cremonense detto Verone. Venice, 1491.
Dante con le esposizioni di Cristoforo Landino e d'Alessandro Vellutello, sopra la sua Commedia dell'Inf. del Purg. e del Par. Con tavole Argomenti e allegorie e riformato riveduto e ridotto alla sua vera lettura da Francesco Sansovino, fiorentino. In Ven. Appresso Giovanbatt. Marchio Sessa e fratelli, 1578.
Quaestiones Camaldulenses (also Disputationes). About 1470. 4 books.—I, De Vita activa et contemplativa. II, De summo bono. III and IV in Publij Virgili Maronis Allegorias. Ed. Mathias Schürerius, 1508.

LANDO, O. Confutazione del libro de'Paradossi nuovamente composta et in tre orationi distincta. (No date or place.) Paradossi. Lyon, 1543.
LAURIE, S. S. Studies in the history of educational opinion from the Renaissance. Cambridge, 1903.
LAZZARI, A. Ugolino e Michele Verino. Imola, 1895.
LEE, SIR SIDNEY. Shakespeare and the Italian Renaissance. Annual Shakespeare Readings of British Academy, 1905.
LEONARDO DA VINCI.
The Literary works of Leonardo. Ed. J. P. Richter. London, 1882.
E. Solmi. La mente di Leonardo.
E. Solmi. Le fonti di Leonardo. G.S., Sup. 10-11, 1908.
E. Solmi. Studi sulla fil. naturale di L. da V. Modena, 1898.
G. Séailles. L. da V. Paris, 1892.
Péladan. La dernière leçon de L. da V. à son académie de Milan. Sansot. Paris, 1904.
James Wolf. L. als Aestetiker. Strasbourg, 1901.
M. Herzfeld. L. da V. der Denker. Iena Diedricns, 1906.
L. Ferri. L. da V. scienziato e filosofo. N.A., February 1873.
L. Venturi. La critica dell'Arte di Leonardo da Vinci. Bologna, 1919.
E. Muntz. Leonardo. Paris.
Trattato della pittura. Lanciano, 1914. English trans. by J. F. Rigaud. London, 1887.
B. Croce. Leonardo Filosofo in Saggio sullo Hegel, pp. 207-32. Bari Laterza, 1927.
B. Croce. L. da Vinci, Conferenze fiorentine. Milan, 1910.
Oswald Sirèn. Leonardo da Vinci. Yale U.P., 1900.
E. Solmi. L. da V. Frammenti letterari e filosofici. Firenze Barbera, 1899.
E. Solmi. Nuovi studi sulla filosofia naturale di Leonardo. Mantova, 1905.
Giulio Urbini. Leonardo da Vinci. Nuova Rivista Storica fascicolo, III, vol. 3, 1919.
Leonardo da Vinci. Bibliography. Società Vinciana, Milan, 1905, in course of publication.
A. Farinelli. Sentimento e concetto della natura in L. da Vinci, pp. 285-367. Miscellanea di studi critici in onore di A. Graf. Bergamo, 1903.
LONDI. Il Classicismo nella pittura fiorentina del' 400. Florence, 1911.

LORENZETTI, P. La Bellezza e l'amore. Annali di Pisa, 1920. Lo intendimento e le cause precipue dei trattati d'amore. Rome, 1913.

LORENZO DE' MEDICI.
Lorenzo dei Medici. Poesie Volgari.
Ed. J. Ross and E. Hutton, 2 vols. London, 1912.
Ed. Carducci. 1 vol. Florence, 1859.
Ed. Crusca. 4 vols. Florence, 1825.
[Pub. Aldus, Venice, 1554.]
Lives and Studies of:
Roscoe. Life of L. de'M. London, 1796.
N. Valori. Vita di L., MS. Cod. Vat. Capponiana, 256.
See also Della Torre. Storia dell'Ac. Plat di Firenze. Florence, 1902.
Garsia, A. Il magnifico e la Rinascita. Florence, 1923.
I del Lungo. Gli Amori del magnifico Lorenzo. Nuova Antologia, May 1913.
N. Scarano. Il Platonismo nelle poesie di L. Nuova Antologia, Aug. 1893, p. 606; September 1893, p. 49.
Carducci. Preface to ed. of Poems. Florence, 1859.

LUIGINI, F. Libro della bella donna. Zonta, 1554. B. Rara 23.

MANACORDA, G. B. Varchi, l'uomo e il poeta. Annali di Pisa, 1903.

MANCINI, G. Vita di L. B. Alberti, Florence, 1882.

MANETTI, G. De dignitate et excellentia hominis. Basle, 1532.

MARCHETTI FERRANTE, G. Rievocazioni del Rinascimento. Laterza, Bari, 1924.

MARIANO, R. La Dottrina dell'Amore. N.A., Vol. XV, 1870, p. 93.

MARSIGLI, L. Commento sulla canzone del Petrarca Italia mia. Soc. di curiosità lettararie. Bologna, 1813.

MARTIN, A. VON. Coluccio Salutati und das humanistiche Lebensideal. Leipzig, 1916.
C. S. Trakst von Tyrannien. Berlin, 1913.

MASSETANI, G. La dottrina filosofica nella canzone de G. Benivieni. Livorno, 104.

MENENDEZ Y PELAYO. Historia de las ideas esteticas en Espagna, Toms. I–II. Madrid, 1890–91.

MESSERI, A. Matteo Palmieri, cittadino fiorentino. Arch. St. It. S.V., Vol. XIII (1894), p. 257.

MICHEL, A. Histoire de l'art. Paris, 1900.

MICHELANGELO.
For bibliography see:
Michelangelo Bibliographie. Ernst Stienmann und Rudolf Wittkower, 1926.
2nd ed., with supplement up to date, 1930. Klinckhardt and Biermann, Leipzig.
Michelangelo.
Poesie. Ed. M. Buonarotti il Giovane. Florence, 1623.
Poesie. Ed. C. Guasti. Florence, 1863.
Poesie. Ed. K. Frey. Berlin, 1897.
Lettere. Ed. K. Frey. Berlin, 1875.
Amico-Mantia A. L'Amore e la Rime di Michelangelo. Messina, 1899.
Capri Cordova G. Il Platonismo nelle rime di M. Cerignola, 1902.
Farinelli. Michelangelo e Dante. Turin, 1918.
Rizzi, F. Michelangelo Poeta. Milan, 1924.
Thomas G. Michel-Ange. Poète. étude sur l'expression de l'amour platonique au moyen âge et pendant la Renaissance. Paris, 1892.
Aurelio Saffi. Michelangelo e la missione del Art. Firenze Bemporad, 1909.
K. Brinski. Die Ratsel Michelangelo. München, 1908.
H. Grimm. Michelangelo. It. trans. Milan.
G. Magherini. M. Buonarroti. Firenze, 1875.
A. Gotti. Vita di M.B. Firenze, 1875.
G. Barzellotti. Dell'animo di M. Buonarrotti. Firenze, 1875.
Cerini. Michelangelo Buonarotti ed i lirici minori del' 500. Turin, Paravia, 1931.

MIRANDOLA PICO DELLA.
Works.
A Platonick Discourse upon Love. . . . Reprinted with introduction by Edmund Gardner in The Humanists' Library, Boston, U.S.A., 1914. [See Benivieni.]
Opera. Basle, 1572, 2 vols.
Sonnets. Nuova Rassegna, August 1894, pp. 97–114.
Lives and Studies.
G. Dreydorf. Das system der G.P. Marburg, 1858.
G. Massetani. Dottrina Cabbalistica di P. Empoli, 1897.

MIRANDOLA PICO DELLA—(*cont.*)
    L. Dorez. Lettres inédites de J.P. della M., 1488-92, G.S., Vol. XXV, 1895, p. 352.
    D. Berti. Intorno a G.P. della M. Cenni e documenti inediti. Riv. Contemporanea, Vol. VIII, 1859, pp. 1-56.
    Vita. G. F. Pico in Opera, Vol. II. Basle, 1572.
    F. Calori Cesis. G.P. della M. detto la Fenice degli ingegni. Bologna, 1872.
    V. da Giovanni. P. della M. nella storia dell Rin. e della Filosofia Palermo, 1894.
    G. Semprini. G.P. della M. Todi, 1921.
    G. Semprini. Le 900 tesi di P. Rivista di Psicologia, n. 3-4, 1920.
    Studies.
    W. Pater. The Renaissance. London, 1873.
    Padovan. Le creature sovrane. Milan, Hoepli, 1891.
    A. Castelnau. Les Medicis, Vol. I, Ch. XIII. Pic de la mirandole. Paris, 1879.
    N.V. Testa. Di G.P. della M. e dei suoi contributi alla lirica del'400. Aquila, 1902.

MONNIER, P. Il Quattrocento. Paris, 1912.

MOORE, E. Dante Studies. Oxford.

MOSCHETTI, A. Dell'idea epica nella poesia e nella pittura del' 500. Gallina, Padua, 1896.

MUNK, S. Notice sur Léon Hebreu in Mélanges de Philosophie juive et arabe. Appendix No. 4, pp. 522-8. Paris, 1859.

MUNTZ, E. Raphael, sa vie, son œuvre et son temps. Paris, 1886.
    Precursori e propugnatori del Rinascimento. Florence, 1902.

NALDI, NALDO. Poems. MSS. Cod. Magl., VII, 1057; Laur., XXXV, 34.

NENCIONI, E. Saggi critici di letteratura italiana. Lemonnier, Florence, 1898.
    La vita italiana nel Rinascimento. Milan, 1893.

NESI, GIOVANNI DI F.
    Poema. Codd. Ricc. 2722, original MS.
    Poema. Codd. Ricc. 2750 [O. IV, 32].
    Canzoniere. Codd. Ricc. 2962.

NIFO, A. De Pulchro et Amore. 1529 ed. used. Leyden, 1641.

NOVATI, F. La Giovinezza di Coluccio Salutati [1331-53] Saggio di un libro sopra la vita, le opere ed i tempi di C.S. E. Loescher, Turin, 1888.

BIBLIOGRAPHY

PALMIERI, MATTEO. Works.
Città di Vita. MSS. Orig. Laur., XL, 53; Magl., II, 11, 41.
Part I and first 15 cantos of Part II printed in Smith College Studies in Mod. Languages, Nos. 1 and 2, with preface by M. Rooke, M.A. Northampton, Mass., 1927.
Della Vita Civile. Giunti, Florence, 1529.
Della Vita Civile. Silvestri, Milan, 1825.
PAOLETTI, G. Delle Questioni Forciane di O. Lando. (See Arch. St. It., N.S., Tom. VI, Pt. II, p. 148.)
PATER, W. The Renaissance. London, 1873.
PELOTTI, A. Poems. Ricc. 834, C. 187, i.
PETRARCA, FRANCESCO. Opera. Basle, 1581.
Lettere Familiari. Ed. Fracassetti, 5 vols. Florence, 1863.
Lettere Senili. Ed. Fracassetti, 2 vols. Florence, 1863.
Studies.
  A. Carlini. Il pensiero filosofico-religioso di F. Petrarca. Jesi, 1904.
  F. Fiorentino. La filosofia di F. Petrarca in Scritti vari di letteratura, filosofia e critica. Naples, 1876.
  G. Gentile. I dialoghi di Platone posseduti dal Petrarca. Rassegna critica della letteratura Italiana. Tom. IX, 1904, pp. 193–219.
  U. Gerosa. Umanesimo agostiniano di F.P. Turin, 1927.
  P. de Nolhac. Pétrarque et l'humanisme. Paris, 1892.
  F. de Sanctis. Saggio critico sul Petrarca. Naples, 1869.
PICAVET, H. Esquisse d'une histoire générale et comparée de la philosophie médiévale. Paris, 1905.
PICCOLOMINI, A. La Raffaella. 1539.
PICCOLOMINI, E. S. Opera. Basle, 1551.
PLATINA. Vita Pontificis. Leiden, 1512.
PLETHO, G. G. De Platonicae atque aristotelicae philosophiae differentia. Basle, 1574.
Oracula Magica Zoroastris. Paris, 1607.
Libellus de Fato. Leiden, 1721.
Traité des Lois. Ed. C. Alexandre. Paris, 1859. Works. Migne, Vol. CLX.
POGGIO, B. Oratio in funere N. Niccoli. [In Martene-Durand, Veter. scriptorum et monumentum. collectio, III, 729. Paris.]
POLIZIANO. Le stanze, l'Orfeo, le Rime. Ed. Carducci. 2nd ed. Bologna, 1911.
Opera. Basle, 1553.

POLIZIANO—(cont.)
    Lives and Studies.
    Carducci. Preface to ed. of poems. Florence, 1863.
    Carducci. Cavalleria ed umanesimo. Opera, Tom..XX, p. 258, 1909.
    de Sanctis. St. della lett. it. [New ed. by B. Croce, 2 vols. Vol. I, pp. 339–442. Bari, 1912].
    del Lungo. I. Florentia. Firenze, 1897.
    Hoffman. P. Lebensbild. Leipzig, 1837.
    Dorez. L'Hellenisme d'Ange Politien. Melanges d'Archéologie et d'histoire. Paris, 1895.
PRATO, G. DA. Paradiso degli Alberti. Ed. Wesselofski. Bologna, soc. di Curiosità lett., 1867.
PUCINOTTI, F. Di M.F. e della Accademie Pl. nel sec XV. Giachetti Prato, 1865.
    Della filosofia di M.F. N.A., V 211, June 1867.
PULCI, LUIGI. Morgante Maggiore. 1900 ed. of G. Volpi. Florence. Based principally on ed. of Matteo di Coecà, 1489. 3 vols.
    Sonnets of Luigi Pulci and M. Franco. Lucca, 1759.
    Lettere a Lorenzo. Ed. S. Bongi. Lucca, 1886.
RALEIGH, WALTER. Introduction to The Book of the Courtier from the Italian of Count Baldassare Castiglione: done into English by Sir Thomas Hoby, 1561. London, 1900.
RAPHAEL. Disegni e lettere. Ed. Leone Zanetti. Bologna, 1924.
RE. C. G. Benivieni, 1452–1541. Città de Castello, 1906.
ROMEI, A. Discorsi divisi in sette giornate. Venice, 1594.
ROSE, G. B. Botticelli. (The Renaissance Masters.) London, 1898.
ROSI, M. Saggio sui trattati d'amore del'500. Recanati, 1889.
    Scienza d'amore. Milan, 1904.
ROSMINI, C. Vita di F. Filelfo. Milan, 1808, 3 vols.
ROSSI, V. Il Quattrocento. Milan, 1878.
    La Vita italiana nel Rinascimento. Milan, 1892.
RUGGIERO, G. Storia della Filosofia: Rinascimento e Riforma. Bari, 1930, 2 vols.
SABBADINI, R. La Vita di G. Veronese. Genoa, 1891.
    La scuola e gli studi di G. Veronese. Catania, 1896.
    La scoperta dei codici nei secoli. XIV e XV. Florence, 1905–14, 2 vols.
SAITTA, G. Filosofia italiana ed Umanesimo. Venice, 1928.
    L'educazione dell'umanesimo. Venice, 1928.
    La filosofia di M. Ficino. Messina, 1923.

SALUTATI, COLUCCIO. Epistolae. Ed. Novati. Rome, 1905.
De Hercule eiusque laboribus. Vatican MS., Urb. Lat. 201.
SALVIATI, L. Dialoghi d'amicizia. Florence, 1564. (Reprinted in Classici Italiani, Milan, 1809.)
SANESI, I. Il Cinquecentista Orténsio Lando. Pistoia, 1893.
SANSOVINO, F. Ragionamento di F. S. nel quale brevemente s'insegna a giovani huomini la bella Arte d'Amore. Mantua, 1545.
SAVINO, L. Di alcuni trattati e trattatisti d'amore italiani. [Studi di let. diretti dal Percopo. Naples, 1909–14, Vols. 9, 10.]
SAVONAROLA. Prediche e scritti. Ed. M. Ferrara. Milan, Hoepli, 1930.
SIEVEKING, A. Die Geschichte der platonischen Academie zu Florenz. Göttingen, 1812.
SOLDATI, B. La poesia astrologica nel' 400. Florence, 1906.
SOLMI, E. Studi sulla filosofia naturale di L. da Vinci. Modena Vicenzi, 1898.
Benedetto Spinoza e Leone Ebreo. Modena, 1905.
SPERONE SPERONI. Opere. Venice, 1740, 5 vols. [Dialogo d'amore. 1528, Vol. I.]
SPRINGER, A., and RICCI, C. Storia dell'arte. Bergamo, 1909–12, 4 vols.
STAMPA, GASPARA. Poesie.
SYMONDS, J. A. The Renaissance. London, 1877.
In the Key of Blue and other Prose Essays. London, 1893, p. 55.
"The Dantesque and Platonic Ideals of Love."
TASSINI, G. V. Franco. Stab. Tip. Fontana, 1888.
TASSO. I dialoghi di T.T. a cura di Cesare Guasti. Florence, 1858–9, Vol. II.
TOLOMEI, CLAUDIO. Rime. Venice, Giolito, 1547.
Lettere. Venice, 1589.
TORRE, A. DELLA. Storia dell'accademia platonica di Firenze. Florence, 1902.
TRAVERSARI, A. Epistolae. Ed. Laurentius Mehus. Florence, 1759, 2 vols.
VALLA, L. Opera. Basle, 1540.
VARCHI, B. Ercolano. Venice, 1565.
Lezioni. Florence, 1561.
Opere. Trieste, 1858, 2 vols.
VASARI, G. Le Opere, con nuove annotazioni e commenti di. G. Milanesi, Firenze, 1878–85, 9 vols.
VAST, H. Le Cardinal Bessarion. Paris, 1878.
VEGIO, M. De educatione liberorum. Maxima biblioteca veterum patrum, Tom. XV, p. 883. Leiden, 1576.

VENTURI, A. Storia dell'arte. Milan, 1901 (in progress).
Botticelli e Dante. Florence, 1922.
VENTURI, L. La critica dell'arte di Leonardo da Vinci. Bologna, 1919.
Il gusto dei primitivi. Bologna, 1926.
La critica d'arte in Italia durante i secoli XIV e XV. [L'Arte, 1917, fasc. 6.]
Dei criteri dell'Arte e della loro esplicazione nei tempi del Risorgimento a proposito di un libro del sig. Carlo Clement, intitolato Michelangelo, Leonardo e Raffaello. Arch. St. It., N.S., Tom. XVII, P. II, 34–53.
VERGERIO, P. P. De ingenuis moribus. Ed. A. Gnesotto. Padua, 1918.
Epistolario. R. Deputazione di Storia Patria, 1887.
VERINO, U. Paradisus. Laur., XXXIX, 40. 1489.
VESCO, A. L.B. Alberti e la critica d'arte. [L'Arte XXII, 1919, fasc. 4–6.]
VIDARI, G. Studi sulla storia del pensiero pedagogico in Italia. Turin, 1924.
VILLARI, P. Machiavelli. Florence, 1877.
Savonarola e i suoi tempi. Florence, 1885, 2 vols.
VISMARA, S. La lirica italiana nel Rinascimento. Florence, 1910.
VITO DI GOZZE, N. Dialogo della Bellezza detto Anthos secondo la mente di Platone. Venice, 1571.
Dialogo d'Amore detto Anthos secondo la mente di Platone. Venice, 1581.
VOIGT, G. Il Risorgimento dell'antichità classica. Trans. Valbusa. Florence, 1888, 2 vols.
VOLPI, G. Luigi Pulci. G.S., Vol. XXII, p. 30.
URBINO. Romanticismo e ricorsi romantici nelle Arti in Italia. N. Riv. St. 1919, fasc. II.
WICKSTEED, P. Dante and Aquinas. London, 1913.
WINDELBAND, H. History of Philosophy. English translation, New York, 1893.
WOODWARD, W. H. Vittorino da Feltre and other humanist educators. Cambridge, 1897.
Studies in education during the age of the Renaissance, 1400–1600. Cambridge, 1906.
ZABUGHIN, G. G. Pomponio Leto. Rome, 1909.
ZIMMELS, B. Leo Hebraeus. Leipzig, 1886.
ZIPPEL, G. Per la biografia dell'Argiropulo. G.S., Vol. XXVIII, p. 94.
ZONTA, G. Trattati d'Amore. Bari, 1912.
Trattati del'500 sulla donna. Laterza, Bari, 1913.
Fil. Nuvolone e un suo dialogo d'amore. Modena, 1905.
ZUMBINI. Studi di Let. straniere. Firenze, 1893.

INDEX

Aglio Peregrino, 61
Alberti Leon Battista, 38–39, 61, 179, 183–187, 217–224
Alexander, 73
Altercazione ovver Dialogo, 96 seq.
Anaxagoras, 73–100
Angelico, Fra, 214
Annunciation (della Robbia), 215
Annunciation (Leonardo da Vinci), 234
Anonimo, Gaddiano, 217
Anthos, 194
Aquinas, St. Thomas, 18, 20
Apostolius, Michael, 47, 49
Aragona, Tullia d', 196, 198, 203–205
Aretino, Pietro, 205, 212, 235
Argyropoulos, John, 46
Ariosto, 137
Aristippus, Henricus, 22
Aristophanes, 82
Aristotle, 21, 50, 51, 53, 100
Ars Amandi, 177
Asolani Gli, 184 seq., 190, 194
Astronomicon, 161, 162
Augustine, St., 17, 18, 21–24, 26, 59, 178
Averroists, 20, 32
Avicenna, 17

Baldini, Baccio, 220
Bandello, M., 205
Bandini, A. M., 139
Barlam, 22
Battle of the Centaurs and the Lapithae, 226
Beatrice, 18, 148, 221, 247
Bellini, Giovanni, 215
Bembo, Pietro, 180, 184 seq., 190–194, 205, 239
Benci, Tommaso, 241
Benivieni, Girolamo, 61, 94, 95, 112 seq., 136, 181, 241, 247

Beoni, 95, 163
Berni, Francesco, 239
Bessarion, Cardinal, 39, 49–54, 57
Betussi, Giovanni, 194 seq., 203
Birth of Venus, 217, 218, 219, 220
Blake, William, 220, 276
Boccaccio, 135, 179, 222
Boccalini, Traiano, 189
Bonincontri, Lorenzo, 136, 137, 161, 162
Botticelli, 136, 216 seq., 224
Bracci, Cecchino de', 243, 254
Bruni, Leonardo, 32, 34
Bruno, Giordano, 13, 40, 75, 270, 271

Callixtus, Andronicus, 47
Calumny (of Apelles), 224
Campanella, Tommaso, 232, 240, 250, 270, 271
Canti Carniascialeschi, 95, 107
Canzone del Amor Divino, 61, 118 seq.
Canzoniere del Amor Divino, 112 seq.
Caro, Annibale, 212
Castiglione, Baldassare, 180, 190 seq., 212, 222, 235
Cavalcanti, Giovanni, 181
Cavalcanti, Guido, 91, 119, 177, 178
Cavalieri, Tommaso, 225, 242, 246–247
Chalchidius, 21
Chrysoloras, Manuel, 31, 34
Cicero, 21, 22, 23, 178
Cimabue, 214
Città di Vita, La, 136 seq.
Colonna, Vittoria, 225, 240, 242, 246, 247, 254
Comparatio Platonis et Aristotelis, 49
Condivi, Ascanio, 241
Convivio, 18
Coppetta de' Beccuti, Francesco, 239
Coronation of the Virgin (Botticelli), 220

Corsi, Giovanni, 61
Cortigiano, 190 seq.
Council of Ferrara, 46
Council of Florence, 46
Crane, T. F., 176
Cusa, Nicholas of, 63

Dante, 18, 19, 97, 135, 136, 139, 178, 220–223, 241, 247
De Amore, 194
Decameron, 222
De Christiana Religione, 59, 63
De excellentia et dignitate hominis, 40, 45
De hominis dignitate, 61
Deifira, 183
Della Barba da Pescia Pompeo, 196
Della Pittura, 224
della Robbia, 215
Della Vita Civile, 138, 150
Delphic Sybil, 246
Democritus, 100
De Monarchia, 135
De Ocio Religiosorum, 28
De Platonicae atque Aristotelicae Philosophiae Differentia, 48, 50
Deposition (Fra Angelico), 214
De Pulchro, 194
De Rebus Caelestis, 137, 161, 162
De Remediis Utriusque Fortuna, 25
De Vita Solitaria, 28
De Voluptate (Ficino), 97
De Voluptate (Valla), 98
Diacceto, Francesco Cattani di, 61, 182 seq., 188, 241
Dialoghi d'Amore, 197 seq.
Dialogum ad Petrum Paulum Histrum, 32
Dionysius (pseudo), 17, 146, 155, 270
Diotima, 84
Dispute of the Sacrament, 229
Divina Commedia, 18, 135–138, 220
Dolce, Ludovico, 222, 235
Dolci, Carlo, 236
Dominici, Giovanni, 179

Donatello, 90, 215
Donati, Lucrezia, 103
Donna mi prega, 177
Doré, Gustave, 220
Dürer, Albrecht, 232
Dying Slave (Michelangelo), 229

Enneads, 59
Epipsychidion, 278
Equicola, Mario, 187 seq.
Erasmus, 139
Evelyn Hope, 277

Ficino, Marsilio, 12, 13, 14, 31, 33, 45, 47, 50, 54, 57 seq., 91, 95, 96, 97, 105, 107, 118, 119, 135, 138, 140, 146, 148, 150, 153, 157, 161, 163, 164, 165, 167, 170, 176, 179, 181, 182, 183, 184, 187, 188, 198, 201, 202, 205, 217, 218, 225, 227, 240, 241
Filelfo, Francesco, 40
Filosofo, Il, 205
Firenzuola, 205
Folengo, Teofilo, 164
Fortezza, 216
Franco, Matteo, 163, 165

Gaza, Theodore, 47, 49, 50
Gennadius (Georgius Scholarius), 47
Gioconda, La (Monna Lisa), 230, 234
Giotto, 214
Giraldi, Cinthio, 196
Gozzoli, Benozzo, 104
Guinizelli, Guido, 119, 177

Hecatomfila, 183
Heptaplus, 61, 64, 71, 92, 272
Hertha, 273
Horne, Herbert, 217
Hugo, Victor, 271, 276

Ilaria del Carretto, tomb of, 215
In Calumniatorem Platonis, 50

INDEX

In Convivium Platonis de Amore Commentarius, 74
Inferno, 220
Infinita d'Amore, 196, 204, 205
In Memoriam, 278
Ion, 223
In Platonis Convivium (Pico), 61
Istitutiones Platonicae, 138

Jacopone da Todi, 111
Judith, 216

Keats, 230
King Lear, 233

Landino, Cristoforo, 44, 61, 97, 98, 136, 217, 220, 221, 223
Lando, Ortensio, 181
Landscape in Rain (Leonardo da Vinci), 232
Lasca, Il, 239
Lascaris, The, 47
Last Judgment (Michelangelo), 228
Last Supper (Leonardo da Vinci), 231
Laude (Lorenzo de' Medici), 96, 102, 107 seq.
Laura, 178, 185, 222
Laws, 49, 54
Leone Ebreo, 40, 75, 176, 197 seq.
Leonora, 194
Leopardi, 243, 273, 277
Leto, Pomponio, 33, 50, 63
Lezioni, 196
Libri d'Amore, 241
Libro di Natura d'Amore, 187 seq.
Lippi, Fra Filippo, 216
Lucian, 224

Macrobius, 28
Madonna of the Magnificat, 219
Madonna of the Rocks, 231, 234
Madonna with Five Saints, 219
Manetti, Gianozzo, 40, 45
Manilius, 161
Marlow, 108

Marsigli, Luigi, 31, 32, 33, 40
Marsilio da Padova, 20
Marsuppini, Carlo, 33, 138
Medici, Cosimo de', 48, 58
Medici, Lorenzo de', 12, 13, 58, 90, 94, 95 seq., 135, 163, 166, 217, 218, 225, 240
Medici, Lorenzo di Pier Francesco de', 217, 220
Medici, Nannina de', 167
Medici tombs, 227, 229, 241
Memmi, Simone, 222
Menendez y Pelayo, 176
Meno, 22
Meredith, George, 273
Metaphysics, 50
Michelangelo, 15, 91, 136, 196, 220, 225 seq., 235, 236, 237, 240 seq, 275
Middleton Murry, J., 270
Mistress of Vision, 275
Molza, 204
Monnica, St., 24
Montgomery, Robert, 137
Morgante Maggiore, 163 seq.
Mystic Crucifixion, 220

Nencia da Barberino, 95, 108, 163
Nesi, Giovanni di Francesco, 136, 153 seq., 161
Niccoli, Niccolo, 32, 135
Nicholas V, 49
Nifo, Agostino, 194
Nuvolone, Filippo, 179

Orazioni, 95
Orcagna, 214
Origen, 139, 140, 168, 270
Orpheus, 48, 80

Pallas and Centaur, 217, 219, 220
Palmieri, Matteo, 136 seq., 159, 161
Panegirico dell'Amore, 183
Paradiso, 220
Paradiso degli Alberti, 32
Paradisus, 136, 159, 160, 161

314　NEOPLATONISM OF THE ITALIAN RENAISSANCE

Paradossi, 181
Pater, Walter, 230
Paul II, 49
Paul, St., 102, 152
Pausanias, 79
Perugino, 233
Petrarch, 11, 19 seq., 33, 34, 35, 178, 182, 185, 196, 222, 239, 241, 243
Phaedo, 22
Phaedrus, 223
Pico della Mirandola, 13, 14, 40, 59, 60 seq., 118 seq., 139, 176, 181, 188, 228, 241, 271
Pico della Mirandola, Giovan Francesco, 188
Piero di Cosimo, 233
Pietà (Giovanni Bellini), 215
Pietà (Michelangelo), 227
Pimandro, 241
Piranesi, 232
Pisani, The, 214
Platina, 188
Plato, 11, 17, 19, 21, 22, 23, 25, 31, 33, 44, 48, 49, 50, 51, 55, 59, 75, 79, 80, 135, 138, 202, 212, 223, 241
Pletho, George Gemisthus, 12, 47–50
Plotinus, 12, 22, 28, 59, 117, 121, 146
Poema Visione, 136, 153 seq.
Polisifo, 179
Politian (Angelo Poliziano), 46, 90 seq., 135, 160, 217, 240, 241
Pollajuoli, The, 216
Pontano, Giovanni, 33, 40, 161, 179
Porphyry, 22, 48, 121
Prato, Giovanni da, 32
Primavera, 217, 218, 219, 220
Proclus, 48
Prometheus Unbound, 276
Pulci, Luigi, 137, 141, 142, 143, 162 seq.
Purgatorio, 220
Pythagoras, 51

Quaestiones Camaldulenses, 44, 61, 96, 97
Rabelais, 164
Raphael, 229, 230, 235, 236, 237
Raverta, Il, 197
Republic, 53
Rerum Naturalum, 161
Resurrection (Michelangelo), 228
Riccardi Chapel, frescoes in, 233
Riccio, Luigi del, 254
Rossi, Roberto de, 32

Salonika, Isidore of, 47
Salutati, Coluccio, 31, 34–39, 45, 179
Salvator Rosa, 234
Savino, Lorenzo, 176
Savonarola, 112, 136, 153, 219
School of Athens, 229
Sebastiano, del Piombo, 227
Secretum, 26, 178
Selve d'Amore, 94, 96, 102 seq.
Seneca, 39
Shelley, 61, 273, 278
Signorelli, Luca, 220
Sistine Chapel, 227, 241
Socrates, 84, 181
Sonnets from the Portuguese, 278
Speroni, Sperone, 198, 203, 204
Spinoza, 75, 198
Sposizione d'un sonetto platonico fatto sopra il primo effetto d'amore, 196
Stampa, Gaspara, 239
Stanza della Segnatura, 229
Stanze per la Giostra, 92, 160
Stanze (Raphael's), 229
Swinburne, 273
Symposium, 75, 92, 118; Ficino's translation, *Convito*, 218, 241

Tansillo, Luigi, 239
Tasso, Torquato, 194, 240
Theologia Platonica de Immortalitate Animae, 59, 63, 138
Thinker (Michelangelo), 246
Thomas à Kempis, 111

INDEX

Thompson, Francis, 276
Timaeus, 18, 21, 148
Titian, 235
Tornabuoni frescoes, 220
Tornabuoni, Lucrezia, 96, 107
Toscanelli, Paolo, 138
Traversari, Ambrogio, 33, 41, 138
Trebizond, George of, 47, 49, 53
Trionfo di Bacco e d'Arianna, 95
Trismegistus, Hermes, 48
Tusculane, 22, 178

Valla, Lorenzo, 39, 40, 45, 46, 98, 179
Varchi, Benedetto, 182, 196, 198, 203, 204, 205, 239
Vasari, Georgio, 217, 222, 235, 236, 243
Vegio, Maffeo, 179
Venus and Mars (Botticelli), 217
Verino, Ugolino di V., 136, 159, 160, 161

Verrio, 236
Verrocchio, 216
Vigny, Alfred de, 273
Villon, 108
Vinci, Leonardo da, 203, 224, 226, 229 seq., 271
Virgil, 97, 135
Virgin and Child and St. Anne (Leonardo de Vinci), 231
Vision of Judgment, 168
Visitation (della Robbia), 215
Vita Nuova, La, 17, 178, 243
Vito de Gozze, Nicolò, 194
Viviani, Emilia, 278
Volpi, 165

Wordsworth, 273, 277
Wuthering Heights, 233

Zambeccari, Pellegrino, 179
Zoroaster, 48

GEORGE ALLEN & UNWIN LTD
LONDON: 40 MUSEUM STREET, W.C.1
LEIPZIG: (F. VOLCKMAR) HOSPITALSTR. 10
CAPE TOWN: 73 ST. GEORGE'S STREET
TORONTO: 91 WELLINGTON STREET, WEST
BOMBAY: 15 GRAHAM ROAD, BALLARD ESTATE
WELLINGTON, N.Z.: 8 KINGS CRESCENT, LOWER HUTT
SYDNEY, N.S.W.: AUSTRALIA HOUSE, WYNYARD SQUARE

For Product Safety Concerns and Information please contact our EU representative GPSR@taylorandfrancis.com
Taylor & Francis Verlag GmbH, Kaufingerstraße 24, 80331 München, Germany

www.ingramcontent.com/pod-product-compliance
Lightning Source LLC
Chambersburg PA
CBHW071156300426
44113CB00009B/1228